THE RICH
WHO OWN
SPORTS

THE RICH WHO OWN SPORTS

Don Kowet

Random House New York

Library of Congress Cataloging in Publication Data
Kowet, Don.
The rich who owns sports.
1. Sports team owners—United States—Biography.
I. Title.
GV719.A2K68   338.4'77960922 [B]   76–53483
ISBN 0–394–49561–6

Manufactured in the United States of America
2 4 6 8 9 7 5 3
First Edition

*To my parents,
without whose cooperation
this author would not have been possible*

Acknowledgments

The author wishes to thank the following for enlarging his understanding of both individual owners and the business of ownership: Glenn Dickey, William Barry Furlong, J. Anthony Lucas, Al Stump, *Dun's Review, Fortune* and *Sports Illustrated.* Thanks also to Stanley Brown, for his early encouragement—and to Begoña Kowet, for the many hours she devoted to research.

Contents

THE RICH
WHO OWN
SPORTS

Prologue

Once upon a time, in the ancient republic of Rome, people were caught up in a fad called *hippomania*—a madness for horses. The leading chariot drivers enjoyed the adulation showered today on Joe Namath and Reggie Jackson and Rick Barry and Bobby Orr. The drivers belonged to four teams—Whites, Blues, Reds and Greens. They dressed in "uniforms"—tunics dyed in their team colors. Nearly every Roman citizen rooted for one team or another; White fans, for example, wore white tunics and white scarves to broadcast their allegiance. Fans at the Circus Maximus sat in groups, shouting encouragement, waving placards and team insignias, just the way fans do today in stadiums and arenas across the country. Each team was owned by a large corporation, similar to those that own, say, the Dallas Cowboys and the Kansas City Chiefs. And all four teams were organized into a league run by the four corporations, just the way modern baseball owners run the major leagues.

3

The Rich Who Own Sports

As the popularity of the races soared, the drivers started making demands. Almost two thousand years before Catfish Hunter got $3.75 million for switching teams, an ex-slave named Diocles got 35 million sesterces ($1.8 million) for switching stables. "Decent men groan to see this former slave earn an income that is one hundred times that of the entire Roman Senate," moaned one contemporary sportswriter.

Eventually, as the empire replaced the republic, the league expanded. Races were increased to twenty-four a day, and eight franchises were added, then another four, for a total of sixteen. The owners of Roman franchises had discovered that by charging millions of sesterces in entry fees, they could turn selling franchises into a profitable business. To make the sport more exciting, as expansion had made it more profitable, the owners began to tolerate, and finally to encourage, violence for its own sake. Just as in modern hockey, the chariot races became marred by collisions and fistfights and deliberate fouls and injuries. The day of the gladiators wasn't far off. In A.D. 79, to attract fans to the newly built Roman Colosseum, promoters staged a bizarre spectacle: a team of Amazon women fought a team of Pygmy men, to the death. Fortunately, the stakes were lower in 1973, when—to attract fans to the newly built Houston Astrodome—an Amazon named Billie Jean King beat a pygmy named Bobby Riggs at tennis.

The Roman franchise owners, of course, didn't have TV to promote their product. Ten years ago the three networks were broadcasting between 540 and 550 hours of sports a year. Now the three commercial networks bombard us with 1,000 hours of baseball and table-top tennis and football and demolition derby and basketball and barrel jumping and ice hockey and dart throwing. TV created a new set of Diocleses, whose cost-accounted grins gleam at us above cans of shaving cream, under a lathery shampoo. It created new leagues. In promoting the modern version of *hippomania,* TV turned our Sundays from days of rest into days of anxiety. It caused Kiwanis clubs and Boy Scout troops and Parent-Teacher Associations to reshuffle their Monday night meetings, so entranced had their members become by the hypnotic monotone of Howard Cosell. As they had in Rome, multimillionaire tycoons infiltrated American sports, joining the old guard who had started

4

their franchises as a hobby, on a shoestring.

The aim of this book is to examine the rich who own sports in America—their motivations, their life styles, their origins, their impact. Some of today's owners were lured by the glamour that pro athletes radiate; others are dyed-in-the-wool fans; many have bitten the bait of tax write-offs and antitrust exemptions. Some are benevolent dictators; others, outright despots. Some live in baroque elegance; a few absolutely detest showiness. But despite their differences one common bond sets them apart from the masses of ordinary men. The poorest of the pro sports owners is very, very rich. Compared to the rich who own sports, even pro athletes are just ordinary men.

Usually the foibles and fantasies of the very rich are concealed by towering gates around palatial estates and frosted-glass portholes of expensive yachts. The rich who own sports have to surrender some of this gold-plated privacy. They have to step into the brilliant spotlight that constantly sweeps across our stadiums and arenas. In doing so, they provide convincing evidence that the rich are *different* from you and me. An owner/oil baron tools around his ranch at the wheel of a gleaming red fire engine; an owner/judge gets trundled up the steps of the Acropolis in a Cleopatran sedan chair; an owner/chewing gum tycoon would rather dig potholes in his backyard than watch his baseball team in a rare pennant drive . . . The owners' passionate, often obsessive fascination with the fantasy factory of pro sports—small potatoes to most of them in terms of dollar profits—is merely the final proof of a profound eccentricity.

Perhaps a kind of dementia has always been a quality of sports ownership. Showman Harry Frazee was labeled downright crazy when, in 1920, he sold Babe Ruth to the New York Yankees to pay for the Broadway fiascos he had financed. Jake Ruppert, who bought Ruth from Frazee's Boston Red Sox, was in turn considered odd because he thought there was a relationship between beer (the beer manufactured by his brewery) and baseball.

The owners in the first chapters of this book are heirs to that older tradition. Art Rooney, an ex-player and ex-coach, purchased one of the early NFL franchises. Phil Wrigley, Horace Stoneham and Wellington Mara all inherited their teams from their fathers.

The Rich Who Own Sports

In comparison with the more recent breed of owners, the manias of these men seem mild. Yet in time each would come to seem odd, too—trapped in an eccentric orbit, their lives forever revolving around the values of a bygone age.

It took Walter O'Malley to bring a modern method to the madness of sports ownership. O'Malley expanded baseball's horizon to the West Coast, and provided an early object lesson to modern owners when he brought the Los Angeles City Council to its knees over the issue of a stadium in Chavez Ravine. Then came two millionaires from Texas: Lamar Hunt, frustrated in his effort to start a new team, invented a whole new *league,* while he was still in his twenties; Clint Murchison, only a few years older, started a new team, then invented a new way to operate it—with computers, and an alert eye for collateral profits. At the same time, Roy Hofheinz, a man with more political clout than cash, was brokering an alliance between Texas and professional baseball; he built the first domed stadium, then saw his empire crumble, all the while indulging his bizarre taste for period furniture.

Perhaps the most striking figure among today's owners is a man who made an unexpected fortune selling health insurance to doctors. Charlie Finley never gained much fame in insurance, but once he bought a baseball team his wildly contradictory behavior made him more famous than most players. He was by turns the advocate of new promotional stunts and fan comfort, deserter of a city, enemy of the Players Association, firer of managers, critic of the press, enemy of the Commissioner and defender of owner rights. And his baseball team happened to be just about the best in the game.

Two other owners who came to wealth late in their lives showed themselves almost as irrepressible as Finley himself. Ewing Kauffman became owner of a baseball team on a fortune made from ground-up oyster shells. And Ray Kroc, whose hamburgers are sold at every crossroads in America, once grabbed the public-address microphone at his team's first home game and denounced his players for their inept performance.

Discounting even their personal foibles and private fantasies, most of the new owners would seem eccentric in one startling respect. Many of them seemed to enjoy losing money—or at least the ounces of red ink spilling over their ledger books didn't dampen their enthusiasm. But there were a few who got into sports to make a fortune, not to lose one. Joe Robbie, a Lebanese-American from North Dakota, used more guile than money to take control of a football franchise. And Al Davis, a football coach from Brooklyn, used his immense energies and muscle as a recruiter to become commissioner of a league, then controlling partner of his team. Others made sports pay by buying up franchises and arenas the way real-estate men assemble lots on a block. Arthur Wirtz and his associates once owned three of the six teams and two of the six arenas in the National Hockey League. Today, Jack Kent Cooke owns indoor sports in Los Angeles—and a big part of a football team in Washington. And one enterprising soul, Gary Davidson, began where Lamar Hunt left off: he fell on the idea of making sports pay by inventing leagues and teams out of whole (some say invisible) cloth; the would-be moguls who bought into his American Basketball Association, World Hockey Association and World Football League were most often exposed to the chill winds of financial disaster, but Davidson himself—and many of the athletes in the league—showed a healthy profit.

The whole boom in sports and the wild increase in the number of teams available to own was the work of the one-eyed monster called television. Noticing this fact, corporate businessmen in the 1960's declared sports a part of the entertainment industry. The Madison Square Garden Corporation, once merely the owner of a malodorous arena and the teams that played there, built a new complex suitable for ice shows, circuses, live musical events, movies and political conventions. Their hockey and basketball players played alternate nights with acrobats and trained seals. CBS, the original patron of televised pro football, even got into the ownership business, paying the bills for the fast-declining baseball Yankees for a few years before selling the team at a loss. The marriage of broadcasting and sports seems more stable on a local level. Cowboy Gene Autry combines interests in radio, television and his sports team, as do several other owners.

Lest anyone get the idea that sports ownership is the last bastion of nonpolitical private enterprise, the book ends with a look at the politics of ownership—the fine art of extracting tax dollars for private ends, chiefly the construction of stadiums for the use of one particular team. If there is a dark side to ownership, this is it —the spectacle, for example, of the New York Yankees "encouraging" a city fast approaching bankruptcy to donate $100 million for the renovation of a stadium touching on one of America's most desolate slums.

History may not spin in cycles. The twentieth-century franchise owner may not, after all, be leading pro sports down the perilous path cleared by his Roman counterpart. But there are some eerie resemblances. The Super Bowl and the World Series seem to have at least as much pomp and pageantry as a Roman circus. The increasing strife between players and owners is mirrored by Diocles' statement two millennia earlier: "I do not care that I am exploited," he said. "I exploit those that exploit me." And an unusual number of the new "emperors" of sport were at one time professional musicians: Ray Kroc and Jack Kent Cooke were dance-band pianists; Gene Autry, a Western singer. We can only be thankful that none of them was a fiddle player.

◀ 1 ▶
The Preserver

It's a typical summer day in Chicago. Eighty-two-year-old Philip K. Wrigley is sitting in his office on the sixteenth floor of the Wrigley Building, memos and reports stacked high on his desk. He scans them page by page. He puts his signature on some, he scrawls comments on others; secretaries will distribute them to executives of the William Wrigley, Jr. Co., makers of Wrigley's Spearmint and Wrigley's Doublemint and Wrigley's Juicy Fruit and—of course—Wrigley's P.K.'s.

As he reaches for another document, Wrigley glances up at a television set. His Cubs are losing, they have been losing with numbing regularity for forty years. His face—mournful as a bloodhound's—turns boyish for a moment, worry lines softening in the excitement of a Cub rally. But, with two on and two out, the Cubs' clean-up hitter strikes out. Glumly, Wrigley returns to his paper work. If he feels any desire to be at the ball park, he refuses to admit it. The assets of the Chicago Cubs franchise, he points out dryly, are worth maybe $10 or $12 million. The assets of his Wrigley's chewing gum empire are worth somewhere around $300 million—earning for him about $10,000 per day. That's why P.K. Wrigley sits in his office throughout the summer; why he has attended only a few games at Wrigley Field in the past twenty years; why he follows his Cubs on TV or the radio.

Still, he loves his franchise and its fans. A few minutes later, at the beginning of the Cubs' half of the seventh inning, the depth of his devotion becomes embarrassingly evident. Philip K. Wrigley pushes aside the documents that link him to the multimillion-dollar empire he inherited from his father. He rises. He solemnly takes communion with Cub fans rising in his stadium a few miles away. No matter where he is—in his office, in his apartment over-looking Lake Shore Drive, in his mansion near Lake Geneva, Wisconsin, or his mansion on Santa Catalina Island—Wrigley al-ways stops whatever he's doing to stand for the Cubs' seventh-inning stretch.

Philip K. Wrigley has achieved a wealth and status beyond the grasp of normal men. He is chairman of the board of the William Wrigley, Jr. Co., holding 115,192 shares of a corporation whose sales reached $176,832,000 in 1970. His 4,000 employees turn out sticks of chewing gum in plants scattered from Gainesville, Georgia, to Melbourne, Australia. He owns a vast estate in Lake Geneva, Wisconsin. He owns 75.7 square miles of a 76-square-mile island in the Pacific—the only major island off Southern California with potential as a mecca for tourists. He owns the Chicago Cubs baseball franchise.

And yet his prime objective has eluded him. Philip K. Wrigley has always longed to be a Nobody, inconspicuous as a Cub fan or a chewing gum salesman. The irony is, this very search for ano-nymity has made Phil Wrigley famous; he has everything money can buy, but money can't buy obscurity.

In contrast, his father, William Wrigley, Jr., always wanted to be a Somebody. William grew up in Philadelphia. Wrigley Sr. owned a soap factory in Wayne Junction. Starting in his father's factory as a soap crutcher, William stirred the bubbling vats of boiling soap with a paddle, for $1.50 a week. At the age of twelve, he convinced his father to send him on the road as a salesman. "I was a full-fledged long-pants traveling salesman before I was thir-teen," he would later boast. He traveled from western Pennsyl-vania to northern New England. He sold scouring soap from a four-horse team with bells on the harness. Despite his youth, he proved to be a genius at outsmarting his competitors. When they lowered their prices to undercut his father's scouring soap, young Wrigley immediately raised the price of his product, from a nickel to ten cents, then gave his dealers baking soda as a premium for every box of soap they sold. Soon the demand for baking soda outstripped the demand for scouring soap. Wrigley decided to sell baking soda, too, giving his dealers chewing gum as a premium. When dealers started clamoring for more chewing gum, Wrigley decided not only to sell it, but to manufacture it. In 1891, at the age of thirty, he settled in Chicago. With a total capital of $32, he formed the William Wrigley, Jr. Co.

In the last decade of the nineteenth century, advertising was still in its infancy. Wrigley became a pioneer. His first two ad campaigns, each for $100,000, produced nothing but debts. His third campaign, for $250,000, started producing profits. By the 1920's, he was spending $4 million a year to advertise his product, while most of his competitors were still spending nothing. His business tripled in a decade, and so did his influence. "Years ago, we used to take double-page ads in *The Saturday Evening Post,*" his son Philip recalls, "really the first color ads ever in magazines. You could always tell when the *Post* was running a Wrigley ad. The cover was red and green, the colors we used in the ad."

Philip Knight Wrigley was born on December 5, 1894, three years after his father founded the chewing gum company. He was raised in the family mansion on Lakeview Avenue, in Chicago, in front of Lincoln Park. As the only son (he had one sister, Dorothy) of a man well on his way to accumulating a personal fortune of $30 million, he was taught the skills befitting his economic class—horseback riding and polo, for example. When it came time for him to go to school, none would do except the exclusive Chicago Latin School. From there, he went to Phillips Academy in Andover, Massachusetts, where he prepared to enter Yale University. At Andover, the five-foot-nine-inch 160-pounder excelled in athletics, particularly in lacrosse. He also became proficient at "craps," a game of dice that taught him a lesson he later applied to baseball: "When the dice are against you, there's nothing you can do about it." Though his father hired a special tutor, Phil never shone as a student. He couldn't read very well, and he couldn't spell properly, either. In 1914, he withdrew from Andover, a year before he was scheduled to graduate.

In retrospect, Wrigley says he was slow to read because his mother and sister always read *to* him. In later years, his wife would do the same—reading aloud from the newspaper or a book while he tinkered over a car engine in his workshop. But there is another explanation for his failure at school. Unlike his outgoing father, Phil was quiet, withdrawn. Even at the age of five, a family acquaintance recalls, he was trying to "live up to his father." In his teens, that urge turned into a subtle form of rebellion. He realized, at some unconscious level, that to grow he would have to plant new roots, in virgin territory. Otherwise, lost in the intimidating shadow of his extroverted—and powerful—father, Phil Wrigley might wither on the vine.

As soon as he learned to sit on a horse, Phil and his father would go riding in the park in front of their mansion, usually at 6:30 in the morning. William Wrigley would chatter about the problems of ruling a chewing gum empire. One of industry's first benevolent dictators, he built a company lunchroom for his employees, devised company life insurance schemes for them and offered them stock-sharing plans. His early-morning discourses on treating company employees as if they were members of the family did not fall on deaf ears.

After dropping out of Andover, Phil embarked on a world tour, one that gave him a chance to demonstrate that even if he hadn't inherited his father's brashness, he had inherited the elder Wrigley's acumen. During a stopover in Australia, he helped establish Wrigley's Australasia, Ltd., in Melbourne, the company's first —and one of its most successful—overseas factories. By the time he came home, Phil was a man, with his own idiosyncratic brand of individualism, and a quiet stubbornness that would cling to him throughout his life. He decided he wanted to study chemistry at the University of Chicago—one chemistry course only. The university told him to enroll as a four-year student. He did, then cut every class except the course he had enrolled for. When he flunked out at the end of the year, Phil Wrigley couldn't have cared less.

He enlisted in the Navy in World War I and discovered he had talent in his hands. He was a natural mechanic. He was put in charge of the aviation-mechanics school at the Great Lakes Naval Air Station. When he got out of the Navy, he continued to march to his own drummer. He developed a reputation for his skill at motorcycle riding, at gliding, at dice-throwing, even at cooking. (One of his proudest possessions is a card in the Cook and Waiters' Union.) His personality now different from, but equal to, his father's, he searched for new ways to exploit the business sense they shared. He decided that airplanes would someday play an important role in commerce. He invested in a tiny airline company that eventually became United Air Lines. In concert with Marshall Field, III, and Edsel Ford, he helped finance that airline's revolutionary all-metal airplane—the precedent-setting Ford Tri-Motor.

In the meantime, the elder Wrigley was enhancing his own reputation as one of America's most successful—and most controversial—tycoons. During the early 1920's, he built his $7,804,000 showpiece, the Wrigley Building. The site he selected was on Michigan Avenue, near the Chicago River, in a shabby neighborhood full of decrepit ma-and-pa groceries and delapidated dwellings. "Everyone thought my father had gone too far," Phil Wrigley recalls. "Everyone thought it was the wrong place for an office building." William Wrigley ignored the critics. He ordered his architects to install four enormous clocks, one on each side of his building's 400-foot tower, "so everybody within seeing distance in the Loop would turn to look to the Wrigley Building to find out what time it was." In an era when buildings were usually erected in each other's shadows, with space for only an alley in-between, he had his architects design a wide plaza. He ordered the side of his building to be coated with white terra cotta tiles. He had floodlights installed, some in parking lots behind the building, some as distant as the far bank of the river. At night, the floodlit terra cotta wall was visible from miles away. The thirty-two-story skyscraper soon became a Chicago landmark. Wrigley was asked to run for mayor of Chicago. He refused.

To promote his Santa Catalina Island, twenty-two miles off Los Angeles, William Wrigley staged a swimming race from the island to the California mainland, with a $25,000 first prize for the winner. One hundred and three swimmers entered. The publicity generated by the race gripped the entire nation. Newspaper columnists debated whether anyone could survive the 52° water temperature—colder even than the English Channel. Wrigley capitalized on the alleged danger. He stacked 100 barrels of hog lard and 200 pounds of axle grease on the beach so the swimmers could smear their bodies to keep warm. Midway between the California coastline and Santa Catalina, he stationed the steamship *Avalon,* converted to a floating hospital. He hired 300 small boats to shepherd the contestants. He made such a fuss, that President Calvin Coolidge ordered the U.S. Coast Guard to stand by, in force.

All the precautions proved unnecessary. The race was won by a seventeen-year-old Canadian, who, Wrigley insisted, had risked his life savings to enter the race, in order to buy his widowed mother a home.

In 1920, Philip Wrigley was named vice-president of the company his father founded. Five years later, at age thirty-one, he took over the presidency, with the elder Wrigley becoming chairman of the board. "I'm not sure I'm succeeding solely on my own merits," Philip said when he became president. "I have a feeling that 'pull' and the fact I'm my father's son had something to do with my election." With this modest disclaimer, he began to demonstrate how his sensitivity could be as effective as his father's boldness. In the midst of the Great Depression, while almost all other corporations were laying off employees by the hundreds, Phil Wrigley arbitrarily gave every one of his employees a 10 percent raise. He also guaranteed each employee a job.

In a further bid to give his employees security in the middle of the greatest financial uncertainty the country had ever known, he introduced a system of full insurance for his workers—twenty years before the labor unions won America's first guaranteed annual wage agreement. Employees earning less than $120 a week were guaranteed thirty weeks' pay per year, even if they only worked a day. "This assures an employee a definite income for a definite period, regardless of conditions beyond his control," Wrigley explained. "It is a backlog for him, just as the surplus of the company is a backlog for the stockholders. Since the surplus of the company is a backlog for the stockholder, it seemed right that he share some of this assurance with the employee." He asked his workers for one favor in return: to keep off the welfare rolls. "It is our idea," he said, "that any company in a position to do so should assume full responsibility of taking care of the people within its own organization, in slack as well as boom times."

He would treat his Cub fans and players with the same benevolence. In 1915, the elder Wrigley had begun investing in the Cubs. By 1925, he had acquired a majority of the franchise's shares. When his father died in 1932, Phil began to increase his personal investment. In 1933, upon the death of club president William Veeck, Sr. (the father of current White Sox owner Bill Veeck), Wrigley—unwilling to step into the limelight—allowed the presidency to go to William Walker. The following year, however, Wrigley bought out Walker and made himself president. "If you own the club," he said then, "you get the blame for what happens, whether you're president or not. So you might as well be president." In the next forty-one years, the Cubs would win the pennant only three times. The last time they won was in 1945, and then only because World War II had severely thinned the ranks of major league baseball. (After the team won the pennant, Wrigley spent three days at his desk, writing letters of explanation to fans who applied for tickets but didn't get any.) The Cubs' profits would be as dismal as their performance. They have lost as much as $902,000 in a single year; their stockholders haven't seen a dividend since 1948.

From the beginning, Wrigley established himself as an absentee owner, felt but not seen. In 1966, when his Leo Durocher–led Cubs brought baseball fans to ecstasy, then despair, with a startling pennant drive that stagnated in the heat of late summer, Wrigley —according to sportswriter Bill Furlong—"was placidly digging potholes. 'For two miles of fencing,' he says. 'A hole every ten feet. A thousand holes—and every hole we dug, we hit a rock or a root.' " On the rare occasion when he does attend a Cub game, he sits in the back rows of the grandstand instead of in his own box seat. "Haven't sat there since they put in an outlet for an electric blanket," he sneers.

Besides the demands of his chewing gum empire, friends point to a more deeply rooted reason why he avoids his ball park. When he does go, they say, ushers and photographers make a fuss over him, and he hates the publicity and the servility. "Besides," he himself says, "I can't hit, field or pitch. The only thing I can do is help out on the business side. If I go out there," he adds, "the best time is in the morning, because in the afternoon you can't find anybody to do business with. They're all out watching the game."

This urge for a low profile extends even to the "business side." Although he is the club president, and owns 8,015 of the franchise's 10,000 shares, Wrigley refuses to preside over the annual stockholders' meeting. He doesn't even attend the meeting. "My ambition," he once said, "is to go live in a cave somewhere, with no telephone, and a big rock over the door."

Wrigley's idea of a good time is to put on his overalls and get his hands dirty. In his spare hours, he invents new tools—a screwdriver, for instance, that can be locked in place and won't slip no matter how it's twisted. "I can remember when he had ten to twelve old cars—a Stutz Bearcat, a Scarab, a Cord, a Locomobile —stored away in machine shops and garages in his homes all over the country," says one of his chauffeurs, "all so he could work on them whenever he pleased." He keeps a garage and workshop behind the Chicago mansion he vacated years ago, and periodically he goes back to visit—not to see the house, but to see the 1957 Cadillac in the garage, the one with 1972 plates. "You can't park your car in an apartment," he says, "and you can't take it apart on the living room rug." Years before Detroit "invented" them, Wrigley's cars had automatic signal indicators, overhead cam shafts and automatic chokes. He always assigns the patents on his inventions to the mechanics who toil alongside him in his garages.

There is, however, one machine he dislikes to handle: the telephone. "He hates to return telephone calls," says his wife Helen, whom he married in 1918. (The Wrigleys have a son, William, now president of the gum company and vice-president of the Cubs, and two daughters, Ada Blanche and Dorothy.) "When he really *has* to make a call," Helen adds, "I'll do the dialing for him."

A tinkerer at home, Phil has been an innovator in the business world. When his researchers were unable to concoct a gum that wouldn't stick to false teeth (it was decades later before someone finally did), he told them to invent false teeth that wouldn't stick to his gum. When his marketing and advertising departments warned him that the name "Wrigley" was a tongue-twister in certain foreign languages, he told them to package the gum with the Doublemint or Spearmint Arrow on the wrapper, but without the brand name. "Sit back," he said, "and see what the people call it." In the Middle East, the gum became known as "White Arrow" gum; in Hong Kong, as "Rider of the Arrow" gum. Problem formulated, problem solved.

The problem put to him concerning mainland China, before the Communists took over, required the insight of an anthropologist. There were many different local dialects. Wrigley's marketing experts didn't know how to explain the important details of their product: that the gum came in single sticks, or in packages of five sticks, and that the cost depended on how many sticks you bought. They presented the problem to Wrigley. He mulled it over, then told his marketing men to manufacture the gum in long, un-wrapped ribbons. Storekeepers would hang up the ribbons. Customers would cut off strips of gum, just as old-time dry-goods stores hung up bolts of cloth and allowed their customers to snip off the quantities they wanted.

Wrigley became an innovator in baseball, as well. He designed a "gummed" belt for his ballplayers that prevented their jerseys from riding up. He designed new knee-length stockings that streamlined their uniforms by removing the bulk from the shirts and pants. Sometimes a penchant for the bizarre would peep through. Back in the 1930's, he quietly hired an "Evil Eye" to put a "whammy" on opposing teams during the height of a pennant race. According to Bill Veeck, who worked for Wrigley at the time, Phil paid the Evil Eye a first installment of $5,000, with another $25,000 guaranteed if the Cubs won the pennant. Even more bizarre than his hiring of the Evil Eye was the fact that Wrigley didn't do it for publicity. He ordered Veeck to keep the deal a secret from the press.

Other innovations were more far-sighted, if no more successful. At the start of the 1938 season, Wrigley hired Coleman Robert Griffith, director of the Bureau of Institutional Research, to study his ballplayers' reflexes. "We figured," says Wrigley, "if we could measure the physical characteristics and reflexes of an established ballplayer, we could test prospects and know what to look for. If you want to make the best knives in the world, you buy the finest steel. You can go out and spend $250,000 for a ballplayer, and he may not be able to cut butter. But if you know what makes a player who does come through in the majors, you have something. It's surprising how many players can play Triple A ball, but still not make it in the majors." His attempt to apply scientific principles to baseball was frustrated by the players, and by sportswriters. The players refused to cooperate with the psychologist. The sportswriters heaped so much abuse on the idea that Wrigley abandoned it. Later, Ewing Kauffman, owner of the Kansas City Royals, would try a similar technique, with some success.

A school for teaching baseball was another idea Kauffman borrowed from Phil Wrigley. In 1940, two decades before Kauffman opened his Baseball Academy in Florida, Wrigley was running a school at the Chicago Cubs' summer training camp, where youngsters, paying a daily fee, could learn the game.

He also anticipated the day—now upon us—when the courts would strike down the reserve clause that indentures players to specific teams. In the late 1930's, he had his staff work out an alternative to the clause. Then, at the start of World War II, he invented a testing ground to determine if his system of player control was workable. It was called the All-American Girls Baseball League, and Wrigley hoped it would become popular as a substitute for small-town baseball during the war years, when many male players were inducted into the Armed Forces. He dressed the girls up in a Forties version of the miniskirt. To make sure they looked like women, and not men in drag, he sent every girl for a course of instruction at a Helena Rubenstein school. The league failed after the war ended, and Wrigley's alternative to the reserve clause proved unworkable. But at least he had raised the question of player control, in an era when players were considered —both by their owners and by themselves—as little more than chattel.

In business, he had been an early proponent of automation and computerization. (He had, at the same time, designed a complex program to make sure his employees wouldn't be made superfluous by these new time-saving devices.) He then became the first to introduce the computer into baseball. Three decades before Clint

Murchison, Jr., began asking a computer to make his Dallas Cowboys' draft picks, Wrigley was feeding baseball statistics into a machine that coughed up punch-card analyses of who played best in any given situation.

Most of Wrigley's innovations, in business and in baseball (in Wrigley's mind the two were different spheres of activity), were designed not to make his organizations more efficient, but to make people happier and more secure. Soon after he took over the chewing gum company, he decided that people who reach the age of sixty-five are not necessarily senile, or obsolete. He devised a scheme which permitted his employees to keep on working after their sixty-fifth birthday. The only stipulation was that they take on-the-job training to prepare them for retirement. In their first year of "retirement training," they had to take one full month off from work; in the second year, two full months; in the third year, three full months. The schedule would continue until they were mentally prepared to take off the rest of their lives.

Wrigley has always been just as concerned about the nameless millions who purchase his gum. During World War II, when shortages of high-grade materials limited chewing gum production, the Wrigley company sent its entire output of Juicy Fruit, Spearmint and Doublemint to servicemen in the Armed Forces. To satisfy civilian demand back home, it manufactured a gum using artificial ingredients. But instead of advertising a product of inferior quality under the company trademark, Wrigley devised a new name—Orbit—and wrapping. Then he created a series of ads showing empty packages of Juicy Fruit, Spearmint and Doublemint, bearing the motto: "Remember This Wrapper." When the board of directors urged that the ingredients used in Orbit be used after the war in all Wrigley brands of chewing gum, he resigned as president of the company. Not until a new board was chosen—a group who promised to uphold the quality of Wrigley's chewing gum—did he consent to resume his position.

In everything he did, Phil Wrigley demonstrated an incorruptible integrity. On one occasion, he was eating lunch in the elegant restaurant in his Wrigley Building when a friend casually mentioned that the double-martini glasses did not hold twice as much liquid as a single. Wrigley was indignant. He ordered the head waiter to bring him two empty glasses. He poured water from one glass to the other. He found, *by God,* that a double *did* contain less than twice the liquid as a single. Wrigley marched up to the bar. He supervised personally while every double-martini glass was smashed on the spot, and replaced with authentic double double-martini glasses.

He makes sure his Cub fans get the same square deal. Years ago, he decided that the chairs in Wrigley Field's box seats were too narrow. He installed wider, more comfortable seats, even though this meant that each section now had eight seats instead of ten, cutting his box seat revenues by 20 percent. And he didn't stop there. He concluded that fans sitting in the box seats farthest away from home plate (down the first and third base lines, near the left and right field corners) had a better view of the outfield grass than of the action around the batter's box. "A man who pays for a box seat has a right to see the game without getting a pain in his neck," he announced. Then he backed up his words with a couple of million dollars. He had the concrete foundations for those box seats ripped out. He installed new seats, aligned on an angle, so that everyone sitting in a box seat faced home plate, not the outfield.

He mounted loudspeakers in the grandstands so that fans could hear the play-by-play chatter they enjoyed at home. At a loss of millions of dollars, he had the advertisements torn off the walls and scoreboards, then replaced with hundreds of clinging vines. When he discovered that batters were being blinded by the glare from white shirts in the center field bleachers, he shut down an entire section permanently, and had it painted green. His scoreboard was the first ever to flash the ball-and-strike count, to signal either "error" or "hit" on a controversial play. At the cost of further millions, he installed moving ramps to convey the lowest-paying patrons to the highest regions of the ball park. Worried about his pitchers' health on windy, cold days in spring, he tried wiring their warm-up jackets for heat. He introduced discounted tickets for women and children. He made tickets easily available to fans at every Western Union office in the city.

Unlike the owners who followed him into major league baseball, he was always willing to sacrifice a potential profit if the gain meant hurting the overall interests of professional baseball. "A

more honest and selfless man would be hard to find," says Bill
Veeck. "He's one owner who wouldn't hesitate to vote against his
own best interests if he felt it was in the interest of the game."
When the Boston Braves' owner, Lou Perini, wanted to move his
near-bankrupt franchise to nearby Milwaukee, Wrigley encour-
aged him, even though a National League franchise in Cub territory was sure to siphon off fans from his own team; Wrigley argued
that baseball needed to avoid another bankruptcy more than he
needed those extra customers. He fought for Walter O'Malley's
right to move his Brooklyn Dodgers to Los Angeles, even though
O'Malley would displace Wrigley's top minor league franchise,
located in that same city. In fact, Wrigley helped finance the studies
that proved the move feasible. Then he sold O'Malley his Wrigley
Field in Los Angeles. He believed firmly that baseball, to flourish,
had to expand to the West Coast. And for the same reason that he
favored Perini's move, and O'Malley's move, he protested vehemently—although privately—when the Milwaukee Braves' franchise was shifted to Atlanta. Even though that move was executed
by Bill Bartholmay, the son of an old family friend and neighbor,
Wrigley fought it bitterly. There was nothing, he argued, more
damaging to baseball than a rash of cynical franchise shifts, in
search of ever-increasing revenues. At a 1951 Congressional committee hearing to investigate baseball's antitrust restrictions, Wrigley incurred the enmity of his fellow owners by criticizing baseball's hierarchy and arguing that its monopoly should be shattered.

Ironically, despite his innovations on the field and in the
stands, despite his lack of self-interest and his overriding concern
for the well-being of his fans, one controversial decision would
eventually earn him the reputation of being baseball's most stub-
born, and stodgy, conservative: his refusal to install tower lights for
night games at his ball park. "You wouldn't like to live where you
have twenty thousand or thirty thousand people yelling and holler-
ing up to midnight every night," he says. Night baseball could have
reduced the Cubs' operating deficit substantially, but Wrigley was
more concerned with the quality of life around his stadium than
with his personal profit. "What we needed was good baseball," he
says, "not night baseball." He has ignored all pleas for him to
reconsider. Once sued by a Cub stockholder on the issue of tower

lights, Wrigley won the case in the Illinois Supreme Court, at the cost of $40,000 in legal fees. In 1962, the National League owners pressured Wrigley "to review your thinking in regard to night baseball," because competing teams might be disappointed with their receipts from dwindling Cub daytime attendance. His answer to them was: "Number one, I don't think lights are necessary. If you'll check the figures, I think you'll see that lights are just a novelty shot-in-the-arm. If you have a winning team, I think you'll draw as many people in the long run without lights. And number two," he added, characteristically, "we're in a residential neighborhood."

Wrigley has, of course, been less successful as a motivator than as an innovator. In 1935, his first full year as president of the club, the Cubs won a pennant. They finished second in 1936 and 1937, then won the pennant again in 1938 and 1945. It was all downhill from there. From the mid-1940's till the present, the Cubs have rarely been contenders in the pennant race. Wrigley has tried every strategem possible. He revamped and expanded the Cubs' farm system. He instituted a head coach system based on three coaches managing the team in rotation, instead of one omnipotent field manager. He hired one "field director" whose only claim to talent was his ventriloquism; when a Cub hit a pop fly to the infield, he would throw the words "I got it!" into the mouth of the opposing second baseman.

Then Wrigley reeled toward the opposite extreme. He hired one of the most fiery, and autocratic, field managers of all time to replace his rotating coach system. Leo Durocher took over the club in 1966, and by 1967 had turned the Cubs into contenders. But by 1969 it became obvious that all Durocher could do was postpone the Cubs' annual collapse, not prevent it. In 1969, the Cubs led the Eastern Division of the National League from opening day to Labor Day. Then, in the last few weeks of the season, they skidded from nine and a half games ahead of the New York Mets to eight and a half games behind. In 1971, as the season drew to a close, Wrigley took an ad in the Chicago newspapers defending Durocher against the cruel criticism leveled against him by his players and the press. Wrigley accused some of his ballplayers of failing to hustle. Then, without any warning, he fired Durocher before the start of the 1972 season.

Yet, in a way, being the owner of a losing franchise probably suits Wrigley's temperament. It's difficult enough avoiding the limelight when your name is carved into the most famous building in Chicago, when it appears on a ball park and on millions of sticks of chewing gum each year, without becoming the owner of a world champion baseball team. Phil Wrigley would rather stay at home than attend a World Series. He'd rather tinker with his antique cars. He'd rather make a batch of fudge for the Lake Geneva Garden Show and Bazaar.

"You can double the recipe if you want," he declares, summing up his philosophy of life as well as fudge-making, "but any more than one pound and it ceases to be *homemade* fudge."

◀ 2 ▶
The Founder

Seventy-four-year-old Art Rooney, Sr., is sitting in the back seat of a Cadillac, an Irish priest on one side of him, an Irish politician on the other. He's en route to an Irish wake in Pittsburgh's First Ward, where he grew up. Later this afternoon, he'll stop off at an Irish saloon, just like the one his father Dan started almost a century ago. This evening, he'll board an eastbound airplane to watch his Thoroughbreds run at Aqueduct in New York. Tomorrow, he'll be in Philadelphia, watching his trotters. His friends and his family may not know where he is, but they'll know where he's just been. He always writes post cards.

On Sunday, there's no question as to his whereabouts. No matter where his Pittsburgh Steelers are playing, at home or on the road, Art Rooney will be in the stadium, watching them from the owner's box. If they win, he'll be ecstatic. If they lose, he'll be inconsolable. It's always been that way. "I had this standing rule in my house when our five boys were growing up," he says. "Nobody was allowed to mention the Steelers for two days after we'd lost. That's how much it bothered me. I didn't want to read about it. I didn't want to see the films. I didn't want to have to have anybody tell me we gave it a good try."

29

The Rich Who Own Sports

In the forty-three years following his purchase of the franchise, that two-day gag rule was often in effect. Art Rooney's Pittsburgh Steelers lost almost as consistently as Phil Wrigley's Chicago Cubs. During thirty-nine seasons, from 1933 through 1971, their wins exceeded their losses only eight times. They didn't finish in first place until 1972. Yet, like Wrigley, Rooney never lost his enthusiasm, nor his loyalty to his players and fans. With his broad Irish face, his frosty white hair, a cigar propped between his lips and a laugh bubbling up at the least provocation, he endured to become the most beloved figure in all of professional football.

Art Rooney, Sr., has hardly altered his life style since he started his franchise in 1933. He and his wife Kathleen still live in the same three-story Victorian house at 940 North Lincoln, across the street from where he grew up. The area has deteriorated. The old Rooney house was torn down long ago. The saloons and one-family homes are giving way to parking lots and rooming houses. But Rooney stays on, clinging stubbornly, like Phil Wrigley, to the mores of another age.

Art Rooney was born in Coulterville, Pennsylvania. His father's family worked in a steel mill; his mother's, in a coal mine. Art's father, Dan, moved to Pittsburgh and opened Rooney's Saloon, soon the favorite haunt of the city's old-guard Irish sportsmen. As a boy, Art spent six days a week on playing fields with his six brothers. He spent Sunday in church. Sports gave him an identity in the neighborhood; the church gave him a sense of belonging in the universe at large.

After high school, Art attended Duquesne, Indiana State Normal and Georgetown, when he could manage to take time off from sports. Knute Rockne once invited him to play football at Notre Dame, but Art turned down the invitation. Baseball was Art's forte. "In the early 1920's, I remember playing for Indiana State Normal against Duquesne," he says. "It was the last inning, with the score nothing to nothing. I got to first base, then I stole second and third. Their pitcher was a big guy named Bevil Boone. Their coach was a priest I'd known for years, named Father McWiggin. Well, as soon as I stole third, the Father went out to the mound. 'Don't wind up,' he told Bevil, 'in case that Rooney decides to steal home, too.' Bevil listened, then he took a windup anyway. I stole home for the winning run. The Father," Rooney adds with a chuckle, "did not react with the vocabulary of a saint."

One Rooney anecdote is merely the prelude to another. "I used to run a team for the neighborhood kids," he says, "and one day I took them to play Duquesne High School. Duquesne had this priest who coached the high school team—sort of a mild-mannered fellow. They also had that same Father McWiggin, who had been a fine athlete himself, and now was coaching the Duquesne college team. Well, by the top of the ninth inning, we were losing. Then we got three boys on base, and I decided it was time to put myself in the line-up as a pinch-hitter. Now, immediately the mild-mannered priest becomes not so mild-mannered. He starts telling the umpire that I shouldn't be allowed to pinch-hit. But Father McWiggin, he says, 'Let the big bum hit. He can't hit, anyway.' Their pitcher gave me his best fast ball, and I hit that first pitch right out of the ball park. Father McWiggin never forgave me."

Rooney was a boxer, too. He defeated Sammy Mossberg, later an Olympic welterweight champion; twice he reached the quarter finals of the National AAU boxing championships, in the days when that competition was held in Boston's Fanueil Hall. "I could have gone to the 1920 Olympics," he says, "but instead I turned pro. In may first fight, I beat a kid named Joe Azevedo, on a Pinky Mitchell–Tommy O'Brien card in Milwaukee. Dick Guy, my manager, had ideas about matching me with Benny Leonard, the world professional champion. I never quite made it that far," he adds, "which turned out to be a good thing. The kind of wide-open brawler I was, I probably would have wound up with a few screws loose."

Rooney was also proficient at swimming, a skill that came in handy one memorable day when the future owner of the Pittsburgh Steelers almost drowned. He was seventeen, out for a romp at Exposition Park, where Three Rivers Stadium now stands, and where that particular day three feet of water still stood after a torrential rain. "Me, my brother Dan [who later became a Franciscan missionary in China] and a fellow named Squawker were paddling across the park in a canoe—the park was just sort of a big hole in the ground," Rooney says. "Well, this Squawker just wouldn't sit down, even though I kept warning him he was going to tip the canoe. Finally, he got the message. He sat down, but so clumsily, that he tipped the canoe. Squawker and Dan got their coats and boots off in a hurry. I got my coat off, but my boots stuck fast. So I had to swim all the way to the nearest bleachers, weighed down in back by my boots. It was a long swim, and for a while there I didn't think I was going to make it. I was almost right."

By his early twenties, Art was drifting toward politics, drawn both by aptitude and by environment. Rooney's Saloon was a focus of local political activity, particularly after one of those not-so-solemn Irish wakes, when the bigwigs on Pittsburgh's North Side would gather to drown their sorrow for the dead—and then celebrate the living. "Sometimes the mourners would get so happy from drinking, they didn't go home until the next day," he remembers. "One time, the wake lasted so long, we ended up just putting the deceased outside the door, in the street."

When the local members of the Republican party weren't congregating at his father's saloon, they were puffing cigar smoke toward the ceiling of his mother's living room. "Everybody came out to our house," Rooney says. "My mother never knew who we were going to bring home to dinner—and she didn't care, either. Sometimes she must have felt she was running a rooming house, except that she got paid in compliments instead of coin. We'd bring friends home overnight, and they'd stay a week. We'd bring friends home for a week, and they'd stay for a year."

Rooney became a ward leader, the right-hand man of State Senator James J. Coyne, Republican kingpin in Pittsburgh during the 1920's and 1930's, and it was in local politics that he first demonstrated the quality he would lavish on a hapless franchise years later: loyalty. "Art is a true-blue guy who will be with you when you die," said former governor David Lawrence, during his time in the White House as a Presidential assistant to Lyndon Johnson. "His deep loyalty to Senator Coyne when he was a leader on the North Side made a lasting impression on me. When Coyne was on the way out and the rats were jumping ship to join the Democrats on the way in, Rooney stuck with Coyne to the bitter end. That's the quality I admire most in a man."

Once, Rooney slipped out from the saloons and caucus rooms

to stand for elective office. The Republican party had asked him to run for the post of Registrar of Wills—a sacrificial Republican lamb on the altar of a predicted FDR-led onslaught. Rooney lost the election, but got the chance to put on public display another of the qualities that would endear him to generations of football fans and football players: a disarming candor. From the start, he told every crowd he addressed that he knew absolutely nothing about being Registrar of Wills; he didn't even know where that office was located. "But," he said, "if I'm elected, I promise to put someone in the job who *does* know what he's doing."

When Rooney wasn't playing some sport, he was promoting one. On Pittsburgh's North Side, being a promoter was only one step away from being a politician. Rooney was often called on to raise funds for a variety of campaigns; his particular expertise was raising money by staging semi-pro football games. Usually, a semi-pro contest featured either the Rooney Reds or the Hope-Harveys —each managed by the same Art Rooney. None of these encounters mimicked the martial precision that would later characterize the NFL. Once, for instance, Rooney's Hope-Harvey team was scheduled to face a semi-pro outfit named West View. To bolster his squad, Rooney hired the Duquesne football coach, Joe Bach, for $75. "Early in the first quarter," Art recalls, "we blocked a punt, and naturally that started a brawl. After a while, the crowd got into the spirit of the thing and poured onto the field, so instead of a fight we now had a riot. Well, Joe Bach decided that the game would never be finished. He was right. Bach walked off the field and went home. The next day, I sent someone to Joe's house to pay him his $75. Bach refused to take it, until my guy told him, 'Go ahead. The Hope-Harveys haven't finished a game yet!' "

In 1933, Rooney purchased his franchise in the struggling NFL, for $2,500. It didn't look like a particularly promising venture: franchises had already failed in Canton, Decatur, Hammond, Pottsville and Racine. But NFL operating costs back then were modest—around $125,000 a year. The league was informal, with the owners making rules and decisions on an ad hoc basis that would shock their modern counterparts.

"At one time," Rooney remembers, "the league had an executive committee of three, rotated among the owners, to screen proposed legislation before each league meeting. One year, Charley Bidwell [of the Cardinals] and George Marshall [of the Redskins] and I were on the committee, and we met in Chicago, just before the league meeting. As usual, Marshall had about a hundred proposals to make to the league. Charley and I agreed with every one of them, and we got finished in less than an hour. Marshall said it was a great thing that the league finally had a progressive executive committee. Charley and I just wanted to get out to the race track.

"We did," Rooney adds, "but the next day we met again with Marshall and just as calmly voted *against* every one of the things he had proposed the day before. And that was the end of *that* executive committee."

In the early days, Rooney ran his fledgling franchise from an office on the first floor of the Fort Pitt Hotel in downtown Pittsburgh. In a sense, the office was merely an extension of his father's saloon and his mother's living room. Political cronies and gamblers and priests would shuffle in and out, any hour of the day. The room had windows that opened onto the street. Rooney visitors were often the kind who preferred to enter and exit through those windows, rather than be spotted in the hotel lobby.

Pie Traynor, the baseball player, was one of Rooney's bosom cronies, and a regular at Rooney's regular nightly card games. When the franchise moved to a new office on the fourth floor, Rooney recalls, Traynor refused to show up any more. He was afraid—with some justification—that one night, in the heat of a card game, and flushed with alcohol, he might forget that the Steelers had moved up three floors, and exit to the street through a fourth-floor window.

"Once upon a time, I suppose, the Fort Pitt had been a high-class hotel," Rooney says. "My room on the first floor had windows that went up to the ceiling and down to the floor." There was, however, nothing "high-class" about the office's location. "I can remember guys rushing in, pulling down their flies, and me having to tell them that they had come to the wrong place—that the men's room was next-door."

Many of Rooney's most frequent visitors were those who sloshed daily through ounces of eau de cologne as an antidote to

The Founder

the fiercely clinging fragrance of stale oats and horse manure: touts and tipsters from nearby race tracks. Rooney himself was an expert handicapper, so good he actually supported his franchise from his winnings. In 1936, three years after he had purchased the Steelers' franchise (at first he called them the Pirates), he turned a couple of $20 tickets into a reputed $250,000 payoff in two days of betting —a Saturday at Empire City, and a Monday at Saratoga. And even in the epic mythology that grew up around his gambling exploits, there was room for a clerical collar or two. Once, leaving the track at Bowie, Rooney stopped his car to give a lift to a priest who was waiting for a bus. During the ride into town, the priest casually mentioned that all he needed to build the orphanage of his dreams was an additional $7,500. Rooney immediately took out his wallet and handed over that amount from his winnings. Another priest, upon receiving a $10,000 contribution from the Steelers' owner, said, "I hope you came by this money honestly." To which an indignant Rooney replied: "Of course, Father. I won it playing the horses!"

Rooney, however, denies all acts of charity except one. "I was at the races at Narragansett one day, and I happened to have a winner," he says. "I was coming away from the cashier's window when I noticed a little old lady dressed all in black. She was standing against a wall, crying baby tears. I walked over and said, 'Ma'am, are you ill? Can I do anything for you?' She turned to me, the tears streaming. 'No, sir,' she said. 'Nobody can help me now. I've lost my rent money and the medicine money for my little grandson who's lying there in our furnished room getting weaker by the minute with the whooping cough. I came out to the track praying that I would have a winner to buy medicine for the little tyke. But my horse lost by a lip, and now I don't know what to do. But it's all right, sir. Don't you mind. You're a fine gentleman, and you just go ahead and enjoy your winnings with a champagne and lobster dinner somewhere. I'll get by somehow.' Well, I reached into my pocket and pulled out a one-hundred-dollar bill. 'Take this, my dear lady,' I said. 'Pay your landlord and get the medicine for the little boy. Say a prayer, and I'm sure that some-thing good will turn up for you.' Well, on the way to my hotel, I was riding with a well-known tout and I told him the story. I

35

thought he would laugh himself to death. 'You've been taken by Winnie the Weeper,' he said. 'That old doll has been hanging around the fifty-dollar window and working that act with strangers for years.' "

Rooney shakes his head. "I still think the Weeper deserved the money," he says. "She put on a great performance."

It would be nearly four decades before his Steelers football team scaled an equivalent artistic plateau. Part of the problem lay in Rooney's own character. He usually left the coaching to others. He didn't roar like Chicago Bears owner George Halas, he didn't manipulate like Washington Redskins owner George Preston Marshall. Rooney's character—his generosity and kindliness—was the key to his success as a man, and to his one glaring failure as an owner: he didn't turn out winning teams.

The Steelers gave Johnny Unitas a perfunctory trial, then cut him. "Unitas is just too dumb," said head coach Walt Kiesling. Unitas was only one of many quality players the Steelers released over the years, including Bill Dudley, Byron "Whizzer" White, Lenny Dawson and Bill Nelson. The truth was, the coaches Rooney hired were often "just too dumb." It's not surprising, either. Rooney hired them for their conviviality, not their expertise. Johnny "Blood" McNally was a friend who became a head coach. One Sunday, in 1938, he was in Chicago, watching George Halas' Bears at Wrigley Field. Someone asked him why he wasn't with the Steelers.

"We're playing tomorrow," Blood said.

A few minutes later, the public-address announcer blared, "Final score: Philadelphia, 14; Pittsburgh, 7."

"On most teams," Rooney would later say, "the coach worries about where the players are at night. On our team, the players had to worry about the coach."

Now Art Rooney's five sons have assumed the day-to-day management of the family's sporting enterprises. Together, under the company named Ruanaidh (pronounced "Rooney" in Gaelic), father and sons comprise a total of ten different corporations. Art's second son, Art Jr. ("Artie") is president of the Penn Racing Association; Pat is president of the Green Mountain Park in Vermont and, along with his brother John, runs Liberty Bell Park in

Philadelphia; Tim operates Yonkers Raceway in New York and is general manager of the Palm Beach (Florida) Kennel Club, another of the family properties; Dan, the oldest, runs the Steelers.

It was Dan who hired Chuck Noll, the head coach who would finally lead the Steelers to two successive Super Bowl victories. He and Artie devised and implemented the Steelers' scouting operation—one of the most fruitful in pro football. Dan was born into the organization. At one time or another, while growing up, he performed every menial task extant in a football camp, from collecting socks and jocks to taking tickets. Like his father, Dan was once a promising athlete, a highly regarded high school quarterback. "I quarterbacked North Carolina High School the year we won the city championship," he recalls. "It was a big school, maybe one thousand boys. When the picks came out, I was second-team All-City. I was beaten out by a junior who quarterbacked a little school called St. Justin's. A kid named Johnny Unitas. My friends used to say, 'How can a guy from a little school like that beat you out . . . only a junior?'

"When I was a student at Duquesne, the Steelers practiced there in 1955, the year the Steelers drafted Unitas. I always used to watch practice to see how good Unitas was. He was pretty impressive. Actually, he looked great. Our club never gave him a chance."

As Art Rooney values friendship, so Dan Rooney values efficiency. "All this, the whole organization—my father really made all this possible for us," Dan says. "But I realize I'm going a different route from him. I really never felt I was the same as him. Maybe I never had the same desires or approach. I wanted to make my contribution differently.

"I believe in being businesslike. I think a person has to do his job, hold up his end. My father always worried about everyone's feelings—constantly. Sometimes it infuriated me. But that's just the type of person he is. He really worries about people. For instance, I'll tell the grounds crew that I want the field ready by game time, whether it snows or rains. He'll say, 'It's too bad it wasn't ready, they worked so hard.' I say get the job done and don't tell me about the problems."

"When we were looking for a coach in 1969," says Art Sr.,

"my boys, Danny and Artie, told me, 'When you pick a coach this time, put friendship on the bottom of the list.' It came down to Chuck Noll and Nick Skorich, and we talked to both and then we picked Noll. And, of course, Noll won."

Art didn't smother his sons, but he did demand respect from them—and got it. Once, he was out watching Pat, John and Tim play sandlot ball when Tim, then twelve years old, veered right as he crossed first base after hitting a single. "You're supposed to turn towards second," Art shouted, running over to his son.

"Aw, that's the way you old guys did it," Tim replied.

"Give me those balls and bats," Art roared. "I don't want people to know you're a Rooney!"

Art says he never watched them play ball again. "You'll have to ask them about their athletic abilities," he adds. "For this reason: I never thought much of 'em."

There was another confrontation about ten years later. Tim and John and their father drove from Pittsburgh to Winfield, Maryland, where the Rooneys' Shamrock Farms Thoroughbred stables are located. "My father would sit there in the car saying his rosary," Tim recalls. "He wouldn't talk to you, and he wouldn't let you turn on the radio, and he'd make you leave all the windows wide open in the middle of winter." By the time they arrived, Tim was plenty irritated, so when his father reminded him to take off his boots inside the house, Tim snapped at him. Immediately, Art gave Tim a slap on the head. "Then he turned to John," says Tim, "but John was on the track team—he ran." Both sons were in their twenties; Art Sr. was about sixty.

His sons may have taken the fun out of hiring head coaches, but Art still finds ways to be benevolent. For the 1974 Super Bowl, "the Chief" (as the Steelers call him) took not only his players to New Orleans, but his office personnel, the Three Rivers Stadium ground crew and the coaches' and players' wives. "Some coaches don't want the wives around," he said at the time, "but I never believed in that. I believe the greatest thing for a player is being with his family. I never thought if a guy was with his wife the night before a game that it bothered him. All he had to do was take a glass of milk and he was strong again."

Rooney divides his time between football and horse racing,

pausing in-between to receive awards at banquets. And if there isn't a priest within arm's reach, there's a story about one rolling off his lips. "I remember the Sunday Bert Bell got married," Rooney says. "My Steelers were going to play his Eagles. Well, there on the Eagles' bench is the priest who married Bell that day. It was just like Bell. Instead of giving the priest a free ticket in the stands, he had him on the bench where it didn't cost him even a free ticket. Anyway, that day the Eagles beat us on some lucky play, even though we'd had the upper hand throughout the game.

"The following week, I was there when the Eagles played the Giants—and I was astonished to see that Bert, who was no Catholic, still had this priest sitting on the Eagles' bench. Well, that Sunday, too, the Eagles were losing all the way, then won in the closing moments of the game on some stroke of luck. As soon as the game was over, I strolled up to that priest. Without telling him who I was, I said, 'Father, if you want to convert Bert Bell to Catholicism, you better do it this very week, because next Sunday the Eagles play the Bears, and even with the Pope next to you on the bench, the Bears are going to run the whole lot of you out of the ball park.'

"The next morning, I get a call from Bert. 'Hey,' he says, 'were you the one who went over and talked to my priest after yesterday's game?'

" 'I sure did,' I said. 'I was just trying to give him a piece of good advice, from one Catholic to another.'

"Well, Bert was mad for a while, but the priest thought I was a prophet. That next week, Halas' Bears did run the Eagles right out of the ball park."

Rooney's favorite priest was a man named Jack Slee. "One day in 1952," he remembers, "I was in my office when a girl comes in and says there's a Father Jack Slee to see me. I told her to send the Reverend in, and in comes a tall, good-looking fellow wearing a clerical collar. 'Father Jack Slee here,' he says. 'It's a pleasure to meet you, Mr. Rooney.'

" 'Likewise, Father,' I said. 'What can I do for you?'

"Father Slee didn't beat around the bush. He said, 'Mr. Rooney, I'm a real football fan, and a fan of the Steelers. Could I ask you for a very big favor?'

" 'I'll do what I can for you,' I said. 'What do you have in mind?'

" 'Mr. Rooney,' he said, 'some pro teams have chaplains, but not the Steelers. How about making me the Steelers' chaplain? Give me a tryout. Let me sit on the bench for the Giant game.'

"Now, I went to Catholic schools and have met a few priests in my life. Somehow, Father Jack Slee didn't have the kind of priestly manner I had been accustomed to. So I came right out with it and said, 'By the way, are you a Roman?'

"Jack Slee looked me in the eye. 'No, Mr. Rooney,' he said, 'I am not a Roman, I am an Episcopalian. Does the fact that I'm an Episcopalian mean I can't sit on the Steelers' bench?'

"Well, I told Jack Slee that I was as broad-minded as the next man. It was possible for a man to be both an Episcopalian and the chaplain of my football team. He'd be very welcome to sit on our bench for the Giant game. I didn't go any further than that. Well, Jack Slee was so happy, he started thanking me over and over, saying he wished there was something he could do for me. He was so grateful, I kind of had to ease him towards the door before he started giving me an Episcopalian blessing.

"The following Sunday, Father Slee sat on the bench—and he brought us the best piece of luck we ever had. Playing in the snow at Forbes Field, we gave the Giants the worst licking in their history, sixty-three to seven. Steve Owen, the Giants' coach, came over to me after the game. 'What got into your guys today?' he said.

" 'Why,' I said, 'we got a chaplain. You didn't have a chance.' "

Rooney pauses, his eyes turning inward to a simpler era when owners and players felt like fathers and sons, when a team with God on its side could perform miracles. "Y'know," he says, "we might have won the championship that year, except that Jack Slee was transferred to Los Angeles. He showed up on the bench as chaplain of the Rams.

"And Jack Slee and the Rams beat us, twenty-eight to fourteen."

In summing up his father, Dan Rooney says, "I think what Dad wants most is to be known as a humanistic man. He tries to think of everything in its relation to people. Money doesn't mean that much to him. He tries to be good to people rather than a good businessman or a successful club owner."

"I would rather have Art Rooney's word," said the late Ben Lindheimer, who owned a string of race tracks often frequented by Rooney, "than any other man's bond."

And the word is "loyalty."

"No," Rooney says, "I never thought of moving the club, or selling the club. None of us were ever looking to get out. We were all in the game because it was our life, something we truly loved. When you love something, you don't just walk away from it. After all," he adds, "Pittsburgh is my home. The Pittsburgh Steelers are my team."

Wrigley, the rich one . . . Rooney, the poor one . . . Wrigley, the aristocrat, educated at elite private schools . . . Rooney, the ward-heeler educated in saloons and on the street . . . Both would survive into the 1970's, the last disciples of the personal touch, symbols of an era that, in retrospect, seems innocent.

◀ 3 ▶
The Old New Yorkers

In 1925, Tim Mara, owner of the football Giants, went to Charles Stoneham, owner of the baseball Giants, and asked for a lease on the Polo Grounds. Stoneham agreed, and for the next thirty years the two teams shared the same playing field. In time, Horace Stoneham succeeded his father, and Jack and Wellington Mara succeeded theirs. It seemed certain there would always be two teams of Giants at the Polo Grounds: one owned by a Mara; the other, by a Stoneham.

Then gales of change began to blow, and, unlike Phil Wrigley and Art Rooney, the Maras and Stonehams came unstuck. First the football Giants moved a few miles across the river to Yankee Stadium (1956). Then the baseball Giants, following the lead of Walter O'Malley's Brooklyn Dodgers, moved 3,000 miles across the country to San Francisco (1958). A few years later, the Polo Grounds was demolished to rubble.

Those winds of change pursued the baseball and football Giants relentlessly. In 1974, Wellington Mara announced that he was moving his franchise again, this time across the Hudson River to a sporting complex to be constructed in a New Jersey swamp. At about the same time, Horace Stoneham, grown old and discouraged in wind-swept Candlestick Park, began selling off his assets. He sold his real estate, he sold some of his most cherished ballplayers. Finally, in 1976, a victim of a world he no longer understood, he reluctantly and regretfully sold the Giants franchise itself. Only a few months later, Mara's football Giants began playing their home games in their Hackensack (N.J.) Meadowlands Stadium.

Of the old football team owners, Charley Bidwell and Bert Bell and George Marshall are now dead; Art Rooney and George Halas are easing out of pro football and into retirement. But, aside from Rooney and Halas, one NFL owner still worships the old values—loyalty, fatherliness—even though they often seem out of sync with the attitudes of his fellow owners and his own players. That's why Wellington Mara felt so troubled one day in 1971. He had been devoting a lot of time to affairs of state—the transfer of his New York Giants franchise at some future date to that municipally owned stadium complex in New Jersey. Deep inside, he felt he was letting his Giant fans down. He didn't really think of them as fans, anyway; they were second cousins, invited for a nominal fee to come and visit with the Giant Family on Sundays. And he was worried about his players, too. He felt like a papa who'd been spending too much time at the office lately; he was afraid that the "boys" in the locker room were getting restless. So he called into his office a big thirty-two-year-old defensive end named Bob Lurtsema. Lurtsema was the one the players had chosen to speak to Papa Wellington when, for example, they wanted an increase in their annual allowance, or to stay up an hour later than usual.

"Bob," Mara said, "I want you to make a survey among the players. I want to know how the players feel about me and what they feel about the Giant Family image."

Lurtsema was astonished, but Mara seemed so disturbed, so preoccupied, that he agreed to poll the players. Over the next week, he approached each member of the Family, and got each to express a sentiment. Then, on a Tuesday afternoon at one o'clock, he went back to Mara.

"He asked for an honest report, and I gave it to him with both barrels," says Lurtsema. "I told him, 'You have no rapport with the players, and the Giant Family image is not there.' He was crushed when I told him. I wasn't trying to hurt the guy, but to tell him the truth he asked for. He sat back, maybe asked me a couple of questions, and then shook my hand and said, 'At least I know you gave me an honest answer.' "

That handshake meant not only "thanks," but "goodbye." At 4:30 that same afternoon, defensive end Bob Lurtsema was placed on waivers.

Some owners motivate their players with slogans and status symbols. Others use tyranny to prevent their players from becoming complacent. Wellington Mara wants to be their father—an Old Testament father, however, who rewards loyalty with love and disobedience with revenge. The coordinates of his mind were set back in the era of Phil Wrigley and Art Rooney. He perceives pro football through a fading frame in some late-late movie, where Notre Dame football players in leather helmets still slog through the mud to win one more for the Gipper, and an athlete would rather have a beer in his hand than a breast.

Mara was nine years old when his father, Tim, bought the New York franchise for $500 and founded the Giants. He can still recall standing outside of church after Mass, and hearing his father comment: "Today's the day we see if professional football can go over in New York."

In this one memory are fused the two most influential symbols in his life: his father, Tim, who built the franchise; and the Catholic Church, which gave Wellington a secure road map to Heaven, with no detours or dead ends. With Mara, as with Rooney, football and Catholicism are inseparable. Until recently, he lived in suburban White Plains, a block or so away from Archbishop Stepinac High School. "When the school was built," he says, "a lot of Catholic doctors with large families moved there." The doctors soon became Giant fans, occupying thirty seats in Section 5 of the Yankee Stadium mezzanine. Once, when a friend warned Mrs. Wellington Mara against attending a Giant game in her advanced stage of pregnancy, she replied, "I'm better off in the stadium. We have everything right there—an obstetrician, a pediatrician, a dentist, an internist, a heart surgeon, a chief of surgery and an anesthetist. And in case they fail," Mrs. Mara added, "there are always a couple of priests around."

The Rich Who Own Sports

When Mara met his wife, Ann, she was working for the Jesuit Missions. One day at Mass in the church of St. Ignatius Loyola, they literally bumped into each other when both rushed to the aid of an elderly lady who had fainted.

Throughout the years, Mara—like Wrigley and Rooney—avoided the ostentation characteristic of the newer breed of sports owner. "Ours was a sporting courtship," Ann Mara says. "While all my friends were at the Stork Club, I was at the Fordham gym." When someone suggested that Wellington hung out at P.J. Clarke's (a mecca for New York's sporting crowd), St. Patrick's Cathedral and the exclusive New York Athletic Club, Mara replied, "I've been to Clarke's maybe four times in my life, which is more than I've been to St. Patrick's."

The fifty-two-year-old Mara rises daily at 6 A.M., then attends early-morning Mass, where he regularly receives communion. Afterwards, in the off-season, he'll spend a full day at the Giants' office in New Jersey—taking time out before a light lunch for a workout at the New York A.C. During the regular season, he'll put on his sweatsuit and run laps while his players are practicing. On game days at the Old Yankee Stadium, he sat in a small booth that hung like the bubble on a bomber from the upper stands, around the fifty-yard line. He took Polaroid pictures of the opposing team's formations, then shared that intelligence data with the crew of assistant coaches huddling with him. If the analysts spied something in one of the photos, he pulled out an old sweat sock weighted with football cleats, inserted the photograph and dropped the sock bomb down to the Giants' bench, a couple of levels below. "Actually," Mara insisted, "I just sit up there to stay out of trouble." No one believed him.

Nighttime usually finds him at home. Once in a while, he'll accompany one of his ten children (six girls and four boys) to Madison Square Garden for a Knick game. Once in a while, he and Ann will attend the theater; musical comedy is their favorite. Like Rooney and Wrigley, Mara has retained most of the friendships formed in his youth, "loyalty" being the most cherished word in his vocabulary. Four times a year, he has lunch with Jimmy Dolan, a retired radio executive who regularly met for lunch with Wellington's older brother, Jack. "Since Jack died, we keep it up," he says.

The Old New Yorkers

"A spring, summer, winter and fall luncheon."

Mara's romance with football began when he started attending Loyola, a Jesuit school at 83rd Street and Park Avenue, right across from the Mara home. He won friends at Loyola, and later at Fordham University (a Catholic college), by giving away tickets to the Giant games. Reinforcing this intermingling of God and the Gipper, one of his classmates at Fordham was a Block of Granite named Vince Lombardi, who himself would become a pope in a practice jersey.

In 1937, when Wellington graduated from Fordham, his father Tim, the bookmaker, wanted him to study law, as his brother Jack had. "I had skipped fifth grade," Wellington says, "so I said to my father, 'Let me have this year with the team.' " Tim agreed to let Wellington postpone law school for a year—and Wellington postponed law school for life. In that one year with the Giants, he found a vocation as compelling as the priesthood. "All of the fellows were my age," Mara says. "I was close to them, part of them. There was an entirely different atmosphere in pro football in those days."

And it is with those days still shimmering before his eyes that he peers at the present. Nostalgia is Mara's incurable affliction. He can cough up Giant highlights with the retrieval rate of a computer. He remembers when all the players stayed at the Whitehall Hotel on Upper Broadway, with coach Steve Owen installed in the penthouse—when he wasn't taking the day off to play a round of golf. Boarding a jet with his team, he recalls those interminable train rides, during which players had time to get to know each other and, through poker, each other's weaknesses and strengths. He reveres all these cameos.

Mara became, along with his brother Jack (now deceased), an owner of the Giants through a legal technicality. In 1928, Tim Mara obtained a bank loan to help finance Al Smith in his campaign for the Presidency. Tim thought that after the campaign the loan would be repaid out of the coffers of the Democratic National Committee. But when Smith lost the election, the Democrats denied ever having made such an agreement. The bank took Mara to court and won its case, but it failed to collect a penny. In the interim, Tim had transferred everything he owned, including the

49

Giants, to a corporation composed of his blood relatives, with son Jack the president, and son Wellington the secretary of the Giants.

Over the years, no matter whether the Giants' prospects were bleak or bullish, Mara—like Wrigley and Rooney—never surrendered the trappings of that simpler era when football players had more neck than hair creeping out of their helmets, and a win on Sunday meant God was on your side. Rooney had his Father Jack Slee. Father Benedict Dudley has been a fixture in the Giants' stadiums since a day in 1932 when a friend of Tim Mara's saw him standing in line for a bleacher ticket and handed him one for a box seat right on the 50-yard line. Eventually, Father Dudley became known as the offensive priest, with Father Kevin O'Brien (a professor of physics at Fordham) the defensive priest.

It was with reluctance that Mara rejected, in 1971, New York City's offer to move his Giant football team back into a refurbished Yankee Stadium. But even a renovated Yankee Stadium couldn't match the facilities offered to the Giants by Sonny Werblin.

In 1963, Werblin had purchased the New York Titans of the AFL and renamed them the New York Jets. As head of the Music Corporation of America, Werblin knew the value of a good entertainer when he saw one. He outbid everyone for the services of a quarterback from Alabama named Joe Willie Namath, and the future of the league was secured. Werblin went on to become a major investor in horse racing—owning, among other stalwarts, Silent Screen. In its third start, the horse won $336,075 in the Arlington-Washington Futurity. When a friend asked Werblin, "Would you rather own Namath or Silent Screen?" Werblin replied, "I'd much rather own the horse than Namath. Silent Screen has four good legs." Now, in 1971, the ex-owner of the Jets and current chairman of the New Jersey Sports and Exposition Authority was going to build, for a total cost of $50 million (the figure would later swell to over $300 million), a sports complex that included a 76,000-seat stadium and a race track for Thoroughbreds and harness horses, in time for the Giants' 1976 football season.

Mara's alleged "desertion" of New York City for a home across the Hudson River was generating strong criticism. New York *Post* columnist Larry Merchant (long a thorn in Mara's psyche, having coined, then defined, that special brand of paranoia called "Maranoia"), writing about the shift to New Jersey, concluded with: "This son of a bookmaker. . . . What else can you expect from an *Irishman* named Wellington?" Since criticism from any quarter stings Mara, he issued, in mid-1971, his only public rebuttal ever—at a welcome-home luncheon, with all the Giant Family in attendance.

"I'll tell you exactly what you can expect from an Irishman named Wellington whose father was a bookmaker," he said in a voice thick with emotion. "You can expect that anything he says or writes may be repeated aloud, in your own home, in front of your children. You can believe he was taught to love and respect all mankind—but to fear no man. And you can believe that his two abiding ambitions are that he pass on to his family the true richness of the inheritance he received from his father, the bookmaker—the knowledge and love and fear of God.

"And second," he added, in a tone just as pious, "that the Giants win the Super Bowl for Alex [Alex Webster, the Giants' head coach] and for you."

Many in Mara's audience had a hard time throttling their laughter. Had Art Rooney been among them, he would have had a hard time keeping back his tears.

In 1919, one year before pro football's Founding Fathers met in Canton, Ohio, a former California copper mine pick-and-shovel man named Charles A. Stoneham purchased the New York Giants of baseball's National League, in partnership with a New York City magistrate named Francis X. McQuade and the team's famous manager, John J. McGraw. Stoneham's son Horace grew up like Tim Mara's son Wellington, incurably addicted to the franchise. The Giants' locker room was his nursery; the Polo Grounds was his schoolyard. When the elder Stoneham died in 1936, Horace, then thirty-two, succeeded him, becoming the youngest club president in baseball history. With Calvin Griffith of the Minnesota Twins (the ex–Washington Senators), Stoneham would eventually become a living fossil: an owner who owned nothing but his team and cared for nothing but the game of baseball; an owner whose emotional investment in his franchise meant more than his financial investment.

The Rich Who Own Sports

He would become an anachronism, yet there was a time when he had his share of success—at the box office and on the playing field. Overall, his teams would win one divisional title, five league championships and a world championship. He was an astute judge of managerial talent. In his father's day, he recommended the selection of John J. McGraw's successor, Bill Terry, who led the Giants to a world championship in his first year. In 1948, he lured Leo Durocher away from the rival Dodgers. At Durocher's prodding, he regretfully traded away, in 1949, a roster of stars including Sid Gordon, Johnny Mize, Willard Marshall, Walker Cooper and Buddy Kerr—to make room for Eddie Stanky and Alvin Dark, who, under Durocher, produced the winning teams of 1951 and 1954. He developed a system of scouts and farm clubs that uncovered, then nurtured, future superstars like Monte Irvin, Willie Mays, Willie McCovey, Juan Marichal and Orlando Cepeda, plus a host of near-superstars like Sal Maglie, Whitey Lockman, Bobby Thomson, Larry Jansen, the Alou brothers, Gaylord Perry and Bobby Bonds.

But even back in the 1950's it was becoming increasingly difficult for Stoneham to find owners he could relate to among the beer barons and lawyers and bankers who were infiltrating the board rooms of the major leagues. Unlike Walter O'Malley, the Dodger's owner who served as broker in Stoneham's disastrous marriage with the city of San Francisco, Stoneham was shy, a loner —as much a fan as an owner. Baseball was more than a living; it was his life.

"Horace is loyal beyond the point of good business," Durocher once said. "Personal sentiment never should enter into a baseball judgement, but with Horace it always does. He feels sorry for the run-of-the-ball-park player and rookies that aren't earning big money. Sometimes he's paid them incredible salaries when he could have saved all sorts of money." Stoneham gave Bill Rigney a salary of $18,000, equivalent to $60,000 today, at a time when Rigney wasn't even playing regularly. But there was something about him that Stoneham liked. Later, he hired Rigney as his manager, and cried when he felt compelled to fire him.

"I think it was 1949 when Sid Gordon, one of Horace's all-time favorite players, held out for $30,000 and Horace got him down to $27,500," Durocher recalled. "All year along, Horace fretted about that, fearing that Sid would think he'd been cheated. Just before Christmas, he called the Gordon home and asked Mrs. Gordon what she wanted for Christmas. She told him that since their family was Jewish, they obviously didn't observe the holiday any more than to send cards to Christian friends. Horace told her that this was one year she was going to get a Christmas present. She laughed and told him she didn't think that was going to happen." On Christmas morning, 1949, Gordon received a check from Stoneham for $2,500—even though he'd been traded in the autumn and was by then a member of the Boston Braves.

"He couldn't stand getting rid of a player," Durocher added. "When I was the Giants' manager, Horace was always talking about getting some guy or other back because he missed him after he'd been traded away from the Polo Grounds. I had to beg him to break up that great group of home-run hitters he had assembled in New York in the 1940's. They could only hit the ball. They couldn't do anything else, so they were always in the second division. Horace didn't want to get rid of any of them. The deal for Al Dark and Eddie Stanky that made us a contender just about broke his heart."

The deal that brought the Giants from the Polo Grounds in the Bronx to Candlestick Park in San Francisco finally did break Stoneham's heart. At first, the Giants were idolized, drawing 1,800,000 in their opening season. But it was plain from the start that the stadium's site and design were disastrous. Swirling bayside fogs often turned a ball game into a farce. At 3 P.M. each day, icy Pacific winds would blow in over Candlestick Point, chilling the enthusiasm of the spectators. Despite the fact that the park cost $32 million to build and another $16.5 million to rebuild, Candlestick remained mostly unloved, and mostly vacant.

The Giants did manage to win a pennant from the Dodgers in 1962 (and almost a world championship). When the news of the final out reached San Francisco, ecstatic fans bombarded the financial district with confetti, then performed a snake dance down Powell Street that paralyzed the cable cars. While Handel's *Hallelujah* blared majestically from the organ in Grace Cathedral, in a nearby saloon a tipsy and attractive hooker swore she'd donate her "services" gratis for an entire weekend to the Giant who drove in the winning run against the New York Yankees in the World Series.

By 1967, however, the Giants' attendance had slipped to 1.2 million. In 1968, Charlie Finley moved his franchise from Kansas City to Oakland. The Bay Area couldn't support two major league teams. Faced with declining attendance at the box office, and diminishing productivity from his players on the field, Stoneham began to suffer the same heavy financial losses he had suffered in the Bronx. In 1973, for the first time in modern memory, the Giants paid no dividends. Stoneham started selling his minor league franchises. He chopped his operating budget by some $300,000 a year. He shipped out aging but popular players like Willie McCovey and Willie Mays and Juan Marichal, saving $650,000 but further alienating his fans. By the end of the 1975 season, the Giants were drawing only 519,991 customers—the lowest total in either league. Stoneham told his board of directors that he was willing to sell his interest not only in the Giants, but in his Minneapolis and Arizona real-estate ventures as well.

Yet even when his participation in baseball was nearing the end, when his ball club was suffering heavy and consistent financial losses, Stoneham's guiding principle was sentiment, even more than savings. During the years when Willie Mays was a Giant, Stoneham treated him with tender, loving care. Afraid that Willie wouldn't be able to adapt to life outside baseball after his career was over, Stoneham gave him a contract calling for $50,000 a season for ten years following retirement. The reason Stoneham sent him to New York near the end of his career was that Mrs. Joan Payson's Mets were a healthy franchise and would be able to fulfill that ten-year contract.

He was just as devoted—too devoted to be a good businessman, say his critics—to the old cronies he relied on for both counsel and companionship. In 1974, he called in the head of his speakers' bureau, Walter Malls, age seventy-eight, and his public relations director, Garry Schumacher, age seventy-four. Tearfully, he told them that because of his financial difficulties they would have to retire—at half-salary, for the rest of their lives.

Stoneham was one of the last specimens of an endangered species. Economics left him cold. But, year in and year out, win or lose, the game of baseball paid him enormous psychic rewards.

◀ 4 ▶
The Forty-Niner

Only two decades ago, Chavez Ravine was a barren gully, its tenants some undernourished goats, and squatters huddling in squalid shacks. That was in the Fifties, when the universe was fixed and immutable, and America had forty-eight states and sixteen major league baseball teams. The Giants were in the Bronx. The Dodgers were in Brooklyn.

Walter O'Malley shook that universe and, in the process, turned Chavez Ravine from a publicly owned liability into a privately owned bonanza. In 1957, nearly 110 years after hopeful thousands had trekked to California in a desperate search for gold, he set off a second emigration. He led westward a caravan of Brooklyn Dodgers and their hand-picked playmates, the New York Giants.

The key to Walter Francis O'Malley's character is buried in the rocky, infertile soil of County Mayo, Ireland, a region so impoverished that its inhabitants never utter "County Mayo" without adding "God help us!" County Mayo men are known for their gregariousness, their conviviality, their hospitality—and the sudden palsy that afflicts them whenever it becomes necessary to hand over their hard-earned currency. Walter O'Malley, born on October 9, 1903, was the only son of Manhattan politician Edwin J. O'Malley, himself the son of a County Mayo man. Walter would demonstrate time and time again the love for money, and the reluctance to part with it, that made his ancestors as renowned for their tightness as the most miserly Scotsman. He would wear drab ready-made suits. His wife, Kay, would forgo jewelry and furs. There would be no housekeepers to care for their five-bedroom Alpine-style chalet, built 100 yards from the shore of Lake Arrowhead in the San Bernardino Mountains.

Walter O'Malley's father was the New York City Commissioner of Public Markets, wealthy enough to send Walter for a year of prep at Culver Military Academy after he graduated from Jamaica High School. At Culver, Walter had his first and last fling as a baseball player. He caught a fly ball on his nose. He quit the game forever. Graduating in 1922, he entered the University of Pennsylvania and shunned athletics to become the complete politician. "I believe he was the first man ever to become president of both his junior and senior class," says a fellow member of the Theta Delta Chi fraternity. "It was typical of him that although he didn't dance, he ran the dance classes—and he made money out of them."

Walter graduated with honors in 1926, and enrolled at Columbia University Law School. Then the Depression tripped up his father. "Our family circumstances were above average," he recalls. "My father had been successful. I remember when I was graduated from engineering school at the University of Pennsylvania, he gave me a boat that slept eight. But the stock market crash caught him, and financially he never recovered." His father was no longer able to afford the tuition at Columbia. Walter switched to the law school at Fordham University and attended at night. By day, he worked as an assistant engineer for the Riley Drilling Company.

After graduating from Fordham Law School in 1930, Walter got engaged to Kay Hanson, his high school sweetheart. Pretty and shy, Kay developed cancer of the larynx. In one of the first successful operations of its type, her larynx was removed. Kay was never able to speak again. Walter saw no reason to alter their plans, but his father angrily forbade the marriage. "She's the same girl I fell in love with," Walter insisted. In defiance of his father, he married Kay in 1931. They would raise a close-knit family of two children —Terry, now forty-one, and Peter (who currently runs the Dodgers on a day-to-day basis), now thirty-nine.

The couple began life in the very heart of the Depression. Stockbrokers were swooping out of windows on Wall Street like stunned pigeons. Well-bred matrons who only a few years before had queued only for bargain sales at Saks Fifth Avenue were now queueing in soup lines. "A lot of professional people were selling apples on street corners at the time," Walter recalls, "but I was fortunate in building up an active law practice, handling mostly bankruptcies." Soon he was senior partner in a firm of twenty lawyers. He set up his own engineering firm and earned more than $50,000 (then an enormous sum) in the first year. In 1932, he became a director of the Brooklyn Borough Gas Company. He started chain-smoking cigars. He learned to take two solemn puffs before he answered a question, especially when he was tempted to answer, "Yes."

In 1942, O'Malley was hired as the Dodgers' attorney. (The appointment was as much a testament to his political connections as his legal expertise; the man whom he succeeded was Wendell Willkie.) Almost immediately, O'Malley began to buy up Dodger stock. In November, 1944, he helped to organize a syndicate consisting of Branch Rickey, the late John L. Smith and himself. The syndicate purchased 25 percent of the Dodgers, and less than half a year later it bought 50 percent of the outstanding stock.

If there was anything at all that O'Malley found unpleasant about baseball, it was his association with Rickey. O'Malley was a fun-loving type; Rickey was both a teetotaler and a profanity-hater. The two men never got along. "I'm no psalm-singing Methodist," explains O'Malley, the Roman Catholic, "but I don't know as I ever did anybody any real harm. I'm not knocking Branch for his beliefs; in fact, I've known plenty of daily communicants in my religion who spent the rest of the day thieving. But we never felt we had to apologize to Branch for anything that took place."

Few people were surprised when the showdown came. In 1950, O'Malley and Mrs. John L. Smith bought out Rickey's stock. O'Malley became president, Rickey resigned as general manager.

Critics, Jackie Robinson among them, would later point out that Rickey built the franchise, and O'Malley profited from it. "In the good years preceding 1958," O'Malley says, "I was accused of being a big man on a team that Rickey built. Then, in 1958, when we finished seventh, the team suddenly became mine."

To replace the man who had built the Dodgers into champions (and the St. Louis Cardinals before them), O'Malley hired two vice-presidents: Fresco Thompson, who had directed the Dodgers' farm system, and Buzzi Bavasi, who had managed the Dodgers' Montreal farm club. Fresco was a wit, an old-time infielder with a shrewd eye for talent. Bavasi was a street-smart native of New York City, as comfortable in a seedy billiards parlor as a plush board room. Neither man was immune to the pleasures of alcohol. Their lips, from time to time, formed four-letter words. Now, with power in his hands and cronies he could relate to in the front office, O'Malley turned his attention to more complex problems.

From the very beginning, Ebbets Field had filled him with horror. "We had a ball park in Brooklyn that was over-age," he says. "We had parking facilities for only seven hundred cars. If we wanted to have thirty-two thousand fans in the stadium and we could park only seven hundred cars, a lot of fans would have to come by foot or by subway. Yet subway fares were already falling off. Fewer people were riding the subways because they were riding in automobiles—and we couldn't park them. That was one factor.

"Another factor was the high cost of maintaining our old ball park. We'd patch up one thing, and something else would need attention."

A third reason for his dissatisfaction was the changing social composition of Brooklyn itself. Slums were spreading, towing in their wake the disenfranchised and the destitute—blacks and Puerto Ricans. Critics claimed that the spectators at Ebbets Field, home of the Dodgers since 1913, were beginning to resemble the customers at cockfights. Some fans, it was alleged, were urinating in the aisles.

As far back as 1947, when he was still only a minority stockholder, O'Malley commissioned an engineering firm to design a new stadium with a revolutionary dome. "It was treated facetiously by the press," he says. "But why should we treat baseball fans like cattle? I came to the conclusion years ago that we in baseball were losing our audience and weren't doing a damn thing about it. Why should you leave your nice, comfortable, air-conditioned home to go out and sweat in a dirty, drafty, dingy baseball park? Ball parks then were almost all old. They were built in the poorer sections of the city. The toilets at most ball parks were a germ hazard that would have turned a bacteriologist gray. Why, when I came to the Dodgers, I spent a quarter of a million dollars just to change the urinals, and Branch Rickey, who was general manager, nearly had a stroke. He couldn't comprehend spending that much money on the customers when we could spend it on ballplayers."

But even more pressing than the condition of his dilapidated ball park, or the social composition of the neighborhood around it, was O'Malley's concern for the Dodgers' long-range profitability. Although in the early 1950's the Dodgers were drawing a million paying customers a year, and operating at a profit, he was frustrated by the example of an owner who was doing twice as well. "Yes," he said then, "we are drawing a million people a year, and the Milwaukee club is drawing *two million* people. There's a difference of one million in attendance, right? Lou Perini [who in 1952 had moved his Boston Braves to Milwaukee] is a wealthy man. He is not looking for dividends. If he draws a million people more than we do, at an average admission of two dollars, he has two million dollars a year more to put into his organization for things like absorbing farm club losses, for salaries in the front office, salaries to players, bonus money to attract new players, scouting and all of that.

"Anybody—even a child in public school—can realize that if that disparity between the two best draws in the league, Milwaukee and Brooklyn, is permitted to continue, it will be only a question of two, three, four or five years before Milwaukee will be the Yankees of the National League and Brooklyn will be in Washington. In five years," he warned, "the Perini Braves will have ten million dollars more to spend in baseball than us. They certainly will have a lock on the pennants."

Five years later, of course, the Milwaukee Braves—despite Perini's money—had slunk off to Atlanta, a futile and battered franchise. Still, in the mid-Fifties, Perini's success was a compelling argument for O'Malley. It gave his constant and strident petitions for a new facility a patriotic fervor that no local politician dared to resist. No one wanted to go on record as having helped the Braves outdo the Bums.

Brooklyn was then infamous for the allegiance of its fans, a passionate attachment formed during the decade 1947–1956, when "the Bums" won six pennants, lost out on two in the playoffs, and finished as low as third only once. By 1957, that fabulous team was getting tired, it was getting old. Jackie Robinson, the pioneer, had retired. Captain Pee Wee Reese had lost a step at shortstop. Through hypnotism, pitcher Don Newcombe had conquered his fear of airplanes, but though Newcombe now flew, his fastball didn't. Duke Snider was hobbled with a chronic knee injury, Roy Campanella was paralyzed with a broken neck. And there were no replacements waiting in the wings. Still, the loyalty of the Dodger fans never wavered. Even O'Malley was infected by the passions aroused by the Bums. When someone had the gall to suggest that the nickname had an adverse psychological effect on a team that showed signs of soon playing like bums, O'Malley replied: "I can't lend myself to any squeamish campaign which has as its objective the demise of The Bum. So far as we in Brooklyn are concerned, the lovable little fellow is here to stay. Besides, most of us take ourselves too seriously. It's good for our souls to be lampooned now and then. And one of these days The Bum will have the laugh on everybody again."

The Dodgers weren't merely the heroes of the hoi polloi in the bleachers. They were the darlings of the society figures in the boxes. O'Malley recalls the saga of the late Mrs. I. W. Killam, a lady of fabulous wealth thanks to a husband who made a vast fortune in paper and timberlands. Shortly after O'Malley became president, the widow Killam fell in love with the Dodgers. She attended every home game. Then one day, during spring training, she invited O'Malley, his wife Kay and O'Malley's friends to visit her for cocktails and dinner at her winter home in Nassau, off the coast of Florida. O'Malley accepted the invitation. That very afternoon, he loaded the Dodgers' airplane with as many of his friends as he could round up at a moment's notice.

The Forty-Niner

"It was just the best party I ever saw," he says. "There were so many servants, they outnumbered the ice cubes. Mrs. Killam kept telling one and all about her great devotion to our ball club. Then, in the manner of a charming hostess putting her guests at ease with small talk, she remarked, 'Mr. O'Malley, would you consider an offer of five million dollars for an interest in the team?'

"I was astonished, to say the least. I promptly dropped my drink in the lady's lap. Servants came running from all directions, but Mrs. Killam just acted as if nothing at all had happened. Finally, I recovered from my embarrassment. I told her that I was very sorry, that there was no Dodgers stock presently available. I added that if there ever were stock available, she would be the first to know.

"One day, later on, the same dear lady went to a Giant game," O'Malley continues. "Her arrival at any ball park in New York spread through the grapevine of ushers and attendants even before her chauffeur had time to shut off the motor. She tossed money around so freely that after a while the ushers started regarding a ten-dollar tip as a sort of rebuke for poor service.

"Well, this particular day at the Polo Grounds a young Giant pitcher was pitching a great game. I forget who it was. Along about the eighth inning, he had a two- or three-hitter, and at that point our lady friend pressed a month's income into an usher's hand and asked that Mr. Horace Stoneham be summoned to her box.

" 'Mr. Stoneham,' she said, 'that pitcher of yours is a very attractive young man.'

" 'We consider him to be a promising prospect,' Stoneham said.

" 'What would he be worth to you if you were to sell him?' she asked.

"Stoneham said, 'Well, I have no intention of selling him, but that boy is so promising that I would put a price of possibly seventy-five thousand dollars on him. Maybe one hundred thousand.'

"Mrs. Killam said, 'All right, I'll take him.'

"Stoneham was flabbergasted. He blurted out, 'What do you mean—you'll *take* him?'

65

The Rich Who Own Sports

"The lady drew out her checkbook. 'I'll buy him from you,' she said. 'I'll write you a check right now, for one hundred thousand dollars.'

"Well, Horace was horrified. He said, 'Madam, we do not sell our ballplayers to individuals. I'm sure I don't know what you have in mind, but if you're looking for an escort or a dancing partner, I suggest you look elsewhere.'

"Mrs. Killam looked at Stoneham with absolute loathing. Then she said, 'Mr. Stoneham, I am in no way interested in escorts or dancing partners. I was interested in buying your pitcher as a gift for my friend, Walter O'Malley. He needs pitchers in Brooklyn. Good day, sir!' "

O'Malley got the laugh on Stoneham, and not for the last time, but the New York press were laughing at O'Malley and his "absurd" notion of a domed arena. At that point, in the early 1950's, O'Malley had no idea of building his stadium anywhere but in Brooklyn. He would be content, he said, with the land around the Long Island Railroad station, at the west end of the borough. He knew that the ancient terminal had already outlived its usefulness; it was surrounded by slums that no one would miss, not even the tenants, and the nearby Fort Greene meat market was long overdue for relocation. All he asked was that the city condemn the site, then sell him the land for a pittance. In March, 1955, Owner O'Malley stepped aside for Democrat O'Malley. The politician's son, and Brooklyn powerbroker, had no trouble converting officials of all political persuasions to his cause. The state legislature pushed through a bill setting up the Brooklyn Sports Center Authority. Governor Harriman, whose sports expertise peaked at polo, appeared in person to sign the bill at Borough Hall in Brooklyn, declaring: "I am a Dodger fan." O'Malley could now relax. Almost every conceivable stumbling block had been cleared from his path —except that human "Great Wall of China" called Robert Moses. Moses had very definite ideas about what New York City did and did not need. Walter O'Malley's proposed stadium was, in Moses' mind, an utter expendable.

Before the Sports Center Authority undertook the complicated business of condemnation, O'Malley raised a substantial amount of cash as his share of the venture. "We offered to build the park with our money if the city would provide the site," he says. "To show we meant business, we sold our real estate at Ebbets Field, Montreal and Fort Worth." He sold Ebbets Field for $3,000,000 to a real-estate operator named Marvin Kratter, and signed a lease for the Dodgers to play there for three years more. He sold his Montreal park for $1,000,000, and disposed of his Fort Worth park for another $1,000,000. "In total," he recalls, "we took in five million dollars. So I said to Mr. Moses, the New York Parks Commissioner, 'We've got the money. Now what's the delay?' "

Moses never gave him a satisfactory answer. He let his actions speak for him. While O'Malley was busy rounding up cash and collateral, Moses was busy making sure the Sports Authority died on second. The Long Island Railroad site faded into improbability; politicians suggested other sites, but none of them satisfied O'Malley's criteria. "It was one thing after another," O'Malley says. "One site was between a cemetery and a large body of water. I pointed out that we weren't likely to get many customers from either place. Then they tried to shift us from our site in Brooklyn to Flushing Meadow in Queens. We finally agreed to look at that. But then we decided that going to Flushing Meadow was no different, in a sense, from going to Jersey City or Los Angeles. You would not be the Brooklyn Dodgers if you were not in Brooklyn. And as long as you're going to move, what difference does it make whether you move five miles or five thousand miles?"

It would have made a difference to Phil Wrigley and Art Rooney; it even made a difference to Wellington Mara—moving to the marshlands of New Jersey was a far cry from moving his Giant Family to California. And it definitely made a difference to the New York sportswriters. The slightest hint that O'Malley might leave the city sparked emotional outbursts on the front pages of every local newspaper. Sportswriters wept pints of printer's ink at the thought that O'Malley might "betray the Borough of Brooklyn." The Borough of Brooklyn, O'Malley replied, was already betraying him.

At the winter baseball meetings of 1956, O'Malley conferred with his old friend, Phil Wrigley. He explained his problem—and proposed a solution. He wanted to buy Wrigley's Pacific Coast League franchise in Los Angeles. "I wanted to bring the New York

situation to a head," he admitted later. "I wanted an anchor windward." A few months later, O'Malley announced that Wrigley had
agreed to sell, setting off the noisiest baseball controversy since the
Chicago "Black Sox" scandal: Would the Dodgers really jilt
Brooklyn for the West Coast? O'Malley's critics were convinced by
then that he would, provided someone handed him a large tract of
land ribbed with gold.

Still, O'Malley played coy; just because he had bought the
minor league franchise didn't mean he had definitely decided to
shift the Dodgers to Los Angeles. He insisted that he would remain
in Brooklyn if he could. But between the time he spoke to Wrigley
and the time he announced the deal, he had already visited Los
Angeles. He hardly wasted a glance on the small (23,000 capacity),
antiquated Wrigley Field, where his newly acquired Angels played
their home games. "Absolutely no facilities for parking automobiles," he announced. "Also, in the upper stands there isn't a single
ladies' rest room. You cannot operate a major league franchise
today unless you are very aware of the comfort requirements of
men, women and children."

There was, however, a site that seemed as exciting as Wrigley
Field was depressing. O'Malley visited the sleepy goat pasture
called Chavez Ravine, just north of the heart of the city. He saw
four freeways funneling cars in every direction around the vast
acreage. Publicly, he didn't utter a word. Privately, he bid farewell
to Brooklyn.

Next, Los Angeles Mayor Norris Poulson set about converting Walter's "anchor to windward" into a permanent mooring. In
1957, he formed a posse of the leading officials in his city government and trailed O'Malley to the Dodgers' training camp at Vero
Beach, Florida. Now, spring training always put O'Malley in a
euphoric frame of mind. The weather was warm, the mistakes of
the previous season forgotten. Every morning, O'Malley would rise
early and take breakfast with the team in the big community dining
room. Then he would make a quick trip to the greenhouse at
McKeen Jungle Gardens, where he kept some young flower plants.
A horticulturist and landscaper, O'Malley planted towering palms
in a straight row outside his ball park in Vero Beach. He dug for

artesian wells, creating a beautiful lake which he promptly stocked with fish.

First-time visitors were often favored with a tour in O'Malley's gasoline-powered golf cart. With one hand on the wheel, and the other waving his cigar like a pointer, O'Malley would describe the innovations he had designed, meanwhile astounding the visitor with a roll call of exotic facts—a combination of *Poor Richard's Almanac* and Ripley's *Believe-It-Or-Not.* "You say you have gophers in your backyard?" he might ask, as the visitor passed the hundreds of Navaho willows O'Malley planted around his ball park. "I'll tell you what to do. Get yourself a bunch of white Leghorn chickens. They'll spot the gophers right away and take to roosting in the trees. Then, every time a gopher pokes his head out of a hole, these white Leghorns will pounce on him. There was this fellow who built a castle on one of the Thousand Islands," he would add. "Found the island infested with rattlesnakes. Brought in some white Leghorns and they cleaned out all the rattlers in no time. Now the island is overrun with white Leghorns."

Or else some sight or sound along the tour—a Latin ballplayer speaking Spanish, for instance—might evoke the memory of those unforgettable statuettes he once saw in Mexico City, figurines carved by the mysterious Mayans. "Why, it was the most amazing thing I ever saw. There were baseball players, running, fielding, batting. And—get this now—there was the unmistakable figure of an *umpire.*"

This, undoubtedly, was the Walter O'Malley whom Mayor Norris Poulson met that memorable day when he appeared at the Dodgers' training camp: the garrulous storefront raconteur, the cracker-barrel extrovert—the County Mayo man who regarded every dollar lost in business as an affront to his honor.

Up to the time O'Malley became president of the Dodgers, in 1950, for example, that club's training camp was renowned for its sumptuous dinner menus. Then food prices began to soar, and so did O'Malley's costs. He decided that the children of some players and writers were being wasteful; they weren't eating all they ordered. Privately singling out one offender in particular, the thirteen-year-old daughter of a well-known writer, he posted a sign announcing that no children under fourteen would be permitted in the dining room. The next year, the sign read: NO ONE UNDER 15 ALLOWED IN THE DINING ROOM."

Even the summer sun couldn't warm O'Malley's arctic core. When Mayor Poulson began to wave his arms wildly and spout promises, O'Malley interrupted him. With all the sentimentality of a process server, he handed him a sheet of paper detailing the long list of his demands. O'Malley wanted the 315 acres of Chavez Ravine, but only if the city was willing to make extensive—and expensive—improvements. He wanted Los Angeles to grade the land and build access roads. He wanted the work done quickly. If the city rehabilitated Chavez Ravine to his specifications, he would build a stadium, and was even willing to pay one dollar a year rental on a couple of consecutive ninety-nine-year leases, as long as the property was exempted from real-estate taxes.

A few months later, O'Malley went west again. He was greeted by a welcoming motorcade, escorted through streets bedecked with Dodger pennants. Then he met with Mayor Poulson's brain trust. Point by point, Poulson's aides either rejected O'Malley's demands or substituted demands of their own. "The thing got more and more confusing," O'Malley says. "I finally asked, 'Well, who's the big guy out here? Who do I have to deal with?' "

The answer was: No one. As gangster Mickey Cohen once wailed, when asked who got the political payoff for a syndicate operation in Southern California: "There's no politics in Southern California you can deal with. It's anarchy."

O'Malley began to feel beleaguered on all sides. Back in New York, he couldn't open a newspaper without getting mugged by a journalist. And some of his fellow owners in the National League were complaining bitterly that a franchise in California would make their travel costs exorbitant. The Mayor's men were telling him to tone down his demands, there was already a grass-roots campaign growing to prevent what his critics called a "Chavez Ravine giveaway." O'Malley decided he needed reinforcements. He started looking for an ally. He decided to regroup, recruit new forces and war on two fronts, conducting a two-pronged assault on San Francisco and Los Angeles. If his troops could capture San

Francisco by installing a major league ball club there, traveling costs in the National League wouldn't be so prohibitive. Furthermore, the will of the Los Angelenos—faced with being outflanked by their Northern rivals for glamour—would wither. The only problem was, San Francisco didn't have anywhere near the promise of Los Angeles as a site for major league baseball. What O'Malley needed was an ally.

He needed Horace Stoneham.

At that point, Stoneham was headed for Minneapolis, where there was a ball park waiting for him. "I wanted him in San Francisco," says O'Malley, "so I could turn our interborough feud into an intercity feud. I spoke to Horace and said, 'Do you think you're going to the best location?' When I told him he would do better in San Francisco, Horace was dubious about the kind of ball park he could expect San Francisco to provide. So I asked Mayor Christopher, the mayor of San Francisco, to fly to New York, and when he arrived I sat them down in a room at the Lexington Hotel. Neither Stoneham nor Christopher was clear about what kind of agreement was necessary. So I took an envelope out of my pocket. On the back of it, I wrote out the terms for what became Candlestick Park.

"But remember, I wasn't the one who convinced Stoneham to leave New York in the first place. He had already made that decision. All I did was suggest he had a better chance for success in San Francisco than in Minneapolis."

Even though Stoneham's announcement of his decision to leave New York was made before the 1957 season, it did not spark the hysteria among sportswriters that O'Malley's revelation did later that year. "I think that most of the writers realized that Horace's position was untenable in New York," O'Malley says. "It was almost impossible for him to operate successfully at the gate. On the other hand, the Brooklyn franchise had been successfully operated. I think, too, that the writers were more or less reconciled to the loss of one club in New York. I think they would have been satisfied to have New York reduced to two, the Yankees and the Dodgers. But they never reconciled themselves to just one club, the Yankees."

The Rich Who Own Sports

With Stoneham signed up for the one-way excursion to California, O'Malley had no trouble obtaining the league's permission to move: two clubs in California made travel expenses much cheaper than a single franchise. But O'Malley, even by the end of the 1957 season, had not been able to reach an agreement with the city officials in Los Angeles. Every time he sat down with them, the promised acreage shrank. He surrendered the oil rights in Chavez Ravine; he surrendered any oil deposits that might be lurking under Wrigley Field; eventually, he surrendered Wrigley Field itself. And when finally he did wrench an agreement from the Los Angeles city council—he would get the land virtually free and virtually in perpetuity, but he would pay real-estate taxes—he was ambushed by an opposition movement backed by an oil tycoon named John A. ("Black Jack") Smith. "Black Jack" and his brother wanted to see minor league baseball survive on the West Coast. Not coincidentally, they were the owners of the San Diego Padres, then the leading West Coast minor league franchise.

The opposition had just thirty days to collect 52,000 signatures on a petition to force a referendum on the Chavez Ravine ordinance. In any other state, the task would have been formidable; in the California of the 1950's, for a small fee, collectors could buy all the signatures they needed. The anti-O'Malleys obtained 53,000 signatures—for, according to *Time* magazine, the bargain price of $19,000. But in Walter O'Malley they were dealing with an adversary of the highest order. O'Malley had political heavyweights in his corner. Just how closely he rubbed shoulders with the great and near-great of national politics is illustrated by the story he still likes to tell about the time John F. Kennedy almost became his partner.

"Back in 1950," he recalls, "Jack Kennedy's father made inquiries about buying stock in the Dodgers, a controlling interest if he could get it. At the time, I had just twenty percent of the stock.

"Anyway, it seemed that Joe Kennedy was worried about Jack's health. Jack was then a freshman Congressman, and his back was giving him a lot of trouble. Joe Kennedy said he had high hopes for Jack in politics, but he had begun to wonder if the boy was up to it physically. He said Jack was fond of baseball and, if politics was out, he might like to run a ball club. Joe Kennedy said he was ready to meet anybody's price for a controlling interest, with the idea of putting Jack in as club president.

"Then, while things were still in the early talking stage, North Korea invaded South Korea. Truman sent in troops, the Chinese came in, there were wild rumors out of Moscow, and Joe Kennedy decided that World War III was upon us. He called off everything and predicted that soon there wouldn't be any baseball at all.

"Years later, I saw Jack Kennedy at the White House. I said to him, 'Mr. President, just think. You might have been president of the Brooklyn Dodgers instead.' He laughed and said, 'Walter, there are moments when I wish I were.' "

Proof of O'Malley's political clout, the contract for Chavez Ravine was approved in 1958, although his victory margin was a scant 26,000 votes in a 676,000-vote plebiscite. Much of the opposition stemmed from the contract's generous terms. According to that intricate agreement with the city and county of Los Angeles, O'Malley rented the Los Angeles Coliseum and gave the city Wrigley Field in payment for the 215 acres in Chavez Ravine. He agreed to build the 56,000-seat stadium, and to develop a 40-acre youth recreational facility, but, by the terms of the contract, the city and county would shoulder much of the cost of excavations, land fills and access roadways. In all, preparing Chavez Ravine for the stadium meant moving 7,860,000 cubic yards of earth—one explanation for the building cost's escalation from an estimated $12 million to an eventual $20 million, much of which was paid by local government. Lawsuits and landslides delayed the completion of the project almost three years beyond the original plan. By the time the stadium opened in April, 1962, the new L.A. Angels of the American League were looking for a place to play. As tenants at Dodger Stadium, they would add $200,000 annually to Walter O'Malley's coffers for every million customers they drew, until they built their own stadium at Anaheim.

But even at the Coliseum, a stadium structurally unfit for baseball, it was clear from the start that O'Malley had struck it rich. In their first two years in Los Angeles, the Dodgers drew more than 3,900,000 customers. In nine of the next sixteen years, they would draw over 2,000,000 customers. By the end of 1975, the

Dodgers could boast the highest attendance figure in all of major league baseball (2,271,846). That same year, Horace Stoneham's last full year as owner of the franchise his father had founded, the San Francisco Giants had the lowest figure (440,473).

In every sourdough saga, there's a winner and a loser. Walter O'Malley found his mother lode. Horace Stoneham panned only fool's gold. By the beginning of the 1976–77 season, Stoneham had departed from baseball—the eerie wind in Candlestick Park howling his sad epitaph.

◀ 5 ▶
The Outsiders

In 1959, outdoor sports were still the preserve of the inheritors and the founders. The Halases, Rooneys and Maras still controlled football, and the Stonehams and Wrigleys were struggling manfully against newcomer O'Malley, who had owned a team for only nine years. But while these familiar faces were still prominent at center stage, a new breed, with new ideas about owning a sports franchise, were clamoring from the wings for recognition. Their determination, their cleverness and, most of all, their money would help revolutionize professional sports over the next decade.

Two of the earliest of these interlopers were, fittingly enough, born and raised in Texas, a state that has never lacked the prerequisites for a successful pro franchise—an almost fanatic devotion to sports at every level and an abundance of eager multimillionaires capable of enduring early losses. In Texas, the incest between enormous wealth and overt political power is often blatant. A millionaire is likely to have as much political clout as cash. He can float public bond issues to finance a new stadium. In an otherwise "dry" county, he can obtain a permit to serve liquor in his Stadium Club.

In 1959, two Texas millionaires in particular, both from Dallas, were trying desperately to buy into the National Football League. Clint Murchison, Jr., was thirty-five years old, a formidable business tycoon with a mathematics degree from the Massachusetts Institute of Technology and an engineering degree from Duke. He and his brother, John Dabney Murchison, two years older, had inherited both wealth and a solid education in finance from their multimillionaire father, Clint Sr., a spendthrift who reportedly once said, "Money is like manure. Spread it around."

Lamar Hunt was twenty-six years old, a graduate of Southern Methodist Unioversity. He and his two brothers and two sisters had also inherited both wealth and a solid education in finance from their multimillionaire father, H.L. Sr., a skinflint who reportedly once said, "Money is nothing. It's just something to make bookkeeping convenient."

The Murchison brothers worked together in Dallas, John specializing in finance, insurance and publishing, while Clint Jr., concentrated on real estate and construction. By 1959, they owned or directed enterprises worth more than $1 billion. In other words, by 1959, the Murchisons were the second richest family in Texas— second only to the Hunts, whose total fortune was estimated at more than $2 billion.

Besides their enormous wealth, the two young Texans had in common a love for sports in general and a desire to bring professional football back to Dallas. Clint Jr. had been a 126-pound halfback at MIT. In 1952, he bought twenty season tickets to support the short-lived Dallas Texans of the NFL. When in midseason that franchise foundered, Clint offered to take it over, but the syndicate of hard-pressed Texan owners felt they couldn't afford to wait while he studied their books. In 1954, he arranged to purchase the San Francisco franchise, but one party in the transaction backed out and the deal collapsed. Throughout 1956 and 1957, he negotiated unsuccessfully with George Preston Marshall, owner of the Washington Redskins. Marshall was willing to sell, but with one proviso: Clint would have to guarantee him an executive position with the new franchise. Clint turned to NFL commissioner Bert Bell for advice. Bell told him to negotiate with the Wolfner family, who owned the Chicago Cardinals.

Lamar Hunt had been just as devoted a supporter of the

Texans. Like Clint, he was a frustrated football player, having made an attempt to play college ball at SMU. Like Clint, he thought Dallas could sustain a pro franchise. The problem, he and Clint agreed, was that the Texans' owners had expected too much profit, too soon. In 1957 and 1958, Lamar talked to NFL commissioner Bert Bell about another franchise for Dallas. Bell told him what he had told Clint: to negotiate with the Wolfners.

It didn't take Hunt long to discover that the Wolfners were a dead end. Engaged in a struggle with George Halas' Chicago Bears for the minds and money of Windy City football fans, the Wolfners talked to prospective buyers only in hopes of acquiring either new support for their franchise in Chicago or of driving up the price of the Cardinals. They had no intention of allowing either Texan to ship their football team to Dallas.

Then, one day in early 1959, Lamar Hunt was flying back from Chicago, after a final abortive attempt to convince the Wolfners to sell, when suddenly an exciting idea occurred to him. The Wolfners had boasted that many wealthy sportsmen around the country were interested in purchasing their Cardinals. Why not, thought Hunt, create a new league that would offer pro football to this host of willing millionaires, in major cities untapped by the NFL? In his quiet way, Hunt began to make detailed plans. On August 14, he stunned the NFL establishment by revealing the formation of his American Football League, with franchises in Dallas and Houston.

One-upped by his rival, Clint Murchison intensified his efforts to obtain an NFL franchise in Dallas. In his behalf, he had the enthusiastic cooperation of George Halas, the Chicago Bears' owner, who had his own reason for wanting Dallas in the NFL. Halas wanted the Cardinals out of Chicago. By helping sway hesitant NFL owners in favor of expansion, he could force the Wolfners to move their financially troubled Cardinals—or else face the possibility that choice cities would be claimed by either the fledgling AFL or the expanding NFL. It was no coincidence that 1960, the year the NFL agreed to add two new teams, found the Cardinals playing in St. Louis.

In league with Art Rooney, Halas was finally able to convince even the Wolfners that it was in the NFL's best interest, and in the interest of every individual owner, to expand the league from six-teen to eighteen teams. Only one stumbling block remained—the irascible George Preston Marshall, who was afraid that a franchise in Dallas or Houston might siphon off TV revenues from the South, which his Redskins desperately depended on.

Then George Preston Marshall got a divorce, and Clint Mur-chison got the opportunity he had been waiting for. When Marshall and his wife separated, lawyers divided up the couple's assets. The two parties were informed as to the general provisions of the settle-ment, but the lawyers didn't tell either one the disposition of every trivial item. After the divorce, Marshall's ex-wife, Corinne, discov-ered that she had been awarded the rights to the Redskins' fight song. Fight songs rate well below diamonds and minks at the appraiser's, so when the society bandleader who had composed the song asked to have it back, Corinne sold it to him for a nominal fee. Somehow, Murchison learned of the transaction. Through a business associate named Benny Briskin, he acquired a part interest from the bandleader. Then he telephoned George Preston Mar-shall.

After the usual icebreakers—about the weather, about the family—Murchison reportedly asked Marshall, with all the inno-cence he could feign, if the Redskins expected a substantial crowd that weekend. Marshall replied that he anticipated a big turnout. Murchison asked Marshall if he intended to have the Redskins' band there, entertaining that fine crowd. Marshall replied in the affirmative. Then Murchison asked him if the Redskins' band in-tended to play the Redskins' fight song.

"They sure will," replied Marshall.

"The *hell* they will," Murchison reportedly said. "Nobody plays *my* fight song without my permission!"

A short time later, on January 28, 1960, the National Football League voted (with the consent of George Preston Marshall) to create two new franchises, one in Houston—and one in Dallas. Murchison had obtained his NFL franchise, literally, for a song.

Murchison, his brother John and Bedford Wynne, their busi-ness associate and a member of the prominent Wynne family of Dallas, paid $50,000 for the franchise and $550,000 for players to be drawn from existing teams. The NFL could begin operating in Dallas at the same time as the AFL.

Even more intriguing than the clash between rival leagues was the personal rivalry between Hunt and Murchison. Superficially, their backgrounds were strikingly similar. Both were still young, incredibly rich, heirs to two of the largest fortunes in Texas. Yet the contrasts between them were even more sharply drawn. Each man resembled his own father, and the Texas oil fields never produced two men more unlike than H.L. Hunt, Sr., and Clint Murchison, Sr.

H.L. Hunt, Sr., began his career in 1921, in a gambling house in El Dorado, Arkansas. Using a $50 bankroll, he won an oil well in a poker game. He parlayed that oil well into his Hunt Oil Company, the largest independent petroleum producer in the world. During World War II, Hunt Oil held more petroleum reserves than all other *nations* put together. Right after the war, in 1946, when a strike closed Eastern coal mines, Hunt supplied 85 percent of all natural gas shipped from the Southwest to ease the fuel shortage. Hunt held leases on billions of oil-producing acres in Kuwait and Libya. He also owned ranchland worth $200 million, with 9,000 head of cattle and 12,000 sheep on a single ranch near Cody, Wyoming. His assets included timberland, factories, citrus groves, one of the largest pecan farms in America, food-processing plants and drug laboratories.

And yet, all his life, Hunt prided himself on his contempt for the baubles money could buy. He made his views explicit in his careless dress and decrepit automobile. He trimmed his own hair. He carried his lunch to the office; a guest invited to join him was apt to be served an egg sandwich and a glass of milk, with a piece of white typewriter paper for a napkin.

Hunt's only use for money, outside of making more money, was to wager it. He employed a graduate of MIT as a full-time statistician, to compute the odds on his various bets. He placed those bets through a special communications system, installed in his office, which connected him with the major horse tracks and bookmakers around the country. In the opening game of the 1956 World Series, according to a Dallas friend, Hunt bet on the Yankees over the Dodgers—an error in judgment that cost him a cool $300,000. "Hell," he grumbled irritably, "a whole day and a half's pay!"

At age forty-three, Lamar does not share his father's passion for gambling, but he does cultivate the elder Hunt's contempt for lavish spending. The elder Hunt trimmed his own hair; Lamar trims his own hedges. A habit of having holes in his shoes has led acquaintances to label Lamar, like his father, an eccentric. In the den of his house, beside his 1970 Super Bowl trophy, rests a battered old walking shoe. "That was given to me by a friend, Buzz Kembie," Hunt says. "He had it silvered for me after we climbed a mountain together in Wyoming. I guess he thought it was a first, that I'd actually retired one of my shoes. But I had to. Look at it." The beautifully silvered shoe has four beautifully silvered holes.

The fact is, Hunt says, he wasn't brought up to regard himself as rich, or money as something to be worshiped. "When I was a kid," he says, "I wasn't exactly unaware that we had money, but it didn't impress me. I knew we lived in a big house, and the yardman or the cook used to drive me to school sometimes in our Plymouth and I was embarrassed getting out in front of my classmates. But money was no big deal. If I wanted a little money, I just asked my mother and generally she'd let me have it. It doesn't sound like I was too well-trained, does it? I would have been a lot harder on me than my mother was."

Hunt was born in El Dorado, Arkansas, and brought up in Dallas, although for a time he attended the Hill School in Pottstown, Pennsylvania. As a child, he was nicknamed "Lem" and then "Lemondrop," but the nickname that stuck was "Games." "I'd take a ball and bounce it off a wall and then scratch out a little court with my foot, and there'd be scoring," he recalls. "Even today, I have this tendency to make up games. When fifteen-year-old son, Lamar Jr., and I were on the beach in Hawaii, we scratched a court in the sand and we took a beach ball and we made up a tennis game that we played with our feet, like soccer. I don't know, maybe I have some kind of creative impulse in me. Others paint or write, I make up games."

The game Hunt loved best of all was football. Predictably, when he played on the SMU squad, his teammates razzed him about his wealth. Later, he would be ribbed about playing third-string. "I'm proud I made third-string," he says. "I played behind men like Doyle Nix and Raymond Berry and Ed Bernet. That was a tough team. Players like Forrest Gregg and John Roach. I played football because I loved it; there were only one or two of us on the team who weren't on scholarships, and it was one of the greatest experiences of my life."

But Hunt's biggest challenge was founding the AFL in 1959. "We shuddered on his behalf," a veteran football writer remembers. "You should have seen his first press conference. Here was this poor little rich boy, son of one of the world's richest men, standing up there like he was making a speech in catechism class. He spoke almost in a whisper, without any force or authority. Somebody nudged me and said, 'Wait till George Halas gets ahold of this punk!' It was like watching the first act of a kabuki play. No matter what else happens, you know the last act's gonna be a beheading."

"Sometimes it *was* scary," Lamar says. "My neck was on the line, both financially and personally. I'd have just looked like an idiot if the league had failed. It was tough at first because we had an obviously inferior product and a harebrained idea. We *should* have been scared."

The early years of the AFL were terrifying, but they were also fun. The memory that Lamar cherishes above all others is the one he calls "a golden opportunity missed, a big mistake on our part." It was the last game of the 1962 season. Hunt's Dallas Texans were playing the San Diego Chargers, owned by hotel scion Barron Hilton, at Dallas. Hunt had already decided to move to Kansas City for the next season—the attendance that night would be scanty, the result of the contest meaningless. The night before the game, the two young owners got together and had a talk. Hunt recalls, "I said, 'Barron, I read somewhere about a game in the 1930's when two owners locked everybody out and sat one on one side of the stadium and one on the other and cheered for their teams. Let's do that tomorrow.'

"Barron thought that was a great idea. He said, 'Jeez, they'll *write* about this!' He said, 'Jeez Christ, this'll be great!' Barron has such a natural way of cussin', it doesn't even sound bad. It just comes out like strawberry syrup. 'Jeez Christ,' he said, 'this'll be great!'

"We worked out a way to get the gates closed and go on the radio and refund all the money on the ten thousand tickets we'd sold. But then, at the last minute, we chickened out. It was gutless of us. We should have done it. People would still be talking about it."

After early losses—and the forced move of Hunt's franchise to Kansas City—the new AFL prospered and eventually merged with the NFL. At the same time, Hunt's frugality became legendary. Observers still talk about the time a few years back when Hunt attended a game at Murchison's Texas Stadium in Dallas. He parked his car across the freeway. Then, accompanied by his two sons, he sprinted across the highway, hurdling, on the way, the fence that divided the opposing lanes. Hunt explains that the stadium's access ramps were still under construction, and he wanted to make a quick departure after the game in order to catch a plane. Others remained convinced that Lamar was simply trying to save the two-dollar parking fee.

Hunt's single personal extravagance is his house, the château-style mansion in north Dallas he purchased from another millionaire Texan. Hunt lives there with his second wife, Norma, an ex-schoolteacher, and one of his three children. "Everyone was surprised to hear that Lamar bought it," says a business associate, "because Lamar is unpretentious, to say the least. But he probably bought it because of his wife. Norma works at being a regular person, but sometimes it shows that she's working at it. To Lamar, being a regular person comes naturally."

Friends say that it was Norma who finally convinced Lamar to use the Hunt Oil company jet when he travels. "He used to fly commercial," says one observer, "and because of his heavy schedule, he would cut time too fine. He was always rushing to the airport to catch a plane after his appointments, and she was worried that he would have an automobile accident."

"My husband combines two interesting qualities," says Norma Knobel Hunt, who resembles in face and physique Catherine Deneuve. "He's a hyperactive *calm* person, if you can imagine. He has tremendous inner calm, and no moodiness. His disposition never alters. He's always exactly the same easygoing person, but at the same time he's engaged in constant activity."

"One of my main faults," says Hunt, "is I try to get too much into the average day, whether it's business or working in the yard or sightseeing. I don't ever sit down just to *sit.* I want to do things, and I know that life is short."

When he purchased his eleven-acre estate, Hunt climbed the oak and yaupon and bois d'arc trees that dot his grounds, in order to personally hack off the vines that encircled their trunks. Visitors to the estate were startled to hear a voice calling down from the tops of tall trees: "Hey, y'all, be with you in a minute."

Hunt realizes that many of his wealthy friends can't understand this impulse to constant activity—or his attitude about money. "I probably basically am a cheapskate," he says. "I have a very unusual quirk in me about my things. I just get to likin' them. These old beat-up tennis shoes I have on right now—I use 'em to work in the yard, and I'd rather die than throw 'em away and buy a new pair. I just don't like to spend money on things like shoes, because once they're gone, they're gone, and so is the money. Gone forever. Also," he adds, "I pride myself on being a good businessman, or trying to be, but I'm the world's worst when it comes to handling my personal finances. I very seldom have any money in my wallet, and that causes some misunderstandings."

"He runs out of gas all the time," says Norma. "It's one of the children's favorite subjects, how their daddy is always running out of gas, and the adventures that happen because of it."

"I just don't take the time," says Hunt. "As long as my Chrysler keeps running, why stop?"

"The truth is he's not really interested in anything about cars or machinery," says Norma. "He can hardly tell a Cadillac from a Ford. He just doesn't care."

"But I can tell a Chrysler every time," says Hunt. "They're our sponsors. That's *business.* I drive a Chrysler because they give me one every year free, but cars aren't something that specifically interest me. Now, Norma, she loves cars, and she drives a Corvette. But to me a car's a little like clothing—when it's worn out, it's gone, the money's lost, whereas a good substantial investment in something like an antique retains its value forever. What I hate most is money that's lost and gone forever. I don't know what makes me like that."

A few years ago, Tex Schramm of the Cowboys walked into Hunt's den and noted that it was absolutely bare. "Lamar, what's happened to your furniture?" he asked.

"Heck, Norma's been arguing me about that," Hunt said. "I promised her we could furnish this room when the Chiefs reached twenty-thousand season tickets."

"Well, you've reached twenty-thousand, haven't you?" Schramm asked.

"That's what Norma says, too," Hunt replied. "But she's counting the kid tickets, and I don't think it's fair to include the kid tickets."

Hunt went on to enlarge both his investments and his influence in sports. In 1968, he bought 25 percent of World Championship Tennis. One day soon after, he was suddenly the owner of a 75 percent interest when one of his partners pulled out. He soon injected some radical thinking into the stodgy, feudal world of lob and backhand, proposing to run tennis as a business, and to create, as he told a group of British writers, "the top professional competition in the sport." His bid for power was a direct challenge to the authority of the International Lawn Tennis Federation, which had opened its doors to professionals that same year.

"It was terrible," Hunt says of his early days in tennis. "We made mistake on top of mistake."

"By 1970," says WCT executive director Michael Davies, "it was plain that WCT was going to be out of business within a year. I went to my hotel room for three days and I worked out plans for a World Championship of Tennis, and Lamar and I sat down to talk it over. I said, 'The time is urgent. The time is right now. I want to go out and sign thirty-two players, the best players in the world, and I want to create *the* World Championship of Tennis, and I want one million dollars to do it.' We went over every last detail of the plan for hours, and at the end of that time, Lamar said, 'Okay, let's go.' "

And then, in 1972, the ILTF banned Hunt's contract pros from its tournaments. The ban was intended to force Hunt out of the business of pro tennis, but it failed. On May 14, 1972, Ken

The Outsiders

Rosewall won $50,000 by defeating Rod Laver in the second annual World Championship of Tennis, before 7,800 assembled at SMU's Moody Coliseum and a live TV audience of 21.3 million— the largest ever to watch a single tennis match. That event confirmed the WCT's owner, Lamar Hunt, as the most powerful promoter in tennis. His preeminence in tennis, combined with his other investments, confirmed him as one of the most influential figures in all of pro sports.

Today, Hunt is the sole owner of the NFL Chiefs. He is also assumed to own most of the Dallas Tornado soccer club and World Championship Tennis. But in order to comply with the NFL's rule against majority ownership of more than one pro team, Hunt is listed as a minority owner of both the Tornados and the WCT. The Tornados' "majority" owner is the Texas fruit-cake king, Bill McNutt—an old friend of Lamar's. The WCT's "majority" owner is Lamar's nephew. Hunt also owns 11 percent of the NBA's Chicago Bulls, an investment that has increased in value over recent years. Hunt estimates that the Bulls are worth $4 to $5 million today, making his 11 percent share worth $440,000 to $550,000.

Not all of Hunt's investments have reaped profits. In fact, some of them have turned out badly. Among his failures were a national bowling league, a teenage social center, a commercial fishing lake and a plan to turn Alcatraz Island into an astronaut's Disneyland. "That's just the nature of business," Hunt says. "Sometimes you lose. In the oil business, you frequently have to drill a few dry holes to come up with one that produces oil. Sometimes you get a dry hole in the sports-entertainment business, too."

The only vanity Lamar permits himself is the scoreboard he built in his Kansas City Chiefs' Arrowhead Stadium. The scoreboard was the first to transmit instant-replay, reenacting the glory and gore on the field below. But more often than not the scoreboard's primary reproductive function seems to be to flash the godhead, the visage of Lamar himself, his fingers raised in a V— a luminous secular pope, blessing all the pilgrims who have deposited tithes at the turnstiles.

Apart from an occasional appearance on his scoreboard, however, Hunt cultivates a low profile. His biography in *Who's Who in America* contains as asterisk to signify his noncooperation with the editors. "He just hated to be put in there," says his secretary of ten years, Jean Finn. "He totally dislikes anything that makes him stand out."

"Lamar has nothing at all to do with Dallas high society," says one long-time friend. "He always gets together with those old cronies from SMU—none of them smoke or drink—and they fly to football games and things like that. They're very close, and if there's such a thing as *truly* beautiful people, it's them."

"He's a total zero about food," adds another friend. "Food is a foreign country to all the Hunts. They eat to live. Once, Lamar and his brother Bunker took me to dinner in London, and where do you think we ate? Trader Vic's in the London Hilton! Why, all those Trader Vic's are alike. We could have gone to Stone's Chophouse or Simpson's, but it doesn't matter to the Hunts."

Lamar may not care about what food he eats, but he has definite ideas about drinking. "I'm not against drinking or smoking," he says, "although smoking seems kind of silly in view of what we know about it. But I don't drink for a couple of reasons: I don't like the taste of it, and I can't see any positive value in it. Sure, I'll take a sip of wine. I've gotten to the point where I kind of like white wine, just a few sips. I don't care for a whole glass. My friends say I'm going downhill fast, sipping white wine. But I can't stand the red stuff, and hard liquor is brutal."

Yet, warns one friend, Lamar's plebeian tastes, his bland wardrobe, his air of a small-town Baptist preacher, don't mean he's a Milquetoast. "Lamar comes across to some people like a pantywaist," the friend says, "because he looks so unimpressive and he's so totally unpushy. Ha! Lamar Hunt, in his own quiet, mannerly way, is a very gutsy guy. He's gutsy because he's competitive; he got that from sports. And he's a giant-killer at heart; he got that from his daddy."

Clint Murchison, Jr., Lamar's rival, resembles his father in crucial ways, too. As much as H. L. Hunt, Sr., hated the lavish spending of money, the elder Murchison loved it. For a quarter of a century, Clint Sr. lived in a twenty-five room Dutch Colonial, outside of Dallas, with nine bedrooms, including one with eight beds—"so a group of us boys can talk oil all night." Among his other properties were his Blue-Bird farm, forty miles south of Dallas; El Toro, a 100-acre island in the Gulf of Mexico; the Acuna Ranch, a 75,000-acre spread high in Mexico's Sierra Madre; and a 2,000-acre plot in east Texas, near Athens, the town where he was born. At the east Texas property, he assembled an army of laborers, who cut a road through the woods, leveled a 3,300-foot landing strip, dammed a stream, excavated a lake and planted magnolia, oak and pine trees, plus 10,000 pine seedlings and 10,000 strawberry plants.

"Clint," says a friend, without exaggerating, "did almost everything by ten thousands."

"Figures just didn't scare Clint," says one of his business associates. "In his business, he figured if it was a good deal, it would walk. Like the Lamar Life Insurance Company deal, over in Jackson, Mississippi. I told Clint about that one, it sounded good to Clint. 'Take my plane and go over there to Jackson and buy it for me,' he said. Well, I went over there, but when I got there, it looked like the thing was a little bigger and more complicated than Clint had figured, so I called him up. He was just taking off for a Mexican hunting trip. 'There's nothing complicated about it,' he said. 'A hundred thousand shares at a hundred and five. That's ten million, five hundred thousand. Just a simple business deal. Go ahead and don't worry about it.' "

Clint Jr., now fifty-two, and John, fifty-four, inherited their father's far-flung real estate and oil investments. Clint, in particular, also inherited his father's propensity for doing "everything by ten thousands." To build his home in Dallas—a sprawling mansion that, in comparison, makes Lamar Hunt's rambling chateau look like a bungalow in Levittown—he spent $1 million. Spread over an entire acre, the house contains two dining rooms and a complete children's wing. Twenty-five acres of prime residential land surround the house, dappled with three swimming pools, each of a different depth, all interconnected.

In his private life, Clint is the antithesis of Lamar—one of the central props of Dallas high society, a man who can date a bottle of champagne by its taste, the vintage of a wine by its bouquet. In business, however, the Murchisons project the same low profile as the Hunts. Murchison Brothers occupies the twenty-third floor of the First National Bank building in downtown Dallas. This is the world headquarters for enterprises that include insurance, construction, real estate, finance, sports and energy development. The halls and board rooms are appointed with contemporary paintings and sculpture considered by the brothers as prime investments, and often on loan to various museums across the country.

In their business operations, the Murchisons favor investments easily converted to cash. Their impact is delicate and pervasive. They acquire large assets with little of their own capital—turning $20,000 in cash, say, and an $80,000 promissory note into a construction company worth tens of millions of dollars. And they consider their sports operation—the Dallas Cowboys—a part of their business. Like Lamar Hunt, they do not interfere in the day-to-day operation of their team. They own the Cowboys in order to make a profit. If the business of pro football weren't ultimately profitable for them, they would undoubtedly get out of pro football, despite Clint's love for the game. Profit from the Cowboys in the first ten years was almost $2 million. After that first decade, the franchise was valued at about $12 million—a capital appreciation of 2,000 percent over the $600,000 purchase fee.

Around the time they purchased the Cowboys, the Murchisons sold most of their oil and gas properties to the major oil companies. They still control Delhi International Oil Corporation, and have properties in Ecuador and Thailand, as well as a coal-mining company, but oil has become only a nominal resource in the Murchison portfolio.

While Lamar Hunt was exploring a vast unknown territory by founding a new league, Clint Murchison, Jr., was building an impregnable barony near Dallas. His influence, if more subtly felt, has become almost as pervasive as Hunt's.

First, Murchison engineered a seemingly impossible bridge between the quiet laboratories of his alma mater, MIT, with their long halls full of click-whirring computer banks, and the martial stadiums of the NFL, where the anthem is the crunch of bone against bone, grunts and groans.

In 1962, the Services Bureau Corporation, a subsidiary of International Business Machines, offered to overhaul the Cowboys' complex accounting procedures. Instead, Murchison and Schramm challenged the SBC to devise a computer program that would put scouting on scientific principles. The SBC accepted the challenge. It sent, from its Computer Sciences Division, an Indian statistician from Bombay University named Salam Qureishi. According to the Cowboys' vice-president, Gil Brandt, Salam Qureishi "didn't know whether a football was filled with air or feathers." He did, however, know his science, and was soon declaring, "American football is easily the most scientific game ever invented."

Qureishi's task was to develop formulae to replace the "subjective" hunches of traditional scouts. He and his SBC teammates narrowed down a player's characteristics to eight essentials, three quantitative (weight, height, speed over 40 yards) and five more that depended on judgement (mental alertness, strength and explosion, character, competitiveness, quickness-agility-balance). They then devised a set of "position-specific" skills players need to perform in a given slot. Finally, they constructed a nine-point scale, with a "three" as average.

Then, in 1963, Qureishi ran into a major stumbling block. He discovered that the Cowboys' scouts were unable to collect enough data to formulate a sufficiently large sample for his computer program. He just didn't have enough hard information. To get more data, the Cowboys invited the Los Angeles Rams and the San Francisco 49ers to join them in a combined scouting operation called Troika. Each club would hire a number of full-time scouts and assign them to different areas of the country. The reports of these area scouts, along with reports from unofficial scouts on college campuses, would be shared equally among the three clubs. Meanwhile, the Cowboys would retain exclusive use of the more detailed information collected by Qureishi's crew—data that amounted to about 60 percent of the total collected.

Using the data gathered by Troika, and by the Dallas specialists, Qureishi and his men rated every player available in the 1964 college draft, then fed the data into computers at Optimum Systems, Inc., of Palo Alto, California, a Murchison-owned company. The computer selected the Dallas Cowboy draft picks for that year on the basis of the best athletes available. Three of the Cowboys' top ten draft picks that season—Mel Renfro, Bob Hayes and Roger Staubach—would soon become NFL stars.

Yet some critics remained—and remain—skeptical. Up to 1964, using flesh-and-blood computers only, the Cowboys had invested their top draft picks very wisely, selecting such stars as Eddie LeBaron and E.J. Holub, Bob Lilly and Don Meredith, Lee Roy Jordan and Chuck Howley. Yet convincing proof of Troika's effectiveness is the fact that even after Dallas became a consistent winner, and had to stand in line to get at the top college prospects, the Cowboys still, year after year, managed to come up with two or three draft picks each season who turned into full-fledged Pro Bowl performers.

By 1966, the Bears, Lions, Eagles, Steelers and Vikings had formed their own computerized scouting combine, known by the acronym Blesto-V, while CEPO served the Browns, Cardinals, Colts, Falcons, Giants, Packers and Redskins. In 1967, New Orleans turned Troika into Quadra by joining the Cowboys, Rams and 49ers.

But Murchison—and his alter ego, Schramm—didn't rest at retooling the management techniques of big business and applying them to pro football. Murchison's real mastery was at political gamesmanship. In 1967, when he announced his intention to build a stadium on the Dallas city line, at the junction of four major highways, a public uproar ensued that put his political acumen to the fullest test.

The roots of the Texas Stadium controversy are buried in the character of Dallas itself, and in Dallas' unique political arrangements. Dallas is a perfect reality-principle for an Easterner making his first visit to Texas. The Easterner expects to see ten-gallon hats bobbing by the thousands, to hear the thud of high leather boots and laconic drawls echoing in his ear. Instead, he finds Lamar Hunt and Clint Murchison, Jr.

Just thirty miles away, in Fort Worth, all the trappings of a stereotyped West are still visible. But Dallas is different—essentially a mercantile and corporate town. Its citizens prefer Bill Blass shirts to bandannas, Brooks Brothers suits to buckskins. In the place of lonely mesquite trees framed against stark, craggy cliffs loom plate-glass skyscrapers. Dallas is the banking capital of the

Southwest, boasting prominent financial institutions such as the Republic, First National and Mercantile banks. Dallas has corralled giants of the insurance business such as Fidelity Union Life and Southland Life. Herds of prestigious corporations—Braniff, Texas Instruments, Frito-Lay, Dr Pepper and others—make Dallas their national headquarters.

In sum, Dallas is a city permeated to the core by a corporate psychology. Big business wields enormous influence in every American city, but in Dallas the incest between politics and profits is on public display, thanks to the Dallas Citizens Council, whose membership is a roll call of chief executives of major corporations. It is fair to say that no important decision affecting Dallas has been made over the past forty years without crucial—and often decisive —input from the Citizens Council. Both the site of Murchison's proposed stadium and its method of financing were the result of a schism within that body.

From the beginning, the Dallas Cowboys had played their home games at the Cotton Bowl, in the Texas State Fair Park. By the mid-1960's, Clint Murchison, Jr., had become disenchanted with the Cotton Bowl's archaic facilities—overcrowding on uncomfortable wooden bleacher seats, no protection in the upper decks against the September sun and the December wind, with only semi-open concrete cubicles to serve as VIP and owners' boxes. He was also dissatisfied with the stadium's location—the heart of south Dallas' black ghetto. In 1966, he asked that a new stadium be built, in downtown Dallas, subsidized in part by commercial parking lots nearby.

The Texas State Fair, however, and its elaborate fairgrounds —including, besides the Cotton Bowl, a music hall and eight museums—had long been a pet project of the Citizens Council, of which both Clint and John Murchison were members. The same year Clint proposed a new stadium be built in downtown Dallas, Robert Cullum, president of the State Fair Commission, announced that the Cotton Bowl would undergo a major renovation, including the installation of new theater-style seats, air conditioning in the visitors' dressing room, etc. Then-Mayor Erik Jonsson, a past president of the Citizens Council, and chairman of Texas Instruments, made it known that he favored Cullum's proposal.

Furthermore, he flatly vetoed Murchison's plan, arguing that the city had "more pressing problems."

The debate raged on for months, and meanwhile Murchison started searching for a suitable site outside the Dallas city limits, beyond the political grasp of the Citizens Council. In early 1967, Cowboy officials huddled in secret, at the Dallas Gun Club, with twelve politicians from Irving, a suburb just west of Dallas. The deal they agreed upon (Murchison would buy land in Irving, and the politicians would support his method of financing the stadium) was kept secret until late that year, when Irving's Chamber of Commerce manager inadvertently broke the news in a talk to the Farmer's Branch Lions Club.

The Cowboys immediately followed up the manager's indiscretion with a formal announcement. The new facility was to be called Texas Stadium and was intended to house football, rather than serve as an all-purpose sports arena, like Houston's Astrodome. Initial plans projected 58,000 seats in a $15 million semi-domed stadium.

A season ticket between the 30-yard lines cost $1,000 in stadium bonds, plus a $63 ticket and another $20 for parking—a total of $1,083. And if you didn't purchase four season tickets each year, you lost your option. Less favorably positioned seats between the 30-yard lines and the end zones could be obtained for a $250 bond, while the other half were sold the day of each game, for $7 apiece. And although the price for parking was a standard $2, the price of your seat determined how far away from the stadium you had to park. The end-zoners, at the bottom of the price scale, had to trudge three-quarters of a mile.

At the summit of this carefully graduated pecking order were those who could afford to purchase one of the 158 prestigious Circle Suites that ringed the stadium like brass knuckles on a clenched fist. Most purchasers were Dallas-based corporations, who used the suites to entertain their customers, then deduct the costs from their taxes. It cost $50,000 in stadium bonds to purchase a suite sixteen feet by sixteen, and $100,000 in stadium bonds to purchase a suite sixteen feet by thirty-two.

When the Cowboys moved to Irving, only 22,000 of their previous 32,000 season ticket holders bought tickets at the new stadium, although all 32,000 had been given first choice.

"Yes, I'd say we lost a whole group in the twelve- to twenty-thousand-dollar-a-year salary range," Murchison admits, "who couldn't afford to buy bonds. If we discriminated against them, we discriminated against them. But," he says, with compelling logic, "no more than all America discriminates against people who don't have enough money to buy everything they want."

The formal announcement of the proposed Texas Stadium stirred up vehement protest, particularly in Irving itself. Critics contended that Texas Stadium would be a municipal stadium in name only—in order to obtain real-estate tax exemptions—and would belong, for all intents and purposes, to Murchison and his Cowboys. "Sure, once all the bonds are paid off, in thirty-five years, the stadium revenue will belong to us," a leader of the anti-Murchison faction said. "But by that time old Texas Stadium will be useless. We'll have to pay to get it torn down."

In rebuttal to his critics, Murchison pointed out that many college stadiums had already been financed the same way—say, the city of Miami promoting a public bond issue to finance a stadium, the Orange Bowl, that would be controlled almost in perpetuity by the University of Miami. The idea behind toll bridges, for example, was to make the people who used those bridges pay for their upkeep. What could be fairer, he argued, than asking the people who were going to watch the football games in a stadium built in their community to pay for that stadium?

Apparently, most citizens of Irving agreed with Murchison. In a referendum held in April, 1968, 3,133 voters cast their ballots in favor of the stadium, as long as none of their tax dollars were used in its construction or maintenance, while only 1,925 voted against. A second referendum was held in January, 1969, and this time 5,366 voters were in favor of building the stadium, while only 2,439 opposed. Seven days after that referendum, on January 25, the Cowboys celebrated by holding a groundbreaking ceremony for Texas Stadium.

With a unique method of public financing, Murchison had won more than the right to build his stadium. He had won political power, too. "If you mailed a letter to the mayor of Murchison, Texas," Al Smith, an Irving businessman and long-time foe of the

Murchisons, once observed, "it would be delivered to the City Hall in Irving."

Irving County was, by law, "dry." But a politician friendly to Murchison pushed a bill through the Texas legislature which authorized liquor sales at airports and stadia if the local bodies governing those facilities agreed. Before long, the sale of alcoholic beverages became legal in the Texas Stadium Circle Suites and Stadium Club, while the hoi polloi in that same stadium couldn't even buy a bottle of beer.

Murchison's stadium brought him economic benefits from all sides. Virtually every contract awarded for the stadium's construction and operation proved financially advantageous to him, either directly or indirectly. The contract for constructing the stadium, for example, was awarded to the J. W. Bateson Co., Inc., a Murchison-owned firm, which, in fact, was the only company to submit an offer. "When we asked for bids," says Murchison, "we didn't have the money because the bonds hadn't been sold. Obviously, there was going to be an enormous number of change-orders. It was a risky proposition and anybody else would have been a complete fool to take on the job. There was nobody else to build it but us."

Apparently, no one wanted to risk bidding for the concessions, either. So who got them? The Cebe Corporation—another subsidiary of Murchison's Dallas football franchise.

The insurance contract for the stadium was awarded to the Kenneth Murchison Co., an agent for the Protection Mutual Company. The Kenneth Murchison Co., had been founded by Clint's uncle, and Murchisons—of varying sizes, ages, shapes and Christian names—owned a reported 80 percent of its shares. The logrolling that accompanied this windfall managed to arouse the ire of even the tame local politicians. An Irving businessman, representing the Aetna Life Insurance Co., also put in a strong bid. But, under pressure, Aetna refused to withdraw three fire-safety conditions, and the Murchison Company lowered its unsealed bid. Murchison ended up with all the insurance contracts.

"With all I have wrapped up in this," Murchison says, "I've got to know that the project is run well. And frankly, one can't be sure that any bureaucracy, however good, is going to operate something at optimum level."

Lamar Hunt and Clint Murchison had begun the 1960's as outsiders. But their notion of pro sports' being a *business* rather than an *avocation* was destined to prevail. By the end of that decade, Hunt and Murchison would be central props of the pro sports establishment. The real "outsiders" would be men like Phil Wrigley and Art Rooney—the old die-hard fans, sinking in a sea of accountants.

◀ 6 ▶
The Other Texans

In the late Fifties, while Hunt and Murchison were battling the NFL establishment—and each other—for the right to put a pro football franchise in Dallas, another Texan, Roy Hofheinz, was just as doggedly petitioning the barons of baseball. But the owners of pro baseball franchises could no more reach a consensus in favor of expansion than their counterparts in the NFL. The St. Louis Browns might move to Baltimore, the Philadelphia Athletics might move to Kansas City, the Brooklyn Dodgers to Los Angeles and the New York Giants to San Francisco, but no new owners would be permitted to create wholly new franchises.

So, the same year Lamar Hunt founded his AFL, Branch Rickey started the Continental League, mainly at the prodding of William Shea, who wanted to build a stadium in New York to compete with Yankee Stadium, and of Judge Roy Hofheinz, who wanted to bring pro baseball to his native Houston. That year, 1959, the Continental League set up paper franchises in New York, Toronto, Atlanta, St. Paul–Minneapolis, Dallas–Ft. Worth, Denver, Buffalo and Houston.

Only the New York Yankees would face direct competition from the Continental League, but a number of minor league franchises owned by the majors were also threatened. Furthermore, the new league would be competing on a nation-wide basis for TV revenues. So, after a year or so of public lip service to, and private obstruction of, the notion of a third major league, the majors bought off the Continentals, with a promise to absorb four Continental cities and give the other four top priority in any further expansion. For its part, the National League, at an expansion meeting on October 17, 1959, added two teams, selling a New York Mets franchise to Joan Whitney Payson, and a Houston Colt .45's franchise to Judge Roy Hofheinz.

In the minds of many, the Judge would become a living caricature of every Bunyanesque stereotype ever concocted about Texans, a symbol of unbridled extravagance. Yet, in the long run, Hofheinz would have just as much impact as Hunt and Murchison. His crown jewel, the Astrodome, would become the most newsworthy promotional gimmick of the decade, the prototype for the multipurpose entertainment facilities of the 1970's.

Unlike Hunt and Murchison, Roy Hofheinz was born poor. He was only fifteen years old when his father was killed while driving a laundry truck. Roy had to work to support his family by selling newspapers. He promoted weekly dances when the weekly dance was Houston's most glamorous social event. He passed out the fliers. He posted the handbills. He booked local groups—the Birmingham Blowers, Lee's Owls—into Kensington Hall, an establishment now buried beneath the Gulf Freeway. On at least one occasion, he recalls, "I took home better than one thousand dollars to Mama." More important, he learned a valuable lesson. "Kensington Hall kept the concessions," he says, "and that was regrettable. It taught me the value of these things. And baseball," he adds, "is your best concession sport. That's because it's the only event where the customer always has the time to get rid of one and to take one."

On the side, the young promoter ran an amateur night on a local radio station, ten years before Major Bowes. ("The talent was free and the bands played for nothing, just to get the exposure and the publicity.") He made more money in those years than during the first two years of his legal practice.

The Other Texans

Hofheinz obtained his law degree at the precocious age of nineteen. Three years later, he was elected to the Texas state legislature. He formed a friendship with a young, promising politician named Lyndon Baines Johnson. He became one of LBJ's early campaign managers, and thus a pivotal political figure in the state of Texas. At twenty-four, Hofheinz became the state's youngest county judge. In 1951, when he retired from the bench, he had a reputation for both personal honesty and political intrigue. Those who knew him then say he left the bench with only $18 in his pocket. But, they add, the value of his political IOU's was priceless. In 1952, Hofheinz was elected mayor of Houston.

As soon as he took office, Hofheinz initiated the three major projects that would occupy him throughout his term: overhauling the city's purchasing department; building a city airport; and waging a blood-feud with his city council, in an effort to shake up an entrenched "old guard," wallowing in sloth and corruption. One of the first things he did was to telephone an old friend, Bob Sherill.

"Sherrill," he said, "I want you to be city treasurer."

"I don't know anything about that," Sherrill replied. "How can I be treasurer?"

"You're honest," said Hofheinz. "You can learn the rest."

Hofheinz was making more enemies than friends, but one sector of his constituency never abandoned him. From the beginning, he had been the favorite of black voters. As a county judge, he had integrated Harris County golf courses and buses. "It was ridiculous," he says. "Blacks paid taxes for the golf courses and couldn't play on them. I did it without saying I was going to, and we had no troubles."

As mayor, he continued his quiet desegregating. It was months after his term of office began when someone noticed that Hofheinz had ordered all COLORED and WHITE signs removed from the City Hall rest rooms. When he decided to integrate the public libraries, he invited representatives of both the black and white press to a private meeting. He asked them to surpress the news until integration was a *fait accompli.*

There was a furor when the news that the libraries had been integrated was finally revealed. One memorable day a socially prominent lady came to complain to Hofheinz. "I won't let my children sit by black children in the library," she told him angrily. "I don't know *what* they'd catch!"

"Maybe . . . tolerance," the Judge drawled.

The Judge's racial policies weren't calculated to win friends among Houston's fanatical minority of segregationists. Nor did his fiscal policies earn him praise from the city council. When he started an incredibly ambitious construction program to revitalize the city, the city council—who felt the program was outrageously expensive—attempted to impeach him. Hofheinz, in turn, the Judge, issued a bench warrant for the arrest of any councilman who didn't show up at a meeting he had scheduled. The council retaliated by locking Hofheinz out of City Hall while they prepared the articles of impeachment against him. "That," says Hofheinz, "was like the penitentiary inmates trying to oust the warden."

Hofheinz survived the impeachment proceedings, and the vote for reelection in 1954, even though this time the orthodox Democratic party machinery was mobilized against him. What saved him from defeat was the support of a Texas multimillionaire named Bob Smith, who was able to inject enough cash to sustain Hofheinz's campaign. But even Smith's money couldn't help Hofheinz preserve the mayoral term he won in 1954. With the ranks of his enemies now swelling to include almost everyone in local government in Houston, he was unceremoniously booted out of office, in a special election held in 1955.

The Judge left politics. He purchased a 25,000-watt radio station. Over the next few years, he parlayed that station into extensive radio and TV holdings. With that bankroll, he moved into slag processing; Houston was in the midst of an enormous building boom, and processed slag was an important construction material. Finally, he invested his profits from slag in real estate—and came up a millionaire. Now he had the capital to realize the dream that had haunted him for years—the dream of building his Astrodome.

Hofheinz had conceived the idea for a giant domed sports arena while he and his first wife, Irene, were vacationing in Rome. "Mama and I were standing there looking at the Colosseum," he says. "It was a large, round facility and most of the stadiums in the United States were rectangular, built to conform to the shape of the playing fields. I studied the history of the Colosseum. I found out that on hot days they used to have the slaves pull a cover over the top made out of papyrus, or whatever they used in those days. I guess they didn't want to spoil the lions' appetite with too much heat.

"And I found out, too, that the emperor and the bigwigs all sat at the *top* of the stadium.

"Standing there, thinking back on those days, I figured that a round facility with a cover was what we needed in the United States, and that Houston would be the perfect spot for it."

By 1960, most Houstonians wanted a major league baseball franchise. The fans wanted one so they could watch the superstars perform in person. The oilmen who ran the city wanted one as a matter of pride and prestige. Bob Smith, who had helped finance Hofheinz's second mayoral campaign in 1954, now formed the Houston Sports Association, dedicated to bringing major league baseball to that city. Hofheinz was a natural partner, since Branch Rickey, the year before, had awarded him a franchise in his paper Continental League. "Smith and the others asked me to come in financially," says Hofheinz, "but I went in on the understanding that I would run the show. They could be on the surface running press meetings and talking to the public, and I would be in the basement making deals. And I decided the only way to sell Houston as a major league city was to come up with a stadium that would lure the baseball people."

Hofheinz, Smith and their minority partners bought 497 acres eight miles south of downtown Houston from the men who owned the Shamrock Hilton Hotel. Then they sold 254 acres—targeted as the site for Hofheinz's Astrodomain—to Harris County for $3 million. The State Highway Department then opened construction on Route 90, which passed by the site, and overnight the land appreciated millions more. Hofheinz was awarded his baseball franchise on October 17, 1960. His first major fund-raising effort came on January 31, 1961, when the county voted a general obligation bond of $18 million. Hofheinz celebrated by presiding at a groundbreaking ceremony, at which he fired a Colt .45 pistol into the ground. (His major league franchise would at first be called the Colt .45's, then the Astros.)

The Rich Who Own Sports

Initial success, however, was followed by a number of setbacks. First, a torrential rainfall poured water into the giant hole that had been excavated. A short time later, Hofheinz and Smith discovered, as businessmen who get public funds often do, that they had underestimated their costs. Hofheinz again collected political debts still owed to him. Again, blacks supported him in substantial numbers. His new bond issue won a 42,911-to-36,110 victory at the polls, good for $9.6 million in additional funds.

While the Astrodome was being erected, the Houston Colt .45's played in a temporary stadium that seated 32,000. The players and fans were both fried by a torrid midsummer sun and strafed by squadrons of kamikaze mosquitoes. Soon, the Colt .45's gave up playing day games. The National League even permitted them to play on Sunday nights, until the Astrodome was completed.

And then, on April 8, 1965, one day before the Houston team (now called the Astros) was to meet the Baltimore Orioles in the Astrodome's inaugural game, the stadium was put to the test. Hofheinz flew the Astros' Oklahoma City farm club to Houston to work out with his major-leaguers. It was immediately apparent that something had gone wrong. Outfielders who had up to that day been candidates for Gold Glove fielding awards suddenly developed iron hands—and needed iron heads to survive the fly balls that rattled against their skulls like hail on a windowpane.

"You just can't follow the ball," said a worried Lum Harris, the Astros' manager. "It's impossible because of the glare from the dome. We may be here all day tomorrow," he added, "trying to get that game finished."

The next day, when the Astros and the Orioles met, the contest resembled something Hollywood might have staged in its Golden Age of Comedy, with Charlie Chaplin leading the Orioles, Harold Lloyd leading the Astros, and all their teammates dead ringers for the Keystone Cops. "I'm not going back into the outfield without a batting helmet!" the Orioles' Boog Powell shouted after he had misjudged, in the third inning, an easy pop fly by at least twenty feet. Proof that Powell's error was due to the blinding glare, and not some secret scrambling device the Astros had installed to jam their opponents' radar, in the fourth inning the Orioles' Paul Blair lofted a piddling pop fly to the Astros' outfield and was stunned, as he sprinted around the bases, to see that no one could locate the ball until it had bounced a couple of times. The next inning, John Orsino hit another fly ball to left field—and everyone ran toward right.

Suddenly, overnight, the pop fly had become the most devastating offensive weapon in all of major league baseball.

One critic suggested a revolutionary solution—lift the dome off the stadium and throw it onto the nearest garbage dump. Another cynic advised Hofheinz to cover his giant dome with a giant Venetian blind. Meanwhile, the Astros were trying out fifty different types of sunglasses, and the Judge was chomping the stub of a soggy Havana, telling the press: "Yes, there is no doubt we have a problem here." Finally, before the Astrodome and the man who built it became the butt of every second-rate comedian on the Borscht Belt circuit, Hofheinz ordered his men to apply the only cure possible. A coat of paint over the dome.

That problem solved, another promptly emerged. Hofheinz had financed a study at Texas A&M University to determine which of several strains of grass would best flourish beneath the dome. The scientists chose Tiffway 419 Bermuda, then grew a quantity on a special grass farm in Wharton, Texas, in soil transported from the site of the Astrodome. And good to the scientists' predictions, Tiffway 419 Bermuda did flourish in the filtered sunlight—until, that is, the dome was painted. Then the grass began to die. The Judge's pastoral dream died with it, and he opted wholly for technology, installing synthetic "grass" made of nylon and called Astroturf. It wasn't long before other major league owners realized that Astroturf was both cheaper and more durable than grass. The only thing wrong with it was that the men who had to run on it became less durable, subject—especially in football—to serious knee injuries.

The Astrodomain would in time become the principal source of Hofheinz's wealth. After years of bitter wrangling, the Judge would buy out his main partner, Bob Smith, and gain 100 percent control of the Houston Sports Association, which held, with Harris County, a forty-year lease on the dome and its environs. With its four hotels and its Astroworld, modeled after Disneyland, its park-like surroundings, its technological wizardry, its bowling alley, its

107

restaurants, its domed arena—the Astrodomain was a new concept in total family entertainment, the complete multipurpose leisure facility. In its first year of operation, 1965, the dome and its glitter lured 4,000,000 people (the Eiffel Tower attracted 1,750,000; the Empire State Building, 1,500,000; the Louvre, 1,250,000). Barnum & Bailey's Circus earned 8 percent of its yearly profit in a four-day stand at the Astrodome. Dr. Billy Graham drew 376,419 in ten days, with 61,000 on the final night. (After the evangelist had called the Astrodome "the Eighth Wonder of the World," Bud Adams, whose Houston Oilers football team would become one of the Judge's tenants in 1968, said, "If the Astrodome is the Eighth Wonder of the World, the Judge's price for a lease is the Ninth.") The University of Houston football team, playing small-time schools like Chattanooga and Tampa, averaged 40,000 spectators per game in the arena. The next year, 1966, Hofheinz added even more attractions. In February alone, 372,977 saw the sixteen performances of the world's largest rodeo.

But gradually, over the next year, the novelty showed signs of wearing thin. Even with the addition of bullfights, polo matches, prize fights, auto races, track meets, daredevil motorcycle exhibitions and an occasional political convention, Hofheinz began to see his overall paid attendance decline and his debts mount. He decided to diversify even further. In 1967, for about $10 million, he and two associates purchased 50 percent of the Ringling Brothers' Barnum & Bailey Circus, which—apart from pro sports—had proved to be the Astrodome's most popular attraction. They made two circuses out of one, with the groups touring alternate U.S. cities annually. The scheme made money, and in February, 1972, the Hofheinz group sold the "revitalized" circus to Mattel, Inc., the toymakers, for $47 million in Mattel stock. Hofheinz and family trusts received 1,878,300 Mattel shares, at the time worth $29 million.

But the circus didn't really solve Hofheinz's financial problems. The Astrodomain went into default in 1971 on $34 million of debt, plus interest. The biggest disappointment turned out to be the Astro baseball team. Houston fans soured on the Astros after the team became a consistent divisional doormat. From 1974 to 1975 alone, attendance sagged from 1.1 million to only 860,000.

"At 860,000, the Astros are just not profitable," says one Astrodomain official. Nor did it help matters that the Astrodome's roof leaked almost from the start. In 1975, following a heavy rain, some businessmen were furious to find a foot of water in the exclusive "skyboxes," for which they had paid a season rental of $20,000.

But a major reason for Hofheinz's mounting debt was his own epic extravagance. Consider, for example, the trip he took to Europe in 1971. It began in Athens, Greece, with a small fleet of rented Cadillacs crawling slowly up a hill toward the Acropolis. At the terrace below the entrance, the gleaming caravan halted. To the astonishment of tourists and peddlers, the Cadillacs disgorged first a crew of sturdy men conservatively dressed in ties and suits, then a collapsible curtained sedan chair, and—as cautiously as if his bones were porcelain—hoisted into it was a portly individual with the stub of a cigar propped between his lips. Judge Roy Hofheinz, confined to a wheelchair by a stroke, had come to compare his architectural masterpiece with the work of another master builder named Pericles.

The sheer bulk of his creation gave Hofheinz reason to draw comparisons between himself and history's most ambitious architects. The Astrodome contained 9,000 tons of steel; the Eiffel Tower, only 7,500. It was 710 feet by 710; Rome's Colosseum measured only 617 feet by 512. Its playing surface was 466 feet by 288; the Colosseum's was only 287 by 180. Outside, worshipers of professional sport could park 30,000 piston-driven chariots; inside, the religious rituals of groundball and forward pass were illuminated by 1,906 electric torches, 1,500 watts each. Did the Acropolis have fifty-three "skyboxes," each equipped with its own bar, furniture, closed-circuit TV, bathroom, Dow Jones ticker tape —and leaky roof? A barbershop and a bar whose stools could be raised and lowered by remote control? A bowling alley, a shooting range, an interfaith chapel wherein merely by depressing a button a pilgrim could reproduce on a small window the symbol of one of the world's five principal religions? How could the 523-foot frieze skillfully sculptured on the wall of the Parthenon compare to the Astrodome's right-field patio dappled with imitation orange trees, its Presidential suite with scatter rugs that bore the Presidential seal, its ten-seat movie theater, its three public restaurants, two private clubs, forty-nine concession stands, the scoreboard on which prancing cowboys fired colored bullets and bulls breathed fire through their nostrils, singeing the Texas and U.S. flags flapping from their horns? And all for a mere $40 million.

It is reasonable to assume that, compared to himself, Judge Roy Hofheinz decided Pericles was hopelessly penny ante.

But Hofheinz wasn't making this pilgrimmage to the Continent only to compare himself to Europe's master builders. He intended to decorate his private apartment in the Astrodome with authentic items from different periods of history. In every city he visited, he purchased valuable antiques and artifacts, then had them shipped back to Houston. His method of bargain-hunting was unique, and monstrously typical. Before he arrived in Paris, one of his assistants reserved the Prime Minister's Suite at the George V Hotel—a suite renowned for its furnishings of antiques from the reign of Louis XIV. At Orly Airport, the Judge and his men were met by another fleet of private limos, this time courtesy of the George V. At the entrance to the hotel, he was greeted like royalty, a double file of liveried doormen and "call for Philip Morr-eesss" bellhops bowing as tirelessly as plastic drinking birds on the rim of a glass. The entourage, with the Judge in his sedan chair, flowed across the lobby.

"It is an honor to have you as our guest," the hotel manager kept repeating.

The Judge's only response was to raise a window curtain and fill the manager's face with cigar stench.

The army of servants and the sedan chair moved toward, then into, an elevator, arriving finally at the Prime Minister's Suite, which occupied an upper floor of the hotel. There the Judge was transferred from the sedan chair into a wheelchair. Then, like Montezuma enumerating his treasure for the conquering Cortés, the hotel manager began a roll call of precious antiques, with Hofheinz wheeling along by his side, eyes glued to the floor. Only the regular puffs of smoke issuing from the half-mashed Havana proved he hadn't suffered another—and fatal—stroke.

At last the Judge had wheeled through every room, had been inundated with the pedigree of every piece. "Well, monsieur?"

asked the manager. "Does the suite live up to your expectations?"

"Perfect, sure, just what I need," the Judge drawled in a bored monotone.

"*Merveilleux!*" the manager gushed. "And how long will we have the pleasure of serving you?"

"How long? You mean how long am I gonna be here?" Hofheinz rumbled. "Hell, not more than half an hour, I hope."

The manager was perplexed. "But the accommodations . . . you have found something in error . . .?"

"Everything's just dandy," Hofheinz replied, already propelling himself toward the elevator, where his assistants were preparing the sedan chair. "Perfect. Now just wrap this stuff up, all of it, and I'll have it shipped to Houston."

By 1976, he had surrendered control of his Astrodomain. His successors were trying to sell off some of the Astrodomain's substantial assets to pay off Hofheinz's $38 million in long-term debt. In October, 1976, the Judge sold his Astros to General Electric Credit Corp. and Ford Motor Credit Corp., two of the franchise's largest lenders.

In Houston, the Judge's "domed" stadium was being called the "doomed" stadium.

By 1976, Judge Roy Hofheinz was aging and infirm, a witness to the Decline and Fall of his own empire. But the tradition of outlandish Texans still had a champion in Houston. Bud Adams owns the Houston Oilers football team, five pairs of ostrich-skin cowboy boots, at least one hundred million dollars, and an antique red fire-engine, in which he tools around one of his four ranches. Once, he punched a sportswriter in the nose. Once, he helped create a football league.

Kenneth Stanley Adams, Jr., was born in 1923, not quite as rich as either Murchison or Hunt, but still a millionaire. His father, Boots Adams, was the dictatorial oil baron who ruled Philips Petroleum for thirteen years. His uncle, W. W. Keeler, succeeded Boots; he was chief executive of Philips for six years—and principal chief of the Cherokee Nation for twenty-two years. Bud, age fifty-three, is the only half-Indian (half-German) owner in professional sports. But the Oilers' ballplayers who nicknamed him

"Crazy Horse's Revenge" weren't thinking only about his ancestry.

Bud Adams owns the Ada Oil Company. Ada is the largest distributor of Philips Petroleum products in the Western Hemisphere and the sixth largest gasoline retailer in the Houston market, home base for the U.S. oil industry. Besides the $50 million in revenues Ada generates each year, Adams owns the largest Lincoln-Mercury dealership in the United States, the largest independent automobile-leasing company in Houston, the largest independent travel agency in Houston, four cattle ranches in Texas, an enormous vegetable farm in California, a $1 million hog farm in Texas, and real-estate operations that include an eighteen-million-dollar, twenty-six-story doctors' center in Houston. In total, Adams estimates that these ventures produce more than $100 million a year in revenues. And that sum may swell soon by an additional $200 million. Adams has a 20 percent interest in a seven-partner consortium currently searching for natural gas in the Gulf of Guayaquil, near Ecuador. Adams is the operator of the consortium, which already has two and a half trillion cubic feet of gas behind pipe. He predicts that the total yield may eventually climb to *six trillion cubic feet.*

Like Hunt and Murchison and Hofheinz, Bud Adams became smitten in the 1950's by the siren call of ownership. When Hofheinz and his millionaire backer, Bob Smith, formed the Houston Sports Association, Bud Adams bought 10 percent of the stock. He quickly became disenchanted with the Judge's improvident spending. "They spent six and a half million on the Astros in the first year alone," Adams says.

Adams backed out of pro baseball, and into pro football. Like Hunt and Murchison, he tried to purchase the Chicago Cardinals from the Wolfner family, but had no more success than his competitors from Dallas; the Wolfners were willing to sell him only 4 percent of their franchise. Then Adams got a better offer, one he couldn't refuse. Lamar Hunt asked him if he would help start a new professional league. Adams agreed immediately. He would play a major role both in founding the AFL and in engineering its eventual merger into the NFL.

In those early years of his franchise, Adams barely averted a string of near-catastrophes, mainly the by-product of his long-running feud with Roy Hofheinz. Hofheinz owned the only major league football facility in Houston, the Astrodome; he wouldn't take Bud Adams for a tenant. Houston's one other viable stadium belonged to Rice University, but Rice wouldn't rent to Adams, either. So Adams was forced to install his Oilers in a dilapidated high school stadium, which one newsman immortalized as "an open sewer." Finally, in 1965, Adams and Hofheinz decided to put profits before personalities: the Oilers would move into the Astrodome. "But when I got the lease from Mr. Hofheinz," Adams says, "it was so different from what we had talked about that I just didn't want to sign it." Three weeks before the Oilers' opening game, with thousands of season tickets already sold, Adams convinced Rice to rent its stadium to his Oilers, at $100,000 a year. "The Judge thought he had me over the barrel," Adams says. As it turned out, Adams had the NFL over a barrel. The Judge and Adams would be feuding over that lease till 1969; Adams could keep one foot in Rice Stadium and one in the Astrodome, leaving the NFL no place to put its proposed expansion franchise.

During their first five years, the Oilers had won games but had lost money. In that sixth season, 1965–66, the benefactor who funded much of the sports boom of the 1960's came to Adams' aid. "I was saved by NBC," Adams says. "They gave me a five-hundred-thousand-dollar advance on my television contract." But the solution was only a stopgap measure. Like other AFL owners, Adams was engaged in a bonus war with the NFL. "The last year of the battle, 1966, my bonuses—just bonus money alone—ran eight hundred and fifty thousand dollars," Adams recalls. "I'm still paying off some of them and will be for the next seven years."

In 1967, the year after the AFL and NFL finally agreed to merge, Adams' bonus outlay dropped to $160,000. After having amassed between $4 and $5 million in losses, the Houston Oilers turned a profit for the very first time. That's one reason why Adams was only too happy to pay the NFL a $2 million indemnity, almost eighty times the $25,000 his AFL franchise had cost him in 1959. Two years later, in 1969–70, Adams and Hofheinz came to terms. The Oilers moved into the Astrodome.

In the old AFL, the Oilers had been consistent winners. In the

NFL, they became an immediate and enduring symbol of futility. Recently, however, they have showed signs of becoming a power-house again. Since Bud Adams got much of the blame for the Oilers' failure in the early post-merger years, he deserves a share of the credit for their success since 1974. In any case, win or lose, his guiding—and sometimes imperious—hand has never been off the organization's tiller. In the Oilers' first thirteen years, for in-stance, Adams hired and fired eight head coaches, seven general managers and scores of assistants. The most popular joke around the Oilers' office was: "If the head coach calls, get his name." And when former trainer Bobby Brown opened a health club in Hous-ton, a sportswriter suggested he feature a drink called the Oiler Boiler: "Drink one and you want to fire somebody."

No disciple of Murchison's "passive management," Bud has managed over the years to confound, and sometimes antagonize, his players with an unpredictability matched only by Charles O. Finley's. In 1960, the Oilers won the AFL championship; Adams promised each player a diamond ring. Thirteen years later, the team members bought themselves diamond rings. In 1962, Adams splurged and sent his entire team to train in Hawaii. The next year, he told everyone the Oilers would train in Spain, in a bullring. The only bull the Oilers encountered, however, was Adams' promise to ferry them to Spain.

His relations with the local press corps have been no less stormy. One Saturday afternoon, the AFL owners were concluding a three-day meeting at the Shamrock Hilton in Houston. Adams, who had left after the morning session, returned in his ranch clothes for the afternoon powwow just as Jack Gallagher of the Houston *Post* arrived with a photographer. Gallagher wanted two photos—one with all the owners, the other with all the owners except Adams. Some reporters who witnessed the confrontation insist that Gallagher wanted to avoid embarrassing Adams, the only owner not decked out in a business suit. Adams has a different interpretation. "He was telling me," says Adams, "that I was not dressed for the occasion. So I said, 'Gallagher, you can really hurt a guy.'" Adams then suggested to Gallagher that maybe Jack could use a nose job, and that he, Bud Adams, was willing to perform the surgery, then and there, with his fist. "And Gallagher said," recalls Adams, " 'If you think you're big enough to do it, why don't you try?' Well, that's all I needed. I went over and punched him. I had him down and he hauled off and kicked me right in the you-know-where. With that, I jumped right down on top of him, and I was really going to hurt him real good."

Adams outweighed Gallagher by about sixty pounds, and probably would have succeeded in hurting Gallagher "real good," but for the intervention of Al Davis. Davis (now general managing partner of the Oakland Raiders) had that very day been appointed Commissioner of the AFL. His first official act of arbitration was to separate Houston Oilers owner Bud Adams from Houston *Post* sportswriter Jack Gallagher.

Yet Adams has also shown compassion for the press. Despite frequent run-ins with Wells Twombly, the respected sports columnist, Adams once gave him a two-year-old car to replace his battered auto when he was a newspaper man in Houston. Adams also agreed to sponsor Twombly's radio program. "I told him I would have to rip him on my program just to retain my integrity," says Twombly. "And he said, 'That's okay.' "

Twombly also has an explanation why a multimillionaire like Bud Adams bothers to own a pro franchise at all, and his analysis illuminates not only Adams' motive, but those of other pro franchise owners. In spite of Adams' enormous wealth, Twombly argues, he always craved—and always lacked—public recognition. "Now Bud is someone, because he runs a ball club; the Oilers are his only real contact with fame. That's why rich men buy ball clubs. The little people love you or they hate you; but at least they *know* you."

◀ 7 ▶
The Accidental Millionaire

Charlie Finley sat behind a desk in his tower suite in Chicago—
a deeply tanned, beetle-browed six-footer, with white hair that
barely concealed a bald scalp, and eyes that penetrated like lasers.
He flicked his French cuffs back off his wrists. He tugged irritably
at his vest. Then he picked up an orange baseball lying on his desk.
"Just want to see if the baseball is the same color all the way
through," he told the salesman sitting nearby. The salesman
squirmed uncomfortably, staring at the high ceilings, Oriental
rugs, hardwood floor, the medical scale in a corner behind the desk,
the large phone console standing on top of a tall ashtray. He stared
anywhere except at Finley, who was slicing through the seams of
the orange baseball with a pair of scissors.

The reason for the salesman's discomfort soon became obvious. The baseball wasn't orange all the way through. The cover was
simply dyed orange. Finley didn't stop at the cover. He began
unraveling a mass of string and yarn. He unraveled the ball down
to its core, then held up a mass of compressed cloth strips trium-
phantly. "Why, this is a rag ball," he said, his voice brimming with
indignation. "It says it has a cork-and-rubber center, and it's just
a rag ball!"

"Keep looking," the salesman pleaded. "Rags aren't that

119

unusual. There are some balls that have straw under the string and yarn. And some that are made up of crushed-up carton."

Finley picked the rags apart and finally located a tiny rubberized center. He picked up the cover to read the price.

"That's what we call our major league baseball," the salesman said quickly. "It's our cheapest model."

"Too cheap," Finley snapped, expertly flipping the rubberized center into a wastebasket ten feet away.

Ten minutes later, Finley was sitting in a car, watching his chauffeur negotiate the maze of Chicago's rush-hour traffic. "Get this crate rolling," he snorted. The chauffeur, Howard Risner, weaved through the sluggish traffic toward O'Hare airport. "Shoot the works," Finley called out from the back seat. The chauffeur pressed a button; a musical horn blared stridently. Then Finley himself pressed a button and began speaking into a microphone, calling to startled pedestrians through a loudspeaker hidden beneath the Cadillac's hood. "Hey, Howard," he said to the chauffeur, "now we're *really* going. Hit that horn again!"

By the time his plane landed in Kansas City, where his Oakland A's were to play the Royals, Charlie had invited most of the first-class passengers to be his guest at the ball park. A stewardess —whom he had greeted with, "Hey, baby, you look great!"—was on familiar enough terms by the end of the flight to plant a goodbye kiss on Finley's lips. A Kansas City lawyer offered to drive Charlie to the ball park. Finley accepted. The cab fare from the airport to the park was $20.

In the A's clubhouse, he was greeted by his players: "Christ, Charlie's back again." But Finley was oblivious to their mockery. He was too busy handing out samples of his latest innovation— Day-Glo baseballs. He handed one to pitcher Vida Blue. Blue flicked the orange ball into his locker, a gesture of utter contempt.

While baseball's owners were contending with Branch Rickey's Continental League and trying to pacify the likes of Roy Hofheinz, an even greater threat to their power—and peace of mind—was brewing. An unknown insurance salesman was negotiating to purchase control of a major league team. Finally, in 1960, he succeeded in buying a 52 percent interest in the Kansas City

The Accidental Millionaire

Athletics, a recent expansion franchise in the American League. No one paid much attention, but in hindsight the baseball establishment must rue the day they approved that sale more than any day in modern times.

The insurance salesman's name, of course, was Charles O. Finley. He would spread his brand of havoc to basketball and hockey, but he reserved his best—and worst—for baseball.

Charles O. Finley is a publicity hound, he is contentious, he is a maverick. And, most critics agree, he is probably a genius— the only owner since Connie Mack to act as his team's general manager, chief scout, press secretary and head cheerleader, all with enviable success. "When I came into baseball in Kansas City back in 1960," Finley says, "they told me I'd have to have this and I'd have to have that. I found out one thing about baseball people right away. They like to make the game sound so complex, nobody but them can run it. Well, it doesn't take a genius to run a ball club. Most managers aren't worth a damn," he adds. "They talk about how clever they are and how much strategy they use. In reality, you could get one of the park policemen to stand out there and wave pitchers in and out of the ball game.

"It was the same thing when I bought the hockey team and the basketball team [the California Golden Seals of the NHL and the Memphis Tams of the ABA]. I had some knowledge of hockey, and everybody in Indiana, where I come from, is an expert on basketball. They told me to get men who know all about these sports. I told them I could learn quicker and it would cost me less. I hired Gary Young to run the hockey club, and he spent over eleven million dollars in salaries he didn't tell me about. I can do that myself, and at least I'll know where the money is going."

The roots of Finley's abrasive and flagrant personality lie in his past. Unlike Hunt and Murchison and Hofheinz and Adams, success in life came relatively late to Charlie Finley, as a result of an accident—a near-fatal illness. Much of Finley's impatience with opinions contrary to his own is the accidental millionaire's distrust of a world which has accorded him money, but not respect. Much of Finley's motivation for meddling is the accidental millionaire's need to achieve something in life after his lifelong goals have been realized. The crucial common denominator, the bottom line on

121

The Rich Who Own Sports

Charlie Finley, is that he was born poor. And while most other self-made men who own franchises would rather forget their penurious beginnings, Finley wears his humble origins like a coat of arms.

"My God," says Bill Dauer, the executive vice-president of the Chamber of Commerce when Finley's Oakland A's were still the Kansas City Athletics, "I had to hear the story of how he made his money five hundred times."

Finley made his money the way mules make their reputations for orneriness: by marching to his own drummer, no matter who was calling the tune. Hard work is his religion. "Sweat and sacrifice spell success" is his catechism. "Don't wait, make it happen" is his precipitous lifelong tactic. His fellow owners, whether they inherited their fortunes or made them, have almost all been willing to abide by the protocols of big business. Finley has always remained a machinist at heart—a proletarian rooted in his past.

Charles Oscar Finley was born on a farm, a small, hard-scrabble plot in Ensley, Alabama, on February 22, 1918. (Cynics will revel—and astrologers will despair—over the fact that another great American was born on that date: George Washington.) Charlie was the great-grandson of Protestants from County Offaly, Ireland. He was the son of Oscar Finley, an immigrant who worked in the steel mills of nearby Birmingham to supplement his meager income as a farmer.

During the Depression, the Finleys were forced to give up their farm. They moved to Birmingham. The heartbeat of Finley's youth was steel clanging against steel; the son of a steelworker when steelworkers barely earned enough to eat, he had to work almost from the time he could walk. He sold magazines door-to-door. He bought reject eggs for five cents a dozen and sold them for fifteen. He and a friend picked grapes, then made wine and sold it to neighbors. In the scant leisure left, he played baseball. "First baseball I ever got was a cottonseed ball," he recalls. "You hit it once and it was all over the place. Then you put friction tape all around it. Then you had a *ball.*" By the age of twelve, he had already organized his own sandlot team. Baseball would become his incurable obsession; he would play in semi-pro leagues until he was twenty-nine, and today he still sponsors several Little League and semi-pro teams. "I always wanted to be a player," he says, "but I never had the talent to make the big leagues. So I did the next best thing. I bought a team."

In 1934, at sixteen, Charlie and his family moved to Gary, Indiana. His father got a job at the U.S. Steel works. Charlie attended Horace Mann High School, where he was even better known for his skill with the ladies than with a baseball bat. "We looked on him as quite a dude," recalls one former, and female, classmate, "because he wore a sport coat to school. I'd say the girls remember him more as a good dancer than as an athlete."

Charlie graduated from high school, then followed his father into the the mills—unbearable white heat, a din that could drive you crazy. By day, he taxed his muscles, earning forty-seven cents an hour; by night, he taxed his brain, as a part-time student at Gary Junior College. Somehow, he managed to find time to play first base for the LaPorte Cubs, in a suburb of Gary. His schedule of work, study and play demanded stoicism and self-sacrifice. It limited him to five hours of sleep a night. Three years later, he had completed his engineering course. The degree was good for only a twenty-cent-per-hour raise; he still needed a part-time job. He went to work as a clerk in a butcher shop—and met his future wife. Shirley McCartney would come in and order five dollars' worth of meat. Finley would scan her pretty face and pert figure; he would give her twelve dollars' worth. Shirley's father thought she was a super-shopper. Charlie's employer thought he was a super-sales-man—until he tallied the cash receipts one day and saw they didn't match the total sales. He fired Finley.

In 1941, Charlie had a wife, he had an ulcer, his life seemed to be plummeting hellbent toward mediocrity. Then World War II created a new set of conditions. Finley shook off his lethargy and rushed to join the Armed Forces. The Marine Corps rejected him because of the ulcer. The Army, Navy and Air Force turned him down, too. Spurred on by patriotism, he didn't give up. He searched until he found a job at the Kingsbury Ordinance Plant in La Porte, which manufactured small-caliber ammunition for the government. Soon he was a divisional superintendent, in charge of 5,000 workers. At night, he began selling life insurance, a profession he adopted full-time as soon as the war ended.

The Rich Who Own Sports

He outworked all his competitors. He shattered all records at the Travelers Insurance Company for sales of accident policies in a single year. He also shattered his own health. Destiny intervened, disguised as an illness, and in 1946, at the age of twenty-eight, Finley was told by his doctors that he was suffering from an advanced case of pneumonic tuberculosis, what our grandfathers called "galloping consumption." The malady was supposed to be incurable; at the time, there were no effective antibiotics to combat it. And since both lungs were infected, the only possible treatment, collapsing one lung, was out of the question. His only chance for survival was rest—and prayer.

Finley was transferred to the James O. Parramore Hospital in Crown Point, Indiana. According to his doctors, he was dying. According to his bank book, he was broke. His wife Shirley was forced to take a job as a proofreader on the Gary *Post-Tribune* for $40 a week, to support herself and her two children.

Little by little, Finley wasted away. He shriveled to ninety-six pounds, his emaciated body a frightful echo of the Nazi concentration camps liberated a few years before. He began to suffer from bouts of sweating. For twenty-four days, he grew more and more dehydrated until finally, after a severe attack, a male sanitarium orderly approached him and said, quietly but firmly: "You'd better cut that sweating out. The guy across the hall had those same symptoms. Last night he died."

For the first time, Finley saw Death in all its desolate finality. From then on, he fought back. He downed water like a thirst-stricken camel. When he vomited, he forced himself to swallow more food, repeating the cycle time and time again. Finally, after thirty-two days, the symptoms subsided. Charlie knew he was going to survive. He also knew he was going to be very rich. "Here I was selling insurance, " he says, "and I didn't have any myself. I'd told myself I'd buy some when I was forty. But I was only twenty-nine or so. I was the living proof that professional men needed it. My kids were the living victims. I couldn't wait to get out and preach the gospel."

In 1948, twenty-seven months after he had entered the sanitarium, Finley was released—a healthy man, with a scheme to make a healthy fortune. But he was just where Ray Kroc would be a few years later, when he decided to stake everything on his McDonald's franchises: Finley needed a backer who could put cash where Charlie's mouth was. Finley's efforts to find an insurance company willing to increase the length, and cut the price, of sickness and accident policies for medical men met with rebuff after rebuff. But his perseverance finally paid off. "His first really big customer," recalls a friend, "was a national professional organization of doctors, the American College of Surgeons. Sometime in 1951, they were holding a meeting in San Francisco, and Charlie was dying to get out there. But he didn't even have the price of an air ticket out West. So he went out and got another loan on his car —an old DeSoto, I think it was. Well, as soon as Charlie got that two-thousand-dollar loan, he ran out and bought two suits, and got his first manicure. Then he sped off for the airport. His car broke down on the way, but he still got there in time to buy his ticket and board the plane. When Charlie came home from San Francisco," the friend adds, "he had something like $800,000 in commissions assured to him."

Finley hawked those policies the way, as a kid, he had hawked cracked eggs door-to-door, using guile and enthusiasm—and stubbornness. First he sold the premiums through the Continental Casualty Company, then through his own firm, Charles O. Finley & Company, of Chicago. Within two years, he had made his first million, and eventually his company's gross revenues surpassed $40 million annually. His personal worth is estimated (conservatively) at about $30 million.

Money didn't make Finley content. He realized that for him it was getting to the top that had given life a sense of challenge. Life now seemed somehow anticlimactic. Money, after all, couldn't buy everything. It couldn't restore his youth, or revive the dream he once had of playing major league baseball. But there was one thing money could do. If Finley couldn't be a major league player, he could be a major league owner—and a manager, too.

The first club he tried to purchase was the Philadelphia Athletics; the Athletics' owners felt his three-million-dollar offer wasn't generous enough. He had no luck trying to buy a share of the Detroit Tigers, either. Or the Chicago White Sox. Or the Los Angeles Angels. Only after the Athletics had moved to Kansas

City, and had been converted into a virtual Yankee farm club, was Finley allowed into the major league establishment. In 1960, he bought 52 percent of the Kansas City Athletics for $1,975,000. Just a few months later, he purchased the remaining 48 percent for another $1,975,000. In total, the franchise cost him $3,950,000. (Now, he says, he wouldn't sell for less than $15 million.)

From the start, Finley claims, he was made to feel like an intruder. "The old-time owners didn't accept me then, and I don't expect they ever will," he says. "I didn't inherit a team. I didn't work my way up through the minor leagues as an executive. At the first major league meeting, after I had bought the Athletics and Gene Autry had bought the Angels," he recalls, "Ford Frick presided as Commissioner, but he didn't even have the courtesy to introduce either of us to the National League owners."

When Finley took charge, the Athletics were perennial losers. In twenty-seven seasons in Philadelphia and Kansas City, they had managed only twice to finish in the first division. They had finished dead-last thirteen times. When Parke Carroll (the general manager Finley inhereted when he bought the club) died, Finley hired a respected baseball man, Frank Lane, as his general manager. Finley made speeches around town as if he were running for political office against an invisible, but ubiquitous, foe. In those speeches—to women's clubs, Rotaries, Kiwanises, to any assembly that would listen—he promised that the franchise would become both a winner and a permanent fixture in Kansas City. He was going to move his family down from the Finley farm in La Porte, Indiana, near Gary. He promised to plow not only the club's profits back into the franchise, but his own salaries from baseball as well. He was going to appoint three Kansas City businessmen to the club's board of directors, so the local citizens could be sure he was acting in their behalf.

Then, little by little, the dark side of Charlie Finley began to emerge. Before Finley arrived, fans had been accusing the Athletics' management of turning the franchise into a Yankee farm team, skimming off the cream of Kansas City's baseball talent, shipping men like Roger Maris, Ralph Terry, Clete Boyer and Hector Lopez to New York in "shuttle bus" trades. Soon after he purchased the club, Finley burned a bus behind the left-field wall—a fiery symbol

126

that the shuttle to New York had ended. On June 9, 1961, he reaffirmed his pledge not to trade with the Yankees. "I gave the fans in Kansas City my word we would not trade with the Yankees," he said, "and my word is my bond." Six days later, he defaulted on that bond—trading pitcher Bud Daley to the Yankees for Deron Johnson and Art Ditmar.

After antagonizing the fans, Finley went to work on the local politicians. In 1963, Lamar Hunt arrived with his newly named Kansas City Chiefs in tow. Finley began complaining that he was being charged about $125,000 a year for Municipal Stadium, while the Chiefs were paying a paltry $1 plus a percentage of the concessions—in total, approximately $15,000 a year. The local politicians pointed out that Hunt's Chiefs would use the stadium far less often than Finley's Athletics. Their argument fell on deaf ears.

Finley's abrasive behavior, his conviction that in any situation there is only one correct answer (his) and his willingness to use any means to achieve his ends earned him enemies. His general manager in Kansas City, Frank Lane, is still a sergeant in the anti-Finley brigade. Typically, the power struggle between them ended up in absurd accusations of Indian-giving. The disputed gift was a $10,000 Mercedes-Benz, which Finley had "given" his new general manager when he took the job.

"Lane wanted a ten-gallon hat to go along with the car," Finley says. "So I bought him one for a hundred dollars at Neiman-Marcus in Dallas."

Finley and Lane soon learned they couldn't agree on anything besides ten-gallon hats and ten-thousand-dollar automobiles. Lane departed—at the wheel of that gift car, his ears tucked beneath the brim of that gift hat. It was then, in the kind of apoplectic outburst that mortifies his fellow owners, that Finley ordered Lane to give back the automobile. He argued that the Mercedes went with the job, not the man. Lane refused. To this day, the car sits unused in a garage near Lane's home in Florida.

Finley has the ownership title.

Lane has the keys and the ten-gallon hat.

In the eyes of his public in Kansas City, not only did Finley become a lease-breaker and an Indian-giver, but he had already proven he was no philanthropist. Parke Carroll, Finley's first general manager, died of a sudden heart attack. There was $50,000 owing on Carroll's two-year-contract. Carroll's widow asked Finley for the money. Finley had just spent $80,000 on promotional material, $135,000 on his Fan-O-Gram scoreboard, another $70,000 moving his fences back and an additional $32,000 on firecrackers. Most everyone thought Finley would give Carroll's widow the $50,000. Most everyone was wrong. Finley forced Carroll's widow to sue. She lost the suit. Finley lost the few friends he had left in Kansas City.

Finally, after attempts to move the Athletics to Dallas–Fort Worth, Texas, and to Louisville, Kentucky, had failed,—Finley was allowed to shift his franchise to Oakland in 1968. He had conducted that search for a new site with typical Finley unpredictability. When he decided to transfer his Athletics franchise out of Kansas City, he commissioned a research firm to locate the best city for his new franchise, just the way a Clint Murchison might have done. Then, as only a Charlie Finley would, he surveyed the prospective cities himself, telephoned the research firm and said, "Tell me to move to Oakland."

The A's climbed from sixth place in the American League standings to second place in the league's western division in 1969 and 1970, to first place in 1971 and to the world championship in 1972, 1973 and 1974. But the move to Oakland didn't mellow Finley. His protracted salary dispute with Vida Blue in 1972 left scars on the pitcher's psyche. In the 1973 World Series, he forced reserve second baseman Mike Andrews onto the inactive list as punishment for making a crucial error. That cost Finley $7,000 in fines—and the services of the best manager in baseball, Dick Williams. Williams refused to return to the A's the following season. No one was safe, not even the men Finley employed in the broadcasting booth. The moment Joe Pepitone—the first major-leaguer to let his (store-bought) hair fall past his ears—stepped up to the plate in an Oakland uniform, Finley telephoned his man in the broadcasting booth, John O'Reilly. "He wanted me to introduce the batter as 'Josephine Pepitone,'" O'Reilly recalls. "I told him I couldn't do it. We argued. I resigned before he could fire me."

"Charlie butted into everything," says Bob Elson, a former A's announcer. "He'd sell tickets, hawk programs, sweep out the ball park, anything. He's the hardest-working man in baseball, but Charlie Finley feels that if Charlie Finley should drop dead, the whole world would just stop turning around."

"I'd never known what it was like being a common laborer, until I spent my time with Charlie Finley," says former Golden Seals public relations director Bob Bestor. Finley purchased the NHL Golden Seals in 1970, and for the next three years the Seals finished no higher than sixth in the league standings. His venture into pro basketball was no more successful. In 1972, he bought the Memphis team of the ABA and renamed them the Tams (probably the worst nickname in the history of pro sports), from the initials of the three states they drew support from—Tennessee, Arkansas and Missouri. In 1972–73, the Tams lost sixty out of eighty-four games, and cost Finley $490,000. "I was used to 'Would you please do this?' and 'What do you think of that?' " Bestor adds. "But Charlie is a straw boss on a construction job. He expects a hard day's work for a hard day's pay and reserves the right to chew you out. He's from a different world."

"Charlie has this one little weakness," sums up another ex-A's broadcaster. "He doesn't treat people like human beings."

Finley's relations with the press haven't been any smoother. One day, Finley glanced at his press list. Deciding there were too many freeloaders before night games, he decreed that the first fifty reporters in attendance at the Oakland Coliseum would get fried chicken dinners. The rest could bring their own. Writers who qualify for a free lunch before day games, often find, among the traditional ham sandwich and apple, a couple of oatmeal cookies. Oatmeal cookies are Finley's favorites.

Once, Finley ejected the Oakland *Tribune*'s Ron Bergman from an A's charter flight. Bergman had had the nerve to suggest in print that the Oakland broadcasters were a little too effusive in their praise for Finley. During an Oakland vs. Cincinnati World Series, Finley threw a punch at Chicago *Daily News* columnist Dave Nightingale. The writer had dared to interview Shirley Finley without her husband's consent.

At that same World Series against Cincinnati, Finley had lobsters flown in from Maine for the newsmen. Having flattered them, he then proceeded to insult them, leading his mascot mule,

Charlie O., into the World Series Hospitality Suite. More than one newsman's appetite disappeared when a long mournful snout started chomping on his salad. Finley thought the incident was hilarious. "I just wanted to see what would happen when one mule was confronted by three hundred asses," he quipped. The writers, who take their privileges seriously, were indignant. They appealed to Commissioner Bowie Kuhn. Kuhn ordered the mule barred from the Hospitality Suite. In 1973, when the Series again returned to Oakland, the writers boycotted Finley's Hospitality Suite. They preferred to buy (at their editors' expense, of course) their own dinners in restaurants. Finley was undaunted. He was determined to prove he was a grandmaster of one-upmanship. After the Saturday Series game, a number of baseball writers were dining at Oakland's Elegant Farmer Restaurant in Jack London Square. In walked the Charlie O.'s—mule and man. As the mule passed the tableful of writers, its tail knocked over a drink, staining one journalist's suit. At the time, the writer was pro-Finley. Now he has joined the multitude of Finley's critics. Even a man who knows and respects Finley, and who considers himself a friend, feels obligated to admit: "He has the worst sense of public relations of anyone I ever saw."

And yet the few friends Finley has in baseball are among the most loyal anywhere. They admire his boldness in taking the Kansas City Athletics to Oakland when almost everyone thought such a move would be financial suicide. Finley negotiated a shrewd lease for the Oakland Coliseum. He managed to make owning the franchise profitable.

He has also turned the A's into winners on the field, proving himself an astute general manager. In 1972, he traded home run and RBI leader Mike Epstein, plus catcher Dave Duncan, for a very hittable relief pitcher named Horacio Pina and a weak-hitting catcher named Ray Fosse. The next season, Mike Epstein didn't play. Dave Duncan didn't hit. Pina turned out to be one of the best relievers in the American League; Fosse, a defensive craftsman behind the plate.

And he's not just a shrewd general manager. He's also a cunning manager-by-proxy. In the 1974 World Series, he converted left fielder Joe Rudi into a first baseman; he benched his regular first baseman, Gene Tenace (who had previously been the A's starting catcher), in order to play, in center field, an untried eighteen-year-old named Claudel Washington. Washington responded with a barrage of hits that helped send the Los Angeles Dodgers to defeat.

He's been one of baseball's most creative innovators, too. It was his innovations, in fact, that helped baseball recover from a twelve-year decline. He painted the stadium seats in Kansas City yellow and turquoise. He painted the foul lines a fluorescent pink. In the outfield, he installed a flock of sheep, tended by a shepherd. He set up a picnic area beyond the bleachers, beneath a grove of sugar maples. When the home plate umpire ran out of baseballs, he didn't have to wait for the batboy to bring him new ones; a mechanical rabbit, wearing an A's uniform, popped up from its burrow by the plate with a baseball. Umpires didn't even have to lower themselves to dust off the plate; a mechanical duster called "Little Blowhard" did it for them. "The trouble with baseball," says Finley, "is that it's got its head in the sand. What the game needs is progressive thinking and new ideas. We have got to keep up with the times."

Anyone who disagrees with him he brands as hopelessly anachronistic. "My idea of promoting was to get one more run than the other team," says his former general manager, Frank Lane. "It's the greatest promotion in the world." Finley had other ideas. In 1963, he changed the A's uniform to gold, green and white, with white shoes. ("Kelly green and Finley gold," explained one player.) "When colored uniforms were considered the work of a heretic," Finley says, "I stood up. I knew the system of home whites and road grays couldn't continue. They laughed at the white shoes and said that the Oakland infield looked like a softball team for a gay bar. But I could sense a trend. Now lots of teams have colored uniforms. Our white, green and gold suits are the fashion-setters. When we went to mix-or-match, using green shirts with white pants or white shirts with gold pants or gold-on-gold or green-on-green, they said we were making a farce of the game. Now I see other teams doing the same thing."

He put a roving Dixieland band in the stands, in 1890's outfits, led by a man known only as "the Professor." The band plays only four tunes; it never stops playing them. He hired clowns. He hired dancing bears. He hired equestrian acts. He paid his players $300 apiece to sprout mustaches for a Mustache Day promotion, and the hairy upper lips became, for a while, the Oakland hallmark. He introduced a designated runner; he tried to convince the establishment to start the World Series on a weekend, and to play weekday Series and All-Star games at night. He wants the league to adopt an orange baseball for better visibility; he wants three eight-team regional leagues, interleague play, three pitched balls to count as a walk . . . There is no limit to the innovations he would make, if not held in check by his colleagues.

Finley has no patience for his fellow owners' fear of change. "We in baseball know what our problems are and we can correct them overnight," he is fond of repeating. "Overnight! It's stupidity that we don't. Gross stupidity, which is one hundred and forty-four times worse than plain stupidity. My God, when you're in business and you know sales are slipping and you know why your sales are not increasing with population growth and you do nothing about it, that's stupid."

Despite his egomania, his admirers, be they ever so few, are quick to point out that he is one of the few modern owners who has shown a real concern for the comfort of his customers. On the A's first "Cap Day," for instance, he was driving his wife and seven children to the ball park when he saw a long line of fans queuing outside his ticket booths and several booths with no ticket-takers at all. He stopped his Volkswagen bus, leaped out and screamed, "This is ridiculous, just awful! Look at these people—waiting to give me money!" Storming over to one of the men in charge of the booths, he shouted, "These people won't see the game start, the kiddies won't see the *mule!*" The employee nervously suggested that what was required was more signs directing customers to the proper booths. Finley hissed: "Signs, my ass. Get more ticket-sellers!"

He has also, and with a minimum of fanfare, been generous and compassionate with some of his players. "He helped me with financial problems," says ex-A's pitcher Diego Segui. "He has helped a lot of other players, too, and some of them, after they were traded, turned against Mr. Finley. I don't like that."

The Accidental Millionaire

When pitcher Rollie Fingers was still a minor-leaguer, and was struck by a line drive that fractured his jaw, Finley sent him and his wife to Florida for a three-week vacation.

When the young Catfish Hunter lost a toe in a hunting accident soon after he had signed with the A's for a large bonus, Finley turned up at Hunter's house. Even if Hunter never pitched another game in his life, Finley told him, he shouldn't worry. He could keep the bonus money, and besides, Oakland would make sure he received, free of cost, the best medical care available.

In 1973, Gene Tenace hit four home runs in the World Series. Finley greeted him on the A's charter flight with a check for $5,000 (which cost him an additional $2,500 when the gift was made public, since bonus incentives are prohibited.) "Joe Cronin [whom Finley, in 1973, called publicly "a sanctimonious old fart"] once asked me if it was true I gave my players extra money," Finley explains. " 'You shouldn't do that,' he told me. 'It makes it hard on the other owners.' Why, if I can't do that for my players, I should get out of baseball."

Still, the nice things Finley does get crushed beneath the weight of his epic intransigence, and rudeness, and obstinacy, and arbitrariness. A few years ago, before the A's came east to confront the Baltimore Orioles in a playoff game, infielder Ted Kubiak learned his wife had been shunted to stand-by status on the A's charter flight because the owner had reserved fifteen seats for his friends. During the 1973 World Series, Gene Tenace recalls, "Just before Tuesday night's ball game, my wife came up to me in tears. She and all the other wives were sitting way up in the third deck." Tenace and his teammates were convinced that Finley had exchanged their wives' tickets, giving the preferred set to a group of cronies.

In the 1974 World Series, Oakland vs. the Los Angeles Dodgers, A's manager Alvin Dark's son was barred from the clubhouse by Finley, while Finley's grandson was given more latitude than the working press. Finley also barred Dark's wife from the team charter flights, while Miss California—a tall, willowy blonde from whom the owner was rarely separated during the Series—had a seat up front next to him. On the team charter flight from Los Angeles to Oakland, after the Series opener, Finley inflicted cruel and unusual punishment upon his players by forcing them, under protest, to listen to Miss California exercise her "talent" for singing at 30,000 feet.

And in 1976 Finley again astonished the sports world, this time by auctioning off those of his stars who, under baseball's revised reserve system, were threatening to play out their options and sign with other clubs. For the previous five years, the A's had dominated their division because they had players the caliber of Reggie Jackson, Ken Holtzman, Joe Rudi, Vida Blue and Rollie Fingers. In the winter of 1975, those five decided to play out their options and become free agents, so they refused to sign 1976 contracts. Rather than lose all that valuable talent without remuneration, Finley traded Jackson and Holtzman to Baltimore and sold Blue to the Yankees for $1.5 million and Rudi and Fingers to Boston for $1 million each.

Baseball Commissioner Bowie Kuhn didn't object when Finley traded Jackson and Holtzman, nor was he disturbed when the Twins' owner, Calvin Griffith, received $300,000 for trading *his* best pitcher, Burt Blyleven. But when Finley sold Blue and Rudi and Fingers for $3.5 million, Kuhn said that was bad for baseball and he wouldn't allow it. For once, public sympathy seemed to lie with Finley. Kuhn seemed to be deliberately punishing him because for years Finley had been trying to oust Kuhn as Commissioner. (At the same time, of course, Kuhn had punished pitcher Vida Blue, too. Blue had been playing out his option, till June of 1976, when to facilitate his sale to the Yankees—a trade he desperately wanted—he signed a three-year contract with Oakland. Now, through Kuhn's intervention, Vida would be the property of Oakland through *1978.*) In any case, after the 1976 season, Rudi and Fingers became free agents and departed from Oakland—proof of how little affection Finley's players felt for him. Rudi and Fingers were joined in their exodus by Campy Campaneris, Don Baylor, Sal Bando and Gene Tenace.

In 1973, Finley suffered a severe heart attack, and doctors advised him to cut down on work. He obeyed them by selling the Memphis Tams of the ABA and the California Golden Seals of the NHL, but he couldn't part with the A's. Part of the reason was sentiment; part was economics. Before moving to Kansas City,

The Accidental Millionaire

Finley negotiated a contract with the Oakland municipal government which allows the A's to pay relatively low rent for the use of the Oakland–Alameda County Coliseum and share heftily in TV, concession and parking revenues. (Finley receives 27.5 percent of the parking fees and 25 percent of the concession sales, while paying a minimum annual rental of only $125,000, or 5 percent of the gate up to $1.45 million—a total the A's have never approached. The lease runs for twenty years, a precaution that will probably turn out to be a technicality.) Since the move, the franchise has netted between $600,000 and $1,300,000 a season, making the A's—despite consistently low attendance—one of the more profitable teams in baseball. "I can turn a profit because I don't have too many unessential employees to pay big money to," Finley says. "I put my money into player development and don't worry about paying $20,000 to a public relations man who can't put any extra people in the seats anway."

The heart attack didn't force him to sell the A's, nor did it slow down his hectic schedule. Because of the demands of his insurance business in Chicago, and his baseball team in Oakland, Finley was never able to spend much time with his wife and seven children. Shirley and the unmarried children lived on a 1,280-acre cattle farm in La Porte, with Finley's parents living nearby on a farm Finley purchased for them. Finley, meanwhile, usually spent most of his time either in his apartment in Oakland, overlooking Lake Merritt, or in his apartment in Chicago, overlooking Lake Michigan. "I'm really ashamed of the time I've put in on baseball to the neglect of my family," he told Murray Chass of the New York *Times* in late 1972. "My wife and kids have really sacrificed." In 1974, newspapers across the country announced that Shirley Finley had initiated divorce proceedings. Their thirty-four-year marriage ended in 1975.

Finley's life style is still only slightly less flamboyant than his personality. At his two-bedroom apartment in Chicago, he is never very far away from a telephone. During every A's game, Finley keeps in touch either by calling the press box directly and getting a report from his public relations man or by dialing a special number at radio station KEEN in San Jose to plug in on the play-by-play broadcast. Aside from baseball and business, Finley's

135

main passion is eating. He's an expert cook. He enjoys serving guests his favorite meals: calf's liver and bacon, or avocado stuffed with crabmeat, followed by a two-pound T-bone steak.

His Chicago apartment is cluttered with pennants and trophies; an ironing board stands amid a mass of papers in one unfurnished room. The living room is usually decorated with neighbors and friends, sipping Finley's favorite wine, Liebfraumilch, or Finley's favorite sour mash, Jack Daniel's. Three Playboy Bunnies who live in the building sometimes stop by for a drink when they return home from work at 3 A.M., and Finley will occasionally entertain them with a borrowed guitar. Recently, Oakland *Tribune* columnist Marcy Bachmann selected Finley as one of her "20 Sexiest Men in the Eastbay."

When he leaves his apartment, either in Oakland or in Chicago, he usually travels by cab. If he finds none on the street, he'll simply flag down a police car. "Oh, excuse me," he'll say. "I thought you were a taxi." The cops are usually awed—and anxious to give the celebrity-owner a lift. If his destination is a restaurant, Finley will march straight into the kitchen, select the meat or fish, and tell the cook exactly how he wants it prepared. Even when he dines with friends, he tells everyone where he or she must sit. Nor is he any less autocratic when dealing with his own family. Once, during a recent World Series, a couple of reporters began asking Finley's son Marty what he thought of events up to then. His father moved in quickly. "You smile," he told his son. "I'll answer the questions."

"I have to admit it," says the Yankees' Reggie Jackson, Oakland's most valuable baseball property until Finley traded him to Baltimore before the start of the 1976 season. "Charlie can be a tyrant, but he can be a lot of fun, too. He knows how to raise a little hell. He knows how to have a good time. He would be a great guy to have as a buddy," Reggie adds slyly, "as long as you didn't have to work for him."

◀ 8 ▶
The Salesmen

Like Charlie Finley, Ewing Kauffman of the Kansas City Royals was bedridden with a near-fatal illness when he concocted the scheme that made him a millionaire. Like Charlie Finley, Ray Kroc of the San Diego Padres has always been an ardent baseball fan. All three were survivors of the Depression. They grew up watching their fathers fail, their families humiliated.

The similarities end there. Kauffman and Kroc share an unshakable enthusiasm foreign to Finley's erratic tyranny. Instead of alienating their players and fans, Kauffman and Kroc strive to infect everyone around them with optimism. They move through their locker rooms and stadiums like secular evangelists, delivering upbeat sermons based on the gospel of "can do." They are the prophets of positive thinking, they are the cheerleaders.

Ewing Kauffman, owner of the Kansas City Royals baseball team, owns a twenty-eight-room mansion in the Mission Hills suburb of Kansas City, built during the Depression for the then-formidable sum of $250,000. The house is unusual in a number of ways. When Kauffman purchased it, it already had a pipe organ and a library with Florentine-leather walls and a gilded ceiling. Kauffman and his wife, Muriel, added a swimming pool and a steam bath, plus a set of colored water fountains that spout twenty feet into the air at the press of a button. An art dealer once showed the Kauffmans a few paintings by an obscure artist named Gerrard Roemers, who died in 1965. One hundred of Roemers' paintings now decorate the mansion's walls.

But none of these features is what make that Mission Hills mansion truly remarkable. Its uniqueness, as Kauffman is fond of reminding visitors, goes much deeper—to the foundations of the house itself. "This house," says Kauffman, "was built on oyster shells."

Ewing Kauffman was born poor—on a dirt farm in Missouri. When he was eight, his father gave up trying to draw blood from a rock. He laid down his hoe and tiller. He relocated the family in Kansas City, searching for a better life among tall buildings and paved streets. The only thing he found was survival at subsistence and oblivion. Charlie Finley would make his millions selling insurance; for Ewing's father, his new career as an insurance salesman brought only heartaches. Things went so badly that Ewing's mother had to turn their home into a boarding house. Ewing grew up eating with strangers, who paid for the privilege of passing him the salt.

At the age of twelve, Ewing fell ill with rheumatic fever. He was confined to bed for nearly a year, as doctors prescribed a program of virtual immobility to correct a heart defect caused by the disease. But the curse of illness was in reality a blessing. Kauffman spent his time reading anything he could get—novels, biographies, travel guides, business, psychology, up to twenty books a week. And then, stumbling across a paperback anthology of math puzzles, he discovered something astounding. He could glance at a math problem and solve it almost instantly. He could perform complex calculations in his head. He had a genius for numbers.

Ewing's father had the knack for numbers, too. Now that he saw his son developing that same talent, he spent hours by Ewing's bedside, testing him. "What's thirty-six minus five, plus eight, divided by seven?" he would ask. Then, when Ewing replied, the elder Kauffman would lean back and say, "Okay, now it's your turn to give me one."

Ewing returned to school before his thirteenth birthday. But aside from helping him attain excellent grades in algebra, his mathematical talent proved as little use as his father's had before him. What good did it do if you could solve dollar *problems* in a split second, if you were barred by birth from accumulating *dollars?* It wasn't until he graduated from junior college, during World War II, and enlisted in the U.S. Navy, that he suddenly discovered a use for his math skills he could convert into instant cash. With his retentive memory for numbers, and his ability to perform rapid calculations in his head, he became an eager and fortunate participant in the perennial pastime of sailors with cash and time on their hands. He became a brilliant poker player. When he left the Navy four years later, he had, aside from his severance pay, the neat sum of $50,000.

It took him only one year to dissipate those winnings. After a twelve-month splurge, which proved to him that money, in large amounts, was absolutely indispensable, he went flat broke. He drifted for a while. Then he stumbled into a job as a drug salesman for a small pharmaceutical firm in Illinois. And it didn't take him long to learn that a successful drug salesman needed some of the same skills as a successful poker player. You had to be able to marshal statistics with an instantaneous and overpowering recall. You had to have an insight into the psychology of your opponents. You probed the pharmacist and the doctor for weaknesses; you had to know when and with whom to bluff. Within four months of joining the company, Kauffman had risen to the post of regional sales manager. Two years later, he was earning in commissions more than the company president earned in salary. "That was a mistake," Kauffman says. "They cut my commissions."

Kauffman means *their* mistake. He quit in 1950, convinced that he was only a few years away from becoming a very wealthy man.

The next year, 1951, with a total capital of $5,500, Kauffman founded Marion Laboratories, Inc. He was the sole owner, he was the only employee. The way he devoured those twenty books a week during his confinement, he began devouring medical journals. Then he asked a local manufacturer to make a pill from some standard ingredients he had read about. He bottled the pills in the basement of his home. He marketed his first pharmaceutical concoction—a product called Vicam, which Kauffman claimed would "cure common fatigue." One doctor said that Kauffman's sales literature was the most convincing he had ever read, considering that it didn't contain a single scientific fact.

His personality was even more effective than his prose. Once past a receptionist, he would corner a doctor in his office, detail bag in hand and a spiel spilling from his mouth. "Now, Doctor, I have *just* the thing to rid your patients of that toxicity they're suffering from," he'd spout. "It's called Vicam. It contains *vitamins* and *choline* and *inositol* and *methionine*—three *lipotropics* that will *detoxify* the upper *tract.*"

Before the cowering medical man could gather enough courage and presence of mind to cough up a reply, Kauffman would plunge his hand into his bag and yank out a bottle of enormous yellow pills. "Yes, Doctor, I *know* they look big," he'd continue breathlessly. "They *have* to be big to hold all those ingredients, but they go down *easy,* 'cause they're *shaped like a football.*" Then he would pop that large pill into his mouth. He would swallow it without water, a smile of utter bliss saturating his face.

Unfortunately, Kauffman couldn't use that particular ploy as frequently as he would have liked. Vicam didn't only cure common fatigue. It was a laxative, too.

While Vicam's sales were still booming, Kauffman learned about the work of a bone specialist in Kansas City who claimed fractured bones healed faster when the patient took daily doses of ground oyster shells, full of calcium. Kauffman contacted an oyster processor in Mississippi. The processor was only too happy to sell someone his "useless" supply of shells. Kauffman had them ground up and made pills from the powder. He called his product Os-Cal. And did Os-Cal sell?

At his mansion in Mission Hills, Kauffman serves cocktails with napkins that say:

> If you should meet an oyster
> Be sure you treat him well.
> Because, you see, this house
> Was built from oyster shells.

Twenty-five years after he started Marion Labs with $5,500, Kauffman still owns 28 percent of the company stock and, even in the current market slump, claims he's worth $70 million. From 1968 on, he has been diversifying Marion's holdings, acquiring nine separate companies in the nonpharmaceutical health industry. In 1965, Marion went public at $21 a share. By the end of 1972, each of those shares was worth $636. By the end of 1974, Marion was generating $75 million in sales.

Kauffman's genius transcends his own salesmanship. Called a man who "could sell rubber crutches" by one competitor, and "a man who could breathe life into a bearskin rug" by another, he is an expert at motivating others to sell, too. As Os-Cal's sales increased, Kauffman began to hire and hire and hire. The money and time other companies devoted to discovering new products, Kauffman invested in a search for salesmen. (In fact, Marion Labs spends nothing on original research.) He would interview three hundred applicants to hire half a dozen. He was looking for men who grew up in small towns, true believers in the dogma that success is a function of extraordinary sacrifice. "I hired on promise," he says. "I told people that if they would come to work for me, someday they would have an automobile, hospitalization, profit sharing, stock ownership. They lived on faith."

Candidates lucky enough to be selected were made to feel they had been invited to join an exclusive club. Kauffman believed his men would work as hard for recognition as for dollars. He told them that "they were the best sales force in the world," and the proof was that he had hired them. But he didn't stop at pep talks. He devised a grab bag cluttered with rewards—some material, others psychological. Besides the standard cash bonus, Kauffman gave each successful salesman a Marion ring. If a salesman won rings two years in a row, and a regional or national sales award, he became a member of the Marion Eagles. (It's not coincidental that Kauffman himself was an Eagle Scout.) Membership in the Marion Eagles entitled a salesman to special emblems of prestige —a blazer, calling cards, stationery, all bearing the Marion Eagles' logo—plus extra holidays and a company-owned Buick Centurion. (Salesmen who didn't increase their sales volume had to drive Chevies, Fords or Plymouths.) If a salesman won *three* Marion rings in a row, he graduated from the Eagles into the Marion M Club. That meant he could trade in his Buick Centurion for an

Oldsmobile 98. As a Marion M-er, he also acquired the "bumping privilege": at any company function, any Marion M-er could walk up to any Marion executive, including Ewing Kauffman, and say, "Hey, pal, I want your seat."

In 1956, Kauffman introduced a radical profit-sharing trust fund, with $106,000 worth of Marion stock. (The Internal Revenue Service has since forced Marion to stop selling any more of its stock to the plan.) When Marion went public in 1965, the stock had appreciated to $1.7 million, and by the early 1970's four employees had retired, after twenty-two years of service, with $1 million each.

And all of these motivational catalysts are couched in the vocabulary of trench warfare, where salesmanship is equated with patriotism, and malingering with desertion. A bulletin announcing a promotional contest among salesmen closes, in a parody of Winston Churchill's legendary exhortation during the Battle for Britain, with: "We will fight them [the competitors] in the doctors' offices, we will fight them in the pharmacies, we will fight them in the wholesalers, we will fight them in the streets, but we will never be defeated. If the Marion sales force exists for a thousand years, let it be known that this was their finest hour."

In case any of his troops faltered through lack of ambition (courage under fire), Kauffman made sure he could count on those tough, hard-bitten lieutenants behind the lines: the wives. "If your husband didn't work hard enough to get a bonus last year," Kauffman would often tell wives whom he invited to Marion sales meetings, "he didn't love you."

Besides his twenty-eight-room mansion, Kauffman has converted oyster shells into a private jet, which he employs both on business trips and to satisfy the obsession for gambling that started in the Navy. He owns twenty-two Thoroughbred horses. He has, according to friends, assembled groups of cronies at a moment's notice, herded them into his jet, shot craps on the flight all the way to the gaming tables of Las Vegas, played the tables all night—and returned home in time to keep his 9 A.M. appointments the following morning.

His biggest gamble of all was purchasing the Kansas City Royals in 1969. The American League franchise cost him $6 million. When the city council ran out of funds, he had to spend an additional $8 million to complete the Royals' new municipal stadium. He then paid an additional $2 million to build a twelve-story scoreboard, one of the largest illuminated scoreboards in the country, and a fountain the length of a football field that spurts water seven stories high for a home run. "It's the biggest privately owned fountain in the world. Mrs. K loves fountains," gloats Kauffman, who has so far invested a total of $20 million in baseball.

Mrs. K is his wife Muriel, who, Kauffman insists, taught him to enjoy the things money can buy. Ewing met her in Miami in 1961. He was a widower; she was a widow, a real-estate and insurance broker from Toronto, Canada. Kauffman installed her as treasurer of Marion a full year before he married her. Friends report that she has a quick wit, a sharp tongue—and is fiercely independent. Once, when Ewing decided to fly the American flag outside their home, Muriel started flying the Canadian flag, on a separate, but equal, flagpole. Her influence on him is pervasive; she even buys his clothes. One day not too long ago, Ewing was dressed in a blue herringbone suit, blue pin-striped shirt, blue patterned tie, blue cuff links and a blue undershirt. In his blue Cadillac there is a blue telephone. Blue is Muriel's favorite color.

Immediately after Kauffman bought the Royals, he began to apply the motivational techniques that earned him success in pharmaceuticals. Like Charlie Finley, his innovations are calculated to inspire both his ballplayers and his paying customers. To develop future stars, he founded the world's first—and perhaps last—baseball academy, a junior college to which selected high school graduates went to learn to throw a baseball, and trap it in a leather glove, and smash it with a machined club called a bat. A research psychologist at the Kansas City Royals' Baseball Academy in Florida tested prospective freshman for reflexes, in lieu of college boards. A well-rounded student was a kid who could play third base as well as the outfield. To get on the honor roll, it was enough to hit over .300. A seminar was a gathering in a dugout, where such heady intellectual conundrums were debated as how many California Angels could dance on the head of a Louisville slugger.

In its first year of operation, the Academy team did manage

to win the Gulf Coast League championship—for rookies in organized baseball. But it only produced one authentic major-leaguer, and it closed four years after it opened.

Another motivational technique Kauffman tried was something called "optometherapy," in spring training before the 1972–73 season. Optometherapy was a method (or strategy) devised by an eye doctor named Bill Harrison, in collaboration with his partner, Dr. Bill Lee. "Optometherapy," Harrison explains, "involves learning how to concentrate, how to cope with the negative effect of extra noise and movement." It also involves "the ability to readily obtain visual pictures, the ability to relax and the ability to develop and maintain rhythm and timing. Baseball is strictly a visual game," Harrison adds, "and the batter's two eyes must work as a perfect team."

Harrison was hired to instruct the Royals' hitters in this arcane art. By the end of the season, the Royals led the American League in hitting. By the end of the 1973–74 season, however, the Royals had slipped to fourth place in batting, with only Amos Otis among the league's top fifteen hitters. Optometherapy may be effective, but the consensus among batting coaches and sportwriters around the league was that its main value was psychological.

Ewing Kauffman, of course, is no stranger to placebos.

When Ray Kroc, the owner of the McDonald's fast-food chain, bought the San Diego Padres in February, 1974, for $12 million, he assured everyone who would listen that he wasn't doing it to make money. "To buy a baseball team," he said, "you have to be some kind of baseball nut."

Then he went out and proved it.

At the start of that first season, on an April night in San Diego Stadium, with 39,083 fans in attendance (the largest opening-night crowd in the history of the franchise), Ray Kroc's San Diego Padres prepared to meet Judge Roy Hofheinz's Houston Astros. In their first three contests that season, the Padres had already surrendered a total of twenty-five runs, losing every game. In their five previous major league seasons, the Padres had lost five hundred. It wasn't that the fans weren't grateful for the sideshow Kroc had provided in the grandstand (a "Tuba Man" honking throughout like a horny elephant; a frail dowager in her eighties called the "Bell Lady," who tinkle-tinkled in tandem with the tuba). It was just that, well, winning a game once in a while was entertainment, too.

Before the game, the crowd was officially introduced to the man who had doled out millions to rescue their floundering franchise. To deafening applause, Kroc stood up—a short wiry man, with silvering hair. He clasped his hands over his head like an exulting boxer. He yelled, "With your help and with God's help, we'll raise hell tonight!"

God resisted the temptation to help the Padres' pitchers' curves break extra sharp. By the eighth inning, the Padres were doing what they knew how to do best—losing, 9–2. Well, if the seventy-two-year-old Kroc couldn't get God to intervene on behalf of his hapless franchise, he could get help from a lesser divinity. Ignoring the AUTHORIZED PERSONNEL ONLY sign, he stormed into the public-address booth and told announcer John DeMott to hand over the microphone. "Ladies and gentlemen," he told his San Diego fans. "I suffer with you." And the crowd started cheering. "I've got some good news and some bad news," he continued, his voice beginning to quiver with emotion, just as it would if he were enumerating the countless qualities of a Big Mac. "The good news is that you loyal fans of San Diego have outstripped Los Angeles. They had thirty-one thousand on opening night. We have almost forty thousand tonight, our home opener."

Kroc was about to utter more when an aficionado leaped out of the stands and onto the field, tagged second base, then sprinted into right field, hopping over the wall and disappearing among the crowd. "Get him out of here!" Kroc started screaming, just as he would if some McDonald's patron claimed he'd found a jockey's spur embedded in his Quarter Pounder. "Take him to jail!" Spectators started scrambling, running this way and that, as the emotion of the moment and Kroc's imperious command combined to set them off in a fury of senseless activity. In the midst of the bedlam, Kroc shouted, "And the bad news is that I've never seen such stupid ballplaying in my life!"

The crowd loved it, but the ballplayers didn't. Neither did Players Association chief Marvin Miller. "The players of the San

Diego and Houston clubs," he said, "have demonstrated by their restraint in the face of Mr. Kroc's inexcusable insults that their intelligence far exceeds his." Commissioner Bowie Kuhn demanded—and got—a public apology from Kroc. National League president Chub Feeney declared that the public-address system was off-limits to everyone but the public-address announcer.

"What I regret now," Kroc said later, "is using the word 'stupid.'" Kroc was sitting in a lawn chair, a small, lean man who looks ten years younger than seventy-four. He held a vodka in his hand. A beach umbrella shielded him from the fierce Fort Lauderdale sun. Behind him, towering over his Versailles-style mansion, was a flagpole, with two pennants fluttering in the indifferent breeze. One displayed the emblem of his baseball team; the other, the logo of his fast-food chain. "People who know me realize I meant it, but not in the dictionary sense. I meant it in the sense of 'Okay, we made a stupid move, now let's all smarten up.' That kind of definition. I've even referred to one of the smartest men I know —me—as 'stupid.' I'm a bohunk and that's the way I talk, just like my bohunk friend, George Halas, who owns the Chicago Bears. In fact, George said to me, 'Ray, for the last forty years I've wanted to get on the mike and say the same thing, but I didn't have the guts.'"

Like George Halas, Ray Kroc is a super-fan. Ewing Kauffman and Charlie Finley manipulate and innovate and motivate; running a sports franchise is one more arena in which to prove their talents at salesmanship and organizing and managing. Ray Kroc is and always was a baseball fanatic, as enthusiastic a devotee of "the national pastime" as the most die-hard, beer-swilling bleacher bum. Born on October 5, 1902, in a sense Kroc and baseball grew up together. From the time he was seven years old, he was spending afternoons watching the Chicago Cubs, whose Tinker-to-Evers-to-Chance infield had just led them to a third straight pennant. When he wasn't playing baseball or watching baseball, he was pounding a piano. His mother was a professional piano teacher. His father was a door-to-door salesman, the kind playwright Arthur Miller would immortalize decades later. "When I was a kid, I saw Dad struggling to make ends meet on a meager salary," Kroc says. At an early age, he resolved to make money.

The Salesmen

But the Cubs he loved as much as music or money. Only a world war could keep him away from the 1918 World Series, when the Cubs faced the Boston Red Sox and their star pitcher, Babe Ruth. At age fifteen, after his sophomore year of high school in the Chicago suburb of Oak Park, he convinced U.S. Army recruiters that he was twenty. He ended up in France, in the Ambulance Corps. One of his fellow doughboys was a sixteen-year-old named Walt Disney. "We never figured Walt would amount to much," Kroc says with a chuckle. "He was always sitting around drawing animals." In 1920, Kroc returned to Chicago in time to learn that the White Sox, those Chicago "Black Sox," had fixed the 1919 World Series.

Like Jack Kent Cooke (owner of the L.A. Kings and Lakers, and the Washington Redskins) later on, Kroc survived marginally by playing the piano in local dance bands. He played for Isham Jones—and for Harry Sosnik, who later became leader of the *Hit Parade* orchestra. Kroc enjoyed playing yet disliked the hours musicians had to keep, "working while everyone else was out having fun." When he got married at the age of twenty, he left the music business and became a salesman for the Lily-Tulip Cup Company. But he became restless; there was an exotic lure to the entertainment business that he couldn't resist. He got a job as musical director of the city's first radio station, WGLS. He played the piano, he arranged music, he accompanied singers and hired acts. Even if he hadn't discovered later how to transform a hamburger into a sacrament, or the Padres into a moneymaker, he would be remembered by cultural historians as the man who hired a couple of comedians named Freeman Gosden and Charles Correll, for five dollars, to do a radio show using black dialect. Then they called themselves Sam and Henry. Later they called themselves Amos 'n Andy—those incurable moochers America loved throughout the Golden Age of Radio.

The same nomadic instinct that had driven Kroc to France at the age of fifteen now drove him, in the early 1920's, to Florida. With all the confidence of Dick Whittington's cat (and with about the same amount of collateral), Kroc uprooted his wife and young daughter and headed for the swamplands, to cash in on Florida's land boom. When the boom fizzled to bust in 1926, he stayed on, playing the piano in dreary night clubs to earn the money to send his wife and daughter back to Chicago by train. A month or so later, he drove north in his Model T Ford. "I never will forget that drive as long as I live," he says. "I was stone broke. I didn't have an overcoat, a topcoat or a pair of gloves. I drove into Chicago on icy streets. When I got home, I was frozen stiff, disillusioned and broke."

During those lean Depression years, while his beloved Cubs, under Joe McCarthy and Charlie Grim, were seesawing monotonously between first place and failure, Kroc went back to work as a salesman for Lily-Tulip, eventually achieving the exalted rank of Midwest sales manager. He quit that job in 1937 and obtained the exclusive sales rights to the Prince Castle Multimixer, a machine that could stir as many as six milkshakes at once. Says Kroc: "I wanted adventure." Instead, over the next sixteen years, he got dull, repetitive routine. By 1954, he was fifty-two years old, easing into middle age, frustrated and unfulfilled. And then, as the Cubs entered a decade when they would go absolutely nowhere, Ray Kroc discovered a way to realize his wildest dreams. That year, 1954, while he was plowing through a pile of orders on his desk, his eye caught a startling detail. A restaurant in San Bernadino, California, owned by two transplanted New Englanders named Richard and Maurice McDonald, had ordered eight of the milkshake machines. The McDonalds were obviously doing a booming business in shakes. One day later, Ray Kroc was on route to San Bernadino.

When he reached the hamburger stand of the McDonald brothers, he was stunned. The clientele were literally lined up in the street, each departing customer clutching in one hand a hamburger and in the other a milkshake. "I was amazed," Kroc says. "This little drive-in having people standing in line. The volume was incredible: I figured it at about two hundred and fifty thousand dollars in that single store. I began to do some figuring. If they could have a hundred stores like that one, I could sell them eight hundred Multimixers. The deal would put me in clover."

Kroc approached the McDonalds. He told them he wanted to sell franchises for them. The brothers had already franchised six other stores in California, and weren't very excited about Kroc's offer. They had already turned down an even bigger offer, from someone who had a plan to expand the chain through company-owned restaurants. "A few years before, we would have jumped," Dick McDonald says, "but by now we were netting seventy-five thousand dollars a year from our San Bernadino store, and we were selling franchises without any trouble. The idea of big expansion didn't much appeal to us. It would have entailed a tremendous amount of traveling, and we would have had to neglect San Bernadino." Kroc only got the contract, McDonald says, because his proposal meant less travel and fewer headaches. "It goes to show what a big part fate plays in a man's life," McDonald adds. "After all, what would Ray Kroc's future have been in the milkshake machine business?"

At the time, Kroc still didn't foresee the potential of fast-food franchising. He wanted to expand the chain for one reason: to develop more markets for his Multimixers. Even after he had franchised over 200 drive-ins for the McDonalds, worth more than $37 million a year, his gross cut was only $700,000 annually, and most of that income was eaten up by his milkshake machine business. In the meantime, he had taken a partner, Harry Sonneborn, a former vice-president of Tastee Freez; Sonneborn was drawing $100 per week. Kroc's secretary, Mrs. June Martino, was taking her wages in stock.

He survived throughout the 1950's, working the milkshake machine business and the franchise-selling business in tandem. But as late as 1960, when the White Sox reemerged as a baseball power, Kroc, like his Cubs, was still struggling. That year he got divorced. He had to sell his milkshake machine business for $100,000, to pay off the lawyers. All he had left was the McDonald's franchising rights, the sale of which had always been secondary to the sale of Multimixers. Well, now he had no alternative. He was alone, fifty-eight years old, and flat broke again. He was stuck with the McDonald's franchising operation, and what he needed, even more than the Cubs needed a pennant, was money. About $1.5 million. "My total assets, including my house, were $90,000," Kroc says. "Not much for a man of my age. When I went to see David Kennedy of Chicago's Continental Illinois Bank, I remember he told me: 'You won't find a bank in the country that will make you a loan in your condition. If anyone were willing, you'd have to give him a big slice of the company.' "

The Rich Who Own Sports

He wore out countless pairs of shoes trying to borrow money to expand his franchising business. He was about to quit when a life insurance company (Paul Revere Life, since merged into Avco Corporation) suddenly agreed to take the gamble, giving him a $1.5 million loan for fifteen years; as a premium on the loan, Paul Revere Life took 20 percent of the company. In 1961, Kroc bought out the McDonald brothers for $2.7 million, obtaining rights to the McDonald's name. "I needed that name," he says. "What are you going to do with a name like Kroc? You can't call your stores 'Krocs,' or even 'Half Krocs.' " Then his partner, Harry Sonneborn, sold his 11 percent of the company and retired to Florida. (Sonneborn, who had started at $100 a week, retired with an estimated $10 million in cash, plus $100,000 a year from the company, plus $50,000 for his wife after his death. Kroc's secretary eventually retired with a portfolio estimated at $1 million.) By 1973, Kroc had 600 company-owned stores, as well as 600 franchises. McDonald's had become not just a fast-food chain, but an institution; Kroc had become famous for his enthusiastic brand of restauranteering. His picture regularly appears in newspapers across the country—a Big Mac in his right hand, a shake in his left, a smile of utter bliss on his face, and his personally composed credo printed in large letters alongside:

PRESS ON
NOTHING IN THE WORLD CAN
TAKE THE PLACE OF PERSIS-
TENCE. TALENT WILL NOT:
NOTHING IS MORE COMMON
THAN UNSUCCESSFUL MEN
WITH TALENT. GENIUS WILL
NOT: UNREWARDED GENIUS
IS ALMOST A PROVERB.
EDUCATION ALONE WILL NOT:
THE WORLD IS FULL OF
EDUCATED DERELICTS. PER-
SISTENCE AND DETERMINATION
ALONE ARE OMNIPOTENT

The Salesmen

Every licensed McDonald's operator was required to matriculate, for indoctrination, at Kroc's Hamburger University in Elk Grove, Illinois. Students studied not only the art of cooking hamburgers and the technology of milkshake mixers, but also "Quality, Service and Cleanliness"—the McDonald's "QSC" motto. Degrees were awarded in Hamburgerology (with a minor in French Fries). It doesn't take much imagination to conceive, except for a simple twist of fate, a Ewing Kauffman developing McDonald's along the same bizarre lines and being equally successful in the end.

By 1974, Ray Kroc had accumulated undreamed-of wealth. His *personal* worth was estimated at $340 million. It was time to have some fun, time to buy a baseball team. Naturally, the first team he tried to buy was the Chicago Cubs. "I got hold of George Halas, who is a good friend of P.K. Wrigley," Kroc says, "and I told him I wanted to buy the Cubs, if there was any chance to get them. He said, 'No chance,' so I went ahead looking for some other club to buy." Then, one morning, sitting at the breakfast table with his second wife, Joan Dobbins Kroc, he read that Marjorie Lindheimer Everett's petition to purchase the San Diego Padres for a second time had been rejected by major league baseball. Kroc turned to his wife. "Joni," he said, "why don't I buy the San Diego Padres?"

"You must be nuts," she replied.

In five major league seasons, none of the Padres' previous owners had been able to make the franchise profitable or proficient. Kroc vowed he would do both.

"I just wanted a hobby," he says now, lounging in eighty-degree heat beside his swimming pool in Fort Lauderdale, while one of his staff refills his glass with vodka and tonic. "It's an extravagant hobby, for sure. I could make more money out of one hamburger stand than I can out of baseball. But I love baseball and I have no interest in money. The only enjoyment I get out of making money is from the knowledge that people always say, 'If you're so smart, why aren't you rich?' Well, I'm rich, so I guess you could say I'm smart. Money doesn't have anything to do with it."

Kroc's philanthropy is proof that he no longer cares much for

153

money. Like Charlie Finley, who once raised a record $26.5 million as national chairman of the Christmas Seal campaign, Kroc annually lends his name and influence to charity drives. To celebrate his seventieth birthday, in 1972 he gave $7.5 million in charity and another $9 million in stock to McDonald's employees. When he decided that McDonald's needed a new airplane, he bought it himself for $4.5 million, then leased it to the company for $1 a year. He also paid for the company limousine out of his own wallet, then commented wryly: "I'm just waiting for someone to get up at a stockholders' meeting and complain about my riding around in a company limousine." During his first year as owner of the Padres, when the team opened a home stand against the Montreal Expos, twenty customers were selected by lot, given shopping bags and led onto the field. Kroc gave the signal—and they began to scramble for false one-dollar bills. The idea was to pick up as many false bills as you could in two minutes, then cash them in for real dollar bills.

Finley might know how to turn his players' contempt for him into pennants, but he has never been able to lure fans into his ball park in large numbers. Kroc's enthusiasm, by contrast, had little immediate impact on his players, who continued to flounder on the field, but it did arouse the citizens of San Diego. By his promotional gimmicks, his own contagious euphoria over baseball, he managed to make the franchise a solvent one almost overnight. "I like the San Diego park," Kroc says, scanning the network of canals—the Intracoastal Waterways—that interlink where his lawn ends. "It's beautiful and modern and very clean. Some of these older parks are in neighborhoods out near the vinegar works. I tell you, if I had owned the Cubs, I'd have bought property in that neighborhood and fixed it up. I don't care how good the ball park looks; if the neighborhood looks bad, the park does, too. It's like having a gorgeous painting, then putting it in a frame picked out of the garbage bin."

Kroc looks up, squinting past the blazing sun toward his six-hundred-thousand-dollar yacht, moored at his private dock. In his garage is his forty-five-thousand-dollar Rolls-Royce. His four-and-a-half-million-dollar jet sits on an airstrip nearby. He ponders something silently for a moment, then says, "Y'know, money is an automatic thing to me. It's like . . . turning on a light switch. I take it for granted. What do I need it for? I've never desired to own a harem—anyway, I'm too old for one now. I've never wanted to race a horse, or even a polo pony."

He picks up his vodka and tonic. He takes a sip. "What," says Ray Kroc, "are you gonna do with money?"

High overhead, on that towering flagpole, the Padres' pennant trembles in the light breeze.

◀ 9 ▶
The Upstarts

In the 1930's, the owner of the New York football Giants, Tim Mara, could cover his team's modest losses with profits from his bookmaking business. Art Rooney could sustain his franchise with winnings at the horse track. Until the 1960's, in fact, owning a pro football team was more an avocation than a business. No one made much money, no one lost much money. As late as 1961, the NFL's fourteen teams were filling only half their seats—netting, at best, a little more than $100,000 per year. Then, in 1966, Lamar Hunt's American Football League forced the National Football League into a money-saving merger agreement. Pro football became both popular and profitable. TV revenues and tax write-offs and the indemnities paid to existing teams whenever new teams were invented lured a host of millionaires into pro football. It took a millionaire to survive the inflationary sports boom of the 1960's. In 1939, the payroll of a typical NFL club was about $150,000. By 1961, that sum had escalated to $500,000. By 1969, players' salaries on the average NFL team would swell to $1.4 million per annum.

Still, two men who became prominent owners during the 1960's didn't start out in football as millionaires. Joe Robbie, of the Miami Dolphins, and Al Davis, of the Oakland Raiders, were masters at juggling other men's millions; they didn't have much capital of their own. Eventually, though, each managed to win absolute control of his franchise, on battlegrounds littered with shredded contracts and shattered promises. Today, Robbie and Davis are among the winningest owners in pro football, and the most controversial.

Joe Robbie, owner of the Dolphins, and Art Rooney, owner of the Steelers, both started their franchises on a shoestring; neither one had a corporate empire to cushion his fall if he tripped. The likeness ends right there. Art Rooney is sensitive to feelings; Robbie is sensitive to criticism. Rooney is Irish; Robbie is irate. Rooney is a father figure who finds friends everywhere; Robbie has the irrepressible knack of turning co-conspirators into enemies. For decades, Rooney turned out losers; it took Robbie only six years to build a juggernaut.

Rooney is famous for his generosity; Robbie is notorious for his stinginess. Says one assistant whom Robbie fired a few years back: "When I was there, he even had his nose in the paper clips. For a big man, he's very small. Nobody thinks much of him, especially the partners who are no longer under his hand."

Some of those ex-partners were shrewd and wealthy financiers. Robbie proved himself just a little shrewder—and, thanks to that cunning, is now almost as wealthy. His original investment in a franchise that cost $7.5 million was a mere $100,000. The franchise is currently valued at about $20 million. Joe Robbie is the majority owner, and the absolute dictator.

But he is not popular in Miami, in spite of the fact that his franchise won, in 1973 and 1974, successive Super Bowls. The adults never forgave him for letting Larry Csonka and Paul Warfield and Jim Kiick jump to the World Football League. As for the kids—they remember only one thing: Joe Robbie was the man who fired Flipper.

This tale of intrigue and irony began one historic night in August, 1965, when comedian Danny Thomas flopped flat on the marble floor at Miami's plush Palm Bay Club, lying on his back and pointing at his own enormous, upthrust nose. He pleaded with AFL Commissioner Joe Foss to use his nose as a kicking tee. "With this nose," Thomas quipped for the TV cameramen and the print journalists, "how can we ever miss the point-after-touchdown?"

The "we" referred to Thomas himself, a lawyer from Minneapolis named Joseph Robbie, and the franchise the AFL owners' committee had sold the pair a few days before.

With perfect timing, at the crescendo of laughter, the star of TV's *Make Room for Daddy* leapt easily to his feet, planted his black alligator shoes and flashed a gleaming set of capped teeth. "You can't show me any Lebanese boy raised in Toledo, Ohio, who doesn't want to own a Miami ball club," he said, rolling his eyes theatrically. Then his tone turned sober. "I have confidence in this town," he said. "It's a big city. It's no longer just a citrus grove where people come to escape the winter."

Danny Thomas spoke with conviction. He was a persuasive salesman, but not persuasive enough to convince most onlookers that this new football franchise would prosper. Most reporters thought Thomas' performance—his perfectly executed flop—more prophetic than his sales pitch. The Miami Dolphins, they agreed, would flop, too.

The memory of the last Miami franchise was too vivid in their minds. In 1946, Harvey Hester, from Atlanta, had founded the Seahawks of the All-American Football Conference, the most successful of several leagues begun at the end of World War II by enticing players away from the NFL teams they had left when they were drafted. At the beginning, the NFL ignored the AAFC. Then, when two franchises—one in San Francisco, the other in Cleveland—began to fill their stadiums, the NFL tried to demolish the AAFC by offering membership to the 49ers and the Browns. Both franchises rejected the NFL's offer, and the war for new players, which was doubling and sometimes tripling the payrolls of each league every year, continued until 1949. That year, at the Racquet Club in Philadelphia, the two leagues agreed to a cease-fire. The NFL absorbed three AAFC teams—Baltimore, Cleveland and San Francisco. The other four AAFC franchises disappeared.

The Miami Seahawks had been one of the interleague war's earliest fatalities. The powerful Orange Bowl Committee and the University of Miami had conspired to prevent the Seahawks from using the Orange Bowl on weekends. The Seahawks had to play their home games on Monday nights, and often drew only a few hundred spectators. The franchise had folded at the end of the AAFC's first season, in 1946.

During the next thirteen years, no one attempted to loosen college football's stranglehold on Miami. Then, in 1959, Lamar Hunt founded the AFL, and a millionaire from Detroit named Ralph Wilson tried to bring pro football back to Dade County. But the Orange Bowl Committee and the University of Miami still controlled the only facility in town fit for big-time football; the conditions for tenancy they offered were calculated to discourage the pros. Ralph Wilson installed his franchise in Buffalo instead, where the municipal authorities were more cooperative.

But, in 1965, Danny Thomas and Joe Robbie had a powerful ally in Miami. Mayor Robert High was a reforming David who had already defeated a pair of Goliaths. He had closed some of the worst tourist traps among downtown Miami's night clubs. He had also forced Florida Light & Power, the major utility in the area, to roll back its rates. Mayor High decided that Miami needed the prestige of a big-league football franchise. In Danny Thomas, he saw a magnet who could attract the attention of the media. In Joe Robbie, he saw a crafty manipulator who could shatter the embargo on pro football imposed by the Orange Bowl Committee and the University of Miami.

Like Danny Thomas, Joe Robbie was of Lebanese descent. His father had left Lebanon at age eleven, in 1900, to avoid being conscripted into the Turkish army (the Turks then ruled Beirut). Robbie's grandmother tied a money belt around her son's waist. She gave him letters of introduction to Lebanese exiles in Marseilles and Liverpool. She purchased a ticket for him on a transatlantic steamer. When he reached the shores of the United States, a customs official on Ellis Island asked him his name.

"Arabi," said the boy.

"Sounds like Robbie," the official said. "That's good enough. Make it Robbie."

Sixteen years later, on July 7, 1916, Joseph Robbie was born in Sisseton, South Dakota—population, 3,218. The son of a peddler, he grew up in moderate circumstances, his leisure devoted to sports. But his tongue was far more agile than his feet; he discovered early that talking was his number one talent. At both Northern State College and the University of South Dakota, where he spent a total of seven years and $300 (he swept up and worked behind the counter in cafeterias), he became a debating champion. "I loved to talk," he says. "I learned that it could be a weapon, too. But it was really enjoyment for me. Debating and sports pages were my only distraction.

Robbie went on to law school; he became a member of the South Dakota bar. In 1946, while Harvey Hester's Seahawks were failing in Miami, Joe Robbie was succeeding at politics, one of just nineteen Democrats elected to the South Dakota state legislature. One of the 111 Republicans elected that year was a World War II Congressional Medal of Honor winner named Joe Foss, whom Robbie had befriended years before at the University of South Dakota. Four years later, Robbie won the Democratic nomination for governor, but was defeated in the general election. Foss tried for the Republican nomination that same year, and lost, too.

After he lost the gubernatorial race, Robbie quit politics. He practiced law in Minneapolis. He got married. He fathered eleven children. Then, in the winter of 1964, he traveled to Miami Beach, to confer with a client who wanted to obtain an AFL franchise in Philadelphia. The client knew that Robbie was an old friend of Joe Foss, now Commissioner of the AFL. He asked Robbie to intercede with Foss on his behalf.

Robbie met Foss in Washington. Foss told him that a franchise in Philadelphia was out of the question; the NFL Eagles were too firmly entrenched. But, he said, the AFL might consider a franchise in Miami. Robbie flew south again. His client, a millionaire Miami businessman, was afraid to challenge the jealous authority of the Orange Bowl Committee and the University of Miami. Robbie, a Minneapolis lawyer who had never earned more than $27,000 in a single year, had almost no capital to invest—and therefore almost nothing to lose. He decided to pursue the possibility of a franchise in Miami on his own. The first thing he did was to contact someone who often earned $27,000 in a single week— comedian Danny Thomas, whom he had met years before, when they both did work for Lebanese-American charities. Thomas, a football addict, agreed to back Robbie. Armed with Thomas' money, Robbie announced his intention of starting a Miami franchise.

He didn't get much moral support from the AFL. Ralph Wilson, owner of the Buffalo Bills, predicted that Robbie would have no more success than he had had in 1959. Even Lamar Hunt was pessimistic: if Robbie managed to start a franchise, the Orange Bowl Committee and the University of Miami and their disciples in the Miami city government would make sure it folded.

Robbie ignored their warnings. He met with Mayor High and found in him a staunch ally. But at the same time he encountered a stumbling block. According to High, Melvin Reese, Miami's city manager, claimed that any tenant in the Orange Bowl would have to pay a rental of 17.5 percent of gross receipts—a proviso of the bond issue floated to finance the stadium. That lordly rental had played a significant role in discouraging potential pro franchise owners. Robbie, however, did something other would-be owners had neglected to do. He demanded to see that proviso. He discovered that no such proviso existed and furthermore that the stadium bonds specified no particular rental percentage.

In July, 1965, Robbie attended the AFL's expansion committee meeting at the Monmouth race track, owned by Sonny Werblin of the New York Jets. Robbie argued vehemently in favor of making Miami the AFL's ninth franchise, but lost out to J. Leonard Rensch, ex-Democratic party treasurer and owner of Cox Broadcasting, Inc., who was bidding for a franchise in Atlanta. That same day, however, Robbie got help from an unexpected source. While the AFL owners were convening at Monmouth Park, Pete Rozelle was awarding the NFL's sixteenth franchise to another Atlantan, a personal friend named C. Rankin Smith. The mayor of Atlanta, Ivan Allen, immediately assured the NFL that it would have sole use of the city's new stadium.

That ended the AFL's expansion plans for Atlanta. The owners suddenly decided that Robbie's proposal was very attractive. Without attempting to disguise their condescension, the AFL owners offered to sell Robbie a franchise in Miami for $7.5 million— a full $3.7 million more than they had charged J. Leonard Rensch for a franchise in Atlanta only one day before. Robbie gritted his teeth, counted Danny Thomas' bankroll, and agreed. But instead of showing his gratitude, he demanded that the league give his franchise a $500,000-a-year share of its TV revenues. The AFL owners were stunned by his presumptuousness. They had never intended to give an expansion team a slice of the TV pie. In fact, two years later, when the Cincinnati Bengals entered the AFL, they didn't get a cent in TV revenues. But now, with the collapse of their plans for Atlanta, they needed Robbie as much as he needed them. They gave him what he asked for.

As soon as the deal was approved, Robbie began staffing his organization. In October, 1965, he hired Joe Thomas (now the general manager of the Baltimore Colts) as director of personnel. As player-personnel director for the Minnesota Vikings, Thomas had signed, among others, Fran Tarkenton, Carl Eller, Dave Osborne, Jack Snow and Lance Rentzel. He would provide the raw talent that coach Don Shula eventually molded into a two-time Super Bowl winner.

While Joe Thomas was searching for manpower, Joe Robbie and Danny Thomas were searching for money. In October, the same month in which he hired Joe Thomas, Robbie sold John O'Neil, a Miami businessman, a 10 percent share of the franchise, worth $750,000. The next month, Danny Thomas brought in a friend of twenty-five years, another Lebanese, named George Hamid. Hamid had been discovered as a boy in Beirut by Buffalo Bill Cody, who hired him as an acrobat in his Wild West Show, then brought him to America. Annie Oakley had taught Hamid to read English. Now, at age sixty-nine, Hamid was too busy reading the financial statements of his Hamid-Morton Circus and his Atlantic City Pier company to pay much attention to the Dolphins. His interest in the day-to-day routine of the franchise soon abated, as did the participation of Danny Thomas himself. By the end of the Dolphins' first season, 1966–67, Thomas had slipped quietly back to Hollywood.

"Robbie is a great guy in my book," says Thomas, who was titular head of the Dolphins in that first year of operation. "Joe put the club together. He was the finder and he came to me. We made a deal and went in. I got out a year later. Did I get hurt? Did I

165

lose money? You must be kidding. Did you ever hear of a Lebanese losing money? I don't lose money. I only make money. I trust Robbie implicitly."

Both Thomas' enthusiasm and his involvement peaked on the very first play of the Dolphins' very first season. "I never went into football to make money, only to have fun," he says, expressing motives exactly opposite to Joe Robbie's. "I had all my fun on the first play the Dolphins ever ran. It was the opening kickoff, and I ran fifty yards for a score. Imagine, no other owner ever ran for a touchdown.

"See, this kid named Joe Auer took it back ninety-five yards," he explains. "I'm on the bench, and I pick him up on the forty-five, me and my cigar. Yelling, I go the rest of the way. I fall flat on my face, right in the end zone. What an opening!"

Even the addition of Hamid and O'Neil didn't make the franchise solvent. Robbie's $7.5 million purchase price entitled him to draft thirty-two players from other clubs—in other words, each draftee had cost him about $237,000. His first crisis was a $1 million payment due the AFL by January 1, 1967. In the first of many financial moves that would antagonize his customers in Miami, he told his 12,503 season-ticket holders that they would have to pay for next year's season tickets by December 15, or lose their renewal option. Customers would have to pay for the Dolphins' second season three days before that first season ended.

Robbie desperately needed the operating capital, but the move seemed to most Miamians like unadulterated greed. Even before the season started, in fact, Robbie had begun to acquire the reputation for miserliness that would haunt him into the 1970's. At the Dolphins' first training camp, in St. Petersburg, Florida, for instance, the facilities were inadequate, and so was the food. Players had to put on their uniforms in their rooms, then bus to the ball park, like minor-leaguers.

George Wilson was Robbie's first head coach. That opening season, almost every Californian who tried out for the team made the Dolphins' final roster. It wasn't that Wilson had a preference for Californians. But if a player was invited to camp, and was subsequently cut, Wilson had to pay the money from his own pocket for the player's air fare home. Wilson couldn't afford to cut many Californians.

The practice field itself was a joke, as well as a danger. To save money that first season, the Dolphins accepted an offer from Suncoast Sports, Inc. Suncoast agreed to underwrite $70,000 in expenses for the privilege of being associated with the Dolphins. But when that training camp opened, the sole physical manifestation of that organization turned out to be a man named John Burroughs. It was his task to convert the field into something football players could fall on without suffering lacerations more lethal than crack-back blocks. The problem was, the field was a thick layer of soil over sea shells. After a few days, only the sea shells remained. John Burroughs trotted out his roller and worked on the field daily, trying to get the soil on top again. As an inducement to keep him rolling, Coach Wilson kept Burroughs' son, a candidate for linebacker, around until it appeared he might get crippled. When Wilson finally cut the younger Burroughs, the elder—and his roller —disappeared.

Bud Adams, owner of the Houston Oilers, was soon accusing Robbie of "running a multimillion-dollar-a-year business like a fruitstand." Robbie once wrote a memo ordering every one of his coaches to list any telephone calls they made, for a feasibility study. Robbie once fired the couple who catered food for the press, after he found out that the bill for the press table had reached an awesome $110. He told his new caterer to serve the press hot dogs.

Understandably, Robbie resents his reputation as a miser. "Look," he says, "I've been on the board of governors of St. Jude Hospital for years. I've traveled every place they wanted me to, even on a monthly basis, at my own expense. I've always been actively involved with charities, giving my money and my time."

Later, Robbie would prove his philanthropy more dramatically, paying his football team more in salaries than any other owner in the entire National Football League. But the fans and press in Miami never forgot those early dog days, even after the Dolphins became the most powerful team in professional football. They never forgot how Robbie installed Flipper in a cylindrical tank, eight feet high and twenty feet wide, in the east end zone.

Responding to a buzzer that triggered sound waves, the dolphin would leap into the air every time Miami scored a touchdown. The fans never forgave Robbie for sacking the superstar mascot when the city of Miami and the Seaquarium refused to pay for tank repairs.

Part of Miami's hostility stemmed from Robbie's rough-and-tumble business methods, the infighting that became public when one of his partners or one of his employees became disenchanted. Their complaints and accusations made good newspaper copy. Robbie's rebuttals didn't. The fact was, however, most of Robbie's bad press was connected with the very thing that made him almost unique among modern owners: he didn't come into football rich, and constantly had to search for new capital to shore up his franchise. He felt the pinch particularly hard at the beginning of the franchise's second season, in 1967. With Danny Thomas fading from the scene, Robbie was now running the entire front office. Early in February, he welcomed a new partner into the Dolphin family, a former vice-president of Johnson Wax who had made his millions as a land developer—forty-eight-year-old Willard ("Bud") Keland. Keland bought out Thomas and Hamid, and Robbie felt sufficiently secure economically to announce publicly in March, 1967, that the franchise was not for sale.

Orders for season tickets had increased before that second season. By September, 1967, Robbie had managed to borrow more millions from local bankers, using his ballplayers' bodies as collateral. When Keland saw the enthusiasm of both the local financiers and the local fans, he decided this was a good time to invest more heavily himself. He increased his holdings in the club to an equal half-share with Robbie's. "Bud and I will function with equal responsibility toward the goal of bringing a championship football team to Miami," Robbie declared in September, 1967.

Keland thought "equal responsibility" also meant equal decision-making power, but he was mistaken. Despite the fact that Keland had invested his own money, and Robbie the money of local bankers, it was Robbie who was determined to run the franchise. By December, 1968, Keland was trying to fire Joe Robbie from the post of managing general partner. As an ally, he could count on the support of their other remaining partner, John O'Neil, who, despite his $750,000 worth of shares, had been fired by Robbie from his job as "community relations director" after the 1966 season.

"When we bought out Thomas," Keland says, "Joe didn't come up with the money to buy his half, so I figured I was in control. But it didn't work out that way, and then, when Joe wanted to do some refinancing, he needed me to do it. I said, 'Look, you haven't done your part in this thing.' That's when we decided to let Pete Rozelle handle the matter."

No one knows what issues NFL Commissioner Pete Rozelle took into account during his secret—and lengthy (four months)—deliberations, or why he decided finally to give Robbie ninety days to find new partners—and Keland ninety days to sell his interest in the franchise.

"I bear Joe no ill will," Keland says. "He's all right. I learned a lesson from him. If you're going to run with sharp operators, you've got to be smart. He came up with a group of five from Miami to buy me out, and I guess he's got them doing the same thing for him, supplying the money so he can run the club."

The five Miamians were J. Early Smalley, Wilbur Morrison, Frank Callahan, James McLamore and Harper Sibley, all local millionaires. With Keland's shares now split five ways, Robbie became the majority partner. He kept for himself the sole liability for all outstanding loans and interest. He also retained sole responsibility for making every major decision concerning the franchise.

The key to Robbie's enormous power is something called "the general partnership agreement," which Robbie himself drew up. In spite of the fact that Robbie's original investment in the franchise never exceeded $100,000, the "agreement" left him with control of the Dolphins for a period of twenty years. "I'm where I am now for one reason," Robbie says. "Nobody wanted to take any risks. That's why I have the club. We've had to live by our wits here in Miami. I've been vulnerable because I was not operating from a strong financial position. But let me say this," he adds. "There is not one investor who has ever put one red copper cent into the operations of this club. Every cent that has ever been paid in by an investor has been used to pay the franchise debt to the AFL, and a one-hundred-thousand-dollar annual payment debt to the

NFL. Every bit of operating money has been obtained from income or from banking arrangements that I'm personally liable for. And I'm the only one personally liable in this place."

If Joe Robbie deserves some blame for making more enemies than friends in Miami, he also deserves a lion's share of the credit for turning—in only eight years and under enormous financial pressure—a futile collection of football misfits into the team that went undefeated in 1972, and won the 1973 and 1974 Super Bowls. It was Robbie who hired head coach Don Shula, and it was Shula who turned the players acquired by Joe Thomas into the cohesive unit that became a dominant force in the mid-1970's. Characteristically, in luring Shula away from the Baltimore Colts, Robbie walked a tightrope between deception and decency.

Robbie and Shula timed their first meeting, in 1970, to coincide with a business trip Baltimore owner Carroll Rosenbloom made to Asia. Shula played by the league rules, getting permission to huddle with Robbie from Carroll's second-in-command, his son Steve. Robbie, however, had approached Shula first, without asking anyone for permission. To Pete Rozelle, that constituted tampering. Robbie got Don Shula as head coach, but Rozelle gave the Colts the Dolphins' number one draft choice in 1971. The deal Shula agreed to gave him 10 percent of the Dolphins' stock, plus salary.

Eventually, the relationship between Robbie and Shula deteriorated into bouts of hysterical name-calling. Now Shula almost never refers to Robbie without adding "that ass." Typical of most of Robbie's disputes, the controversy involved millions of dollars. One stipulation of Shula's original ownership agreement was that he could not sell his stock for five years. At the end of five years, however, he could sell his 10 percent back to Robbie at the existing value of the franchise, then subtract the amount of the original purchase value—$750,000 (or 10 percent of the Dolphins' worth of $7.5 million when he arrived). By 1976, Shula was arguing that the franchise was worth $20 million; his 10 percent, $2 million. Robbie was contending that the figure of $20 million was vastly overinflated. He did not intend to let Don Shula become the first opponent to outfox him at finances, no matter how much resentment his haggling generated among the players and fans who idolized his head coach.

Robbie has grown accustomed to being resented. In fact, critics are probably necessary to his psychic survival; if he didn't have any, he'd have to invent them. He perceives himself as an outcast who succeeded in gate-crashing a stuffy and restrictive establishment. "You know," he says, "once people sympathized with the guy who could climb the ladder, the Horatio Alger thing. But I think this affluent society, where lots of people have lots of money, they resent a working stiff making it. That kind of thinking exists particularly in the glamorous area of professional sports, which has always been a rich man's plaything in the past. They're big business now, there's going to be more and more of my kind one day."

Few observers believed that Don Shula the coach would come out on top in his financial feud with Joe Robbie the owner. Only one head coach in modern football had been astute enough to beat the moneymen at their own game—Al Davis of the Oakland Raiders.

In Oakland, California, people who know Al Davis, managing general partner of the Raiders, like to tell this story: Al Davis comes home one night at midnight, after toiling sixteen hours at his office. He goes upstairs. He enters the master bedroom, where his wife Carol is sleeping. While he is undressing, Carol wakes up. She glances at a clock, then murmurs sleepily, "Good God, you're late."

"You can call me Al," her husband replies, without a trace of humor.

A stadium gets built, two leagues merge, the Raiders win more football games than any other franchise over a fourteen-year span —and Al Davis rises from obscure head coach to owner, with dictatorial powers no less absolute than Joe Robbie's. No wonder that in Oakland critics and admirers alike think that Al Davis is a miracle-worker.

In 1963, Davis' first year as head coach and general manager, he led a team that had won three games and lost twenty-five in the previous two seasons to a record of ten wins against only four

171

losses. Three years later, as Commissioner of the AFL, he forced the NFL to agree to a merger by threatening to sign some of its most valuable players. The merger agreement consummated, he returned to the Raiders and became one of the most powerful owners in football—a member of both the NFL's executive committee and its competition committee, which dictates rules and playing conditions.

People have been deploring Al Davis' tough tactics, and applauding his accomplishments, ever since he entered football. Davis was born in Brockton, Massachusetts and raised in Brooklyn. The son of a textile manufacturer, he attended first Wittenburg College in Ohio, then Syracuse University, where he participated in three major sports but lettered in none. In 1950, he began his coaching career at Adelphi College on Long Island. In 1952, he was hired as an assistant coach for the army team at Fort Belvoir, Virginia. He became a recruiter, so successful at signing up pro and college stars who'd been drafted that some unflattering accusations about his methods were uttered from the floor of the U.S. Senate. He slipped quietly away in 1954, to take a coaching job under Weeb Ewbank, head coach of the Baltimore Colts.

A year later, Davis was back coaching college football at the Citadel. General Mark Clark, president of that college, asked Davis if he expected to have a strong team. "You get the money for scholarships," Davis replied, "and I'll get the players."

Clark got the scholarships, and Davis fielded a winner in his first year. In gratitude to the General, Davis named his only son Mark.

Success at the Citadel was a stepping stone to big-time college football. In 1957, Davis went to the University of Southern California, as an assistant to head coach Don Clark. Again, Davis' overenthusiastic recruiting got him into trouble—the Trojans were sanctioned by the NCAA. Davis stayed at USC until Clark retired at the end of the 1959 season. Clark recommended Davis and John McKay as possible successors. The officials at USC chose McKay; they were afraid that Davis would be too controversial. So Davis packed up and departed again, this time moving back to professional football as an assistant coach under Sid Gillman of the San Diego Chargers. At the time, many AFL recruiters were squeamish about signing hot prospects sought after by the NFL. The recruiters of the AFL were afraid that if the AFL eventually folded, the NFL would blackball them. Al Davis wasn't intimidated in the least. He would spirit a prospect away in the dead of night, book him into a hotel in some forgotten backwater and talk until the prospect was dizzy enough to have signed his own death warrant.

Early in 1963, Wayne Valley, owner of the Oakland Raiders, was searching for a savior. "We were losing our war with the San Francisco 49ers," he says, "and we had to do something. We needed somebody who wanted to win so badly, he would do anything. Everywhere I went, people told me what a son of a bitch Al Davis was—hell, that's why I wanted him. Everybody hated his aggressiveness. The AFL people told me that he was too abrasive, too aggressive; they said he'd do anything to win."

Valley, in retrospect, feels he should have gotten deeper insight into Davis' nature right at the start, when he asked Davis to make up a preliminary budget for the Raiders. "I was talking to him at eleven in the morning," Valley told writer Glenn Dickey, in *The Jock Empire,* "and he said he'd get back to me about four that afternoon. At four o'clock, he came in with this complete budget. I said to him, 'Well, Al, now I know what the San Diego Charger budget looks like.' That shook him a little. I figure what he did was to hop a PSA jet down to San Diego, talk one of the secretaries into letting him see the budget and just make a few changes to fit what he thought were our needs. Nobody ever told me what happened, but what can you think when a guy can't talk about a budget at all at 11 A.M., and five hours later he has a complete one, down to the last detail?"

Davis' actions might be controversial, but no one could argue that he lacked ability as a head coach—or as a recruiter. Shortly after he took charge of the Raiders, for example, he flew from Oakland to Toronto. He returned twenty-four hours later with receiver Art Powell in tow. Powell, who had played out his option with the New York Titans, would be a crucial part of Oakland's revival.

Davis the ex-recruiter would do almost anything to gain even a marginal advantage over an opponent. "I often would pass myself off as a sportswriter to inquire into the condition of players on other teams," says Bruce Bishop, in 1963 a young publicist hired by Davis, and now a Pittsburgh executive. But Davis most subtle ploys were aimed at psyching out his ex-boss Sid Gillman's San Diego Chargers. "Once we went to a lot of trouble to give the Chargers a dose of overconfidence," Bishop recalls. "Al had placed in the Oakland *Tribune* a table comparing the two teams. And at virtually every position, the Chargers were given the edge. I picked up some sixty copies of the *Tribune,* and took them down to the Hilton Hotel, near the San Francisco airport, where the Chargers were staying. They were having dinner at the time I arrived. I placed two copies under the door of each room occupied by the players. The Chargers were so overconfident the next day, the Raiders upset them."

Davis fired Bishop twice, but Bishop still idolizes his former employer. "He'd look at me with those blue eyes and say, 'I can't pay much, but I have a great opportunity for you,' and I'd come running." When, in 1966, Davis replaced Joe Foss as Commissioner of the AFL, Bruce Bishop was living in Pittsburgh. "I had just bought a new home," he says, "but when I heard his voice, I just simply couldn't resist. My wife thought I was nuts.

"It was so exciting with Davis in the big city. Everyone wanted to know him. I was sort of his man Friday. I did all sorts of jobs for him. I even signed up several of the NFL players and gave them a bundle of bills."

After their amazing turnaround in 1963, Davis' first season as head coach, the Raiders could do no better than 5–7–3 in 1964 and 8–5–1 in 1965. His reputation as a miracle-worker slightly tarnished, Davis saw in the Commissioner's job a chance to regain lost prestige. Ironically, the job offer was made possible by the man Davis had been trying hardest to outdo—Sid Gillman of the San Diego Chargers. "Davis would be the perfect choice for the job," Gillman argued at the time. "He's a smart young man with an endless capacity for work. He's full of ideas. He'll sit up all night scheming and conniving, trying to find ways to improve our league. He's just the kind of man we need to compete with Pete Rozelle. Pete is smart, ambitious and dedicated. But he doesn't have Al's extreme drive. In fact, nobody else has it, either."

The Upstarts

Davis had one qualification that Gillman neglected to mention, but which was uppermost in every AFL owner's mind: a proven track record as a no-holds-barred recruiter. Two months after Davis became Commissioner, the AFL-NFL merger agreement was signed. (The merger itself took place in 1970.) The NFL was forced to agree to that merger when Davis succeeded in signing up some of its top stars, including quarterback John Brodie of the San Francisco 49ers. However, Davis was unhappy about the terms of the settlement, which forced the Raiders and Jets to pay a total of $49 million in indemnities to the 49ers and Giants. He was also unhappy when the owners decided to retain Pete Rozelle, instead of Al Davis, as Commissioner of the merged league.

Before the final decision, Wayne Valley reminded Davis that the NFL owners outnumbered the AFL owners, 16–10.

"I've got friends in the NFL," Davis replied.

"Al," Valley said, "you couldn't even get a majority of *AFL* owners to vote for you over Rozelle."

Davis returned to the Raiders, this time as managing general partner, just like Joe Robbie. His contract was similar to the one Robbie later gave Don Shula—a 10 percent share of the club, plus a salary of $30,000, with a clause that guaranteed him $50,000 a year even if his salary plus his dividends fell short of that sum. But Al Davis was far more ambitious than Don Shula. Shula had been content to take from Dolphins owner Joe Robbie a percentage of the profits. Davis was determined to take from Raiders owner Wayne Valley not only a minority share of the profits, but a lion's share of the power.

The conflict between Davis and Valley started when Oakland wide receiver Warren Wells was jailed for the second time, in September, 1971. Two years before, in September, 1969, Wells had been convicted of attempted rape. He was put on probation, then was arrested again in February, 1971, for drunken driving and illegal possession of a pistol. Again the Raiders managed to get him out of prison on probation, until that September day in 1971 when a girl friend stabbed him after he beat her up.

Davis desperately wanted Wells—who had caught thirty-six touchdown passes over the past three seasons. He was sure that Wayne Valley could intercede on Wells's behalf, since the sentencing judge was Valley's personal friend. Wells was released, but not till the following July—in no condition to play football. According to some Raiders players, Davis made no secret of the fact that Valley was to blame for Wells's unavailability.

Valley, in turn, resented the rumor—and the implication that if Wells had been white, Valley would have flexed his political muscle. He decided to fire Davis as managing general partner when their agreement ended on January 1, 1976. Anticipating just such a maneuver, Davis had the Raiders' attorney, Herman Cook, draw up a new contract, without Valley's knowledge, to take effect the moment in 1976 that the old contract expired. Then Davis and the club's third partner, Ed McGah, signed it, although McGah later said that he hadn't even read the contract beforehand.

In essence, the new contract, signed in July, 1972, assures Davis of a salary of $100,000 a year for twenty years. It also gives him absolute control of the Oakland Raiders, both on and off the field, including the sole right to cast the club's vote at NFL meetings. Valley says he didn't learn about the contract until February of 1973, when a spate of newspapers revealed its existence. He is now challenging the contract in the courts.

In Davis' absence, the Raiders had resumed their old habit of losing more games than they won. "When I arrived," he says, "I realized that we needed a sense of pride in what we were doing, and we needed poise to avoid panic when we found out we didn't have weapons ready for a specific job. The real thrill of life comes from setting goals, from meeting challenges, from overcoming adversity. I felt that for me there could be no greater challenge than that of building a great football franchise in Oakland."

He cleared out the front office and brought in his own men. He negotiated seventeen different player contracts in an effort to strengthen his demoralized club. Toughness was—and is—the key to his approach. He's a hard bargainer and a demanding taskmaster. Anything that does not contribute directly to winning football games he considers trivial. The Raiders' two-story headquarters reflects his obsession. Its offices are decorated in the Raiders' team colors, silver and black. The clothes Davis wears to work are also often silver and black. The building has only one window—the one in Al's office. There are no wall clocks; Raider employees are expected to be on call twenty-four hours a day, and are supposed to suppress temporal thoughts, concentrating only on next Sunday's victory. "Most people have become slaves to time," says Davis, who never wears a watch. "Contrary to this, ours are goal-oriented, not time-oriented. They have jobs that must be done, and they get them done. Ours is an exciting, stimulating field for those with intense competitive instincts. The Raider organization is made up of just this sort of people."

Davis is a handsome man, with thinning blond hair and a powerful torso, but his legs are as skinny as pipe cleaners. He used to wear baggy pants to conceal the fact but gave them up when he realized they only accentuated it. At age fifty-six, to keep in shape, he lifts weights, runs and plays paddle ball in the exercise room he built on the same floor as his office.

This spartan attitude saturates Davis' personality. He doesn't smoke. He eschews alcoholic drinks, and instead sips Seven-Up at parties. His image as a dedicated, if beleaguered, battlefield general conducting a crusade against the forces of defeat inspires in many of his employees an almost religious awe. Del Courtney, the Raiders' administrative director, led a dance band for twenty years before joining the Raiders, and so was prepared for the irregular hours. "It's an education to work around Davis," he says. "He's so intelligent, such an inspirational force. He's so damned enthusiastic. There's no situation he can't cope with." As an example of how Davis copes, Courtney cites an incident early in the 1968 season, when one of Davis' most able platoon leaders, all-pro lineman Ben Davidson, deserted the team. Courtney was heartbroken.

"Del," Davis said, putting his arm around Courtney's shoulder, "you should know how it is. First there was Connie. Then there was Bonnie."

"Al was talking about my singing wives, Connie Haines and Bonnie King," Courtney explains. "I was broken up about my divorce from Bonnie. Al was just making it clear to me that anyone is replaceable."

Davis inspires respect among many of his football players. They feel that he is one of the few owners who knows as much about the game of pro football as they do, having been a successful head coach, league commissioner and recruiter. He combines that technical expertise with the evangelistic persuasiveness of a Ewing Kauffman: "You wouldn't be here if I didn't think you could handle the assignment," he's fond of telling his players.

Davis' charisma is hard to resist. "Al works twice as hard as anyone else," says Bob Bestor, who used to be the Raiders' business manager. "I learned more from him than I ever did in college. For example, he taught me preparedness. I soon learned to think through every plan before I presented it to Al. Once, I gave him a plan for transporting ninety-six people to Denver for a game. I thought I had taken care of every eventuality. Yet Davis at once came up with several things that might happen for which I was unprepared."

"Al's a voracious reader," says Bob McKeen, a former basketball player who became one of Davis' closest friends when they both served on the Oakland City Council, planning the Oakland Coliseum complex. "He often reads an entire book in bed at night. At parties, I've found he can talk on any subject—even though his mind may be on football all the time."

"I think his greatest asset is that he never lets up," echoes Bob Bestor. "He's always thinking. I recall once we were waiting for a team bus in Denver. It was bitterly cold. I was walking around with my hands in my pockets. 'Take your hands out,' Davis snapped at me. 'Let's not have the players think it's colder than it is.'"

Yet there is something unsettling about Davis. Coupled with his enormous grasp, his critics allege, is an equally Bunyanesque insecurity. "He'd always second-guess," Bestor told Glenn Dickey in *The Jock Empire*. "I'd try to get him to commit himself on paper, but it never worked. I'd bring in a piece of paper with everything written out and he'd never even look at it. He'd just say, 'Just do what you think is right, Bobby,' and then, when it went wrong, he'd ask me why I'd done it that way.

"When I was making out the travel schedules in June, 1968, I asked him whether he wanted to charter a plane to San Diego or take the regular flight, which made a twenty-minute stop in Los Angeles. The difference was fifteen hundred or two thousand dollars. He said we'd go on the regular flight. Then, when we made the trip and stopped in Los Angeles, everybody was unhappy. So Davis looks around the cabin and says, 'Why the fuck are we stopping here? Who's responsible for this?' I reminded him of our conversation and he said, 'I don't remember that conversation.' "

"He's lying to you and you know he's lying," Tom Keating, an All-Pro tackle and the Raiders' players' representative, once said. "And still you want to believe him."

But most of the time, his employees are submissive. Caught up in an atmosphere of a cause instead of a career, they willingly sublimate their egos. Davis himself only rarely grants interviews to reporters. During the off-season, he shuns the banquet circuit. "The Raiders win as an organization," he says. "That's the story —the organization. Not the person." When pressed for an interview, he'll tell the writer to do a story on head coach John Madden instead. "Here's a guy who's got the best record in pro football next to Don Shula's," he'll say. "To be head coach, you've either got it or you don't. John's got it. All he does is win."

At the same time, he carefully cultivates a good press in Oakland. No other team has been more generous to the reporters than the Raiders. They often pay sportswriters' traveling expenses. They shower the local press corps with gifts at Christmas. "We've given binoculars, TV's, stereos . . . it's something I want to do," Davis says. "I guess some other teams do it. A little appreciation for the guys who live with us. Instead of a gift certificate, I gave a guy a check once. He showed it to his sports editor. He gave it back. No big deal. He didn't get fired. There was no scandal."

Davis' admirers see in the gifts material proof of his generosity. His critics see in his philanthropy with the local press a subtle form of payola.

"I'm just an organization guy," Davis says. "I like to think I've put together a good thing here. John Madden is a part of that. The players are. We all are. I don't go to workouts," he adds. "I don't send plays down from the top of the stadium. We talk. I talk to John. I tell him some things I know about the team we're going to play. Has he thought of this? Has he thought of that? He usually has."

One of Davis' earliest moves when he revamped the Raiders'

front office in 1963 was to hire a youngster named Ron Wolf. "I hired him when he was twenty-one," Davis says. "He loves college football. He knows every player, every statistic. I needed a guy who would read everything and tell me everything. He gets to know the kids: Is he a leader? What does everyone say about him?"

Davis put Wolf at the head of a scouting system which favors the personal touch over the punchcard. Unlike other NFL teams, the Raiders belong to no scouting combine. Instead, Davis depends on game films. "Ron Wolf, chief scout Ken Herock and our area scouts are totally committed men who work long, hard and enthusiastically within a meticulously designed system," Davis says. "Live-game and practice coverage and extensive film study are all handled by skilled men who know exactly what the Raiders want. The problem of the early days was getting the talent, but today recognition of talent is the key."

Davis never stops evaluating, he never stops working. He spends at least five hours a day on the telephone, probing, urging, seeking. At his home, in the plush Piedmont section of Oakland, he has a twenty-four-hour answering service. He orders extra prints of every Raider game, then screens them in his family room. "Thank heavens for the movies," his wife Carol says. "Otherwise I'd never see Al. It isn't important whether I like football or not, although I do. The important thing is Al likes it."

And it is this issue—the religious devotion Davis exacts not only from his private family, but from the Raider Family—that divides his friends from his enemies. Believing him a god, his friends feel that only with omnipotent control can Davis finally lead the Raiders to total victory—the Super Bowl win which has thus far eluded them. Believing him a devil, Davis' enemies see his checkmate of Valley as one more instance of his deviousness and egomania. Ironically, both friends and enemies cite one anecdote as being symptomatic of his character. One day, when Al was a boy growing up in Brooklyn, he found a screwdriver in the street. A stranger saw him pick it up and place it in his pocket.

"Did you just find a screwdriver?" the stranger asked.

"Yes, sir," young Al replied, then asked, "Did you lose one with a red handle?"

"That's right," the stranger said.

The Upstarts

"The one I found was green," Al said.

When his friends tell the story, it's to show how a precocious kid was smart enough to dodge an adult's con: the screwdriver didn't belong to the stranger. When his enemies tell the story, it's to show how a devious kid was clever enough to con an adult: color the screwdriver handle red.

◀ 10 ▶
The Emperors

In an era when big business is dominated by multinational corporations, the big business of pro sports has come to be dominated by multifranchise owners. Lamar Hunt has been an owner in pro football (the Kansas City Chiefs), pro tennis (World Championship Tennis), pro soccer (the Dallas Tornado) and pro basketball (the now-defunct ABA Dallas Chaparrals). John Basset of Toronto owns the Maple Leaf Garden (home of the NHL Toronto Maple Leafs), the Toronto Argonauts of the Canadian Football League, the Memphis franchise of the defunct World Football League. Nick Mileti owns the Ohio Coliseum, the Cleveland Indians and the Cleveland Cavaliers. Jack Kent Cooke, who used to own a soccer team (the Wolverines of the defunct NAPSL), still owns the Los Angeles Forum, the L.A. Lakers of the NBA, the L.A. Kings of the NHL, and a majority share of the NFL Washington Redskins.

Herman Sarkowsky is a minority owner of the NBA Seattle SuperSonics, and a majority owner in the new NFL Seattle franchise. Ted Turner, the TV magnate and yachtsman, owns the Atlanta Braves baseball team and the Atlanta Hawks basketball team. Charlie Finley at one time owned, besides his Oakland A's, the ABA Memphis Tams and the NHL Golden Seals. Earl Fore-

185

man used to own the ABA Virginia Squires, and is still part-owner of the NHL Philadelphia Flyers. Billy Bidwell owns a part-share of both the St. Louis football Cardinals and the St. Louis hockey Blues. Meanwhile, like Lamar Hunt, George Steinbrenner III, of the New York Yankees, owns 10 percent of the Chicago Bulls, while Bunker Hunt, Lamar's brother, is a minority shareholder in the Yankees. One effect of this interlock is certainly to consolidate the power to make decisions in pro sports in relatively few hands.

Nowhere is this concentration of power more obvious, or significant, than in the indoor winter sports of basketball and ice hockey, where the decisions are often made by the few men and corporations who control the arena in a city or region, and both of the teams that play in it. Arthur Wirtz owns the Chicago Stadium, plus a large interest in the NBA Bulls, while his son, Bill, owns the hockey Black Hawks. Roy Boe controls Long Island's municapally owned Nassau Coliseum, and both the ABA Nets and the NHL Islanders. Jack Kent Cooke owns the L.A. Forum, the Lakers and the Kings. The Madison Square Garden Corporation owns the Garden itself, plus the Knickerbockers and the Rangers. Nick Mileti owned, until recently, both the NBA Cavaliers and the WHA Crusaders, plus the Cleveland Arena, where the Cavaliers used to play, and the Ohio Coliseum, where both teams now play. The late Robert Schmertz owned the NBA Celtics and the WHA Whalers; John Wilcox, Jr., of Atlanta had ownership interests in both the NBA Hawks and the NHL Flames . . .

It would take a computer to unscramble and identify every instance of interleague incest, but one fact is evident. The interlock between the two winter sports in a particular city can be a source of conflicts of interest.

It was in the 1930's, while Americans by the millions were watching baseball and ignoring pro football, that the seed was sown for a boom in indoor sports. Arthur Wirtz, having graduated from the University of Michigan in 1922, formed, with a pair of partners, the real-estate brokerage firm of Wirtz, Hubert and Little. Soon the firm owned or managed some eighty buildings, with a total of 3,000 rental units around Chicago's North Side lakefront (the bulk of which Wirtz still owns). With those real-estate holdings as a springboard, Wirtz, the son of a Chicago policeman, would eventually gain control of five wholesale liquor distributorships (whose estimated annual sales exceeded $150 million), two banks (with assets worth more than $140 million), two radio stations in Milwaukee, and a string of movie theaters. Plus, of course, a handful of pro franchises and indoor arenas across the country.

But, in the early 1930's, he was still far from being a millionaire—until he met, in the course of a business transaction, a transplanted Canadian named James Norris who had already made a fortune as a grain speculator and a dealer on the Board of Trade. Norris, like most other Chicagoans who encountered Wirtz, was impressed by the way Wirtz was maneuvering his way past the debris of the Depression. According to *The Wall Street Journal,* Wirtz's forte was just what a Depression called for: "He could take a faltering building corporation, reorganize it, lop off most of its debts, and prevent it from going bankrupt."

In 1933, at age thirty-two, Wirtz entered into a partnership with Norris. "Mr. Norris pretty quickly realized that Wirtz had the head for business that his son Jim lacked," a business associate recalls. "Jim was, back then, a charming guy who loved having a good time and hanging around with the sort of people who frequent race tracks and prizefights. The old man saw he needed someone to keep young Jim from spending every cent he had. After a while, Jim rarely made a move without clearing it with Arthur. If it wasn't for Arthur, God knows what would have happened to young Jim."

"The elder Norris saw in Wirtz a bright young man who could assist in making money in real estate," says another acquaintance. "Wirtz saw in Norris someone who had a couple of million dollars in cash."

The elder Norris was a fanatic for hockey. He thirsted for a team of his own—and the Depression was a good time to buy things cheap, especially when you had an astute real-estate expert like Arthur Wirtz to guide you. In 1933, both the Detroit hockey franchise and the Olympia, the arena where it played its home matches, were, like many corporate entities throughout the U.S., suffering severe financial traumas. Wirtz/Norris purchased the franchise and the arena at a bargain price: in 1927, just six years before, the arena had been built at a cost of $2.5 million; Wirtz/ Norris bought it for ten cents on the dollar; another $100,000, and the sellers threw in the Detroit Red Wings hockey team, too. Next on their shopping list was the 17,000-seat Chicago Stadium. Today, the arena stands in a dismal neighborhood. Before a game, patrons are liable to be propositioned by prostitutes—and, if they're foolish enough to dawdle long after a game, by muggers. But in 1929, when it was built at a cost of $7 million, Chicago Stadium was reputed to be the biggest and best indoor sports arena in the entire country. In 1935, Wirtz and Norris bought it for $300,000. They didn't stop at Detroit or Chicago, either. At one time or another during the next twenty years, Wirtz and the Norrises (Jim, his sons Jim Jr. and Bruce, and his daughter Margurite) held leases on indoor arenas in Omaha and Indianapolis, and owned the St. Louis Arena and 40 percent of New York's Madison Square Garden. In 1946, the trio financed the purchase of the Chicago Black Hawks by an outside party, thus avoiding the appearance of a conflict of interest with their ownership of the Detroit Red Wings. (It wasn't until 1954 that they actually assumed control of the Black Hawks.) So pervasive was their influence that, according to New York columnist Dan Parker, "NHL meant Norris House League."

The Norrises and Wirtz virtually ran the NHL for four decades—along with a colorful promoter named Conn Smythe. Smythe was a World War I hero who organized the first New York Rangers team in 1926, only to be fired before that first season by owner Colonel John Hammond. A year later, he owned the Toronto Maple Leafs franchise and Maple Leaf Gardens. "When Smythe or Norris—or both—snapped their fingers," Stan Fischler wrote in *Slashing!,* "Campbell [long-time NHL President Clarence Campbell] jumped." For example, Smythe, the Norrises and Wirtz did not believe the NHL should expand; they felt the league should stay small and exclusive, with only six teams—the Boston Bruins, Chicago Black Hawks, Detroit Red Wings, Montreal Canadiens, New York Rangers and Toronto Maple Leafs. Such was their power that until 1966 they managed to scuttle every proposal to expand the NHL from six teams to eight, ten or twelve—while baseball, football and basketball were adding new franchises as fast as they could be invented. Ironically, it was Conn's son, Stafford (he took over the Maple Leafs when Conn retired), who led the successful fight against Jim Norris, Jr., that resulted in the NHL's adding six new teams in 1966. However, the elder Smythe's legacy is still with us, in the form of broken heads and bloody brawls. "Yes," Conn once said, in reply to critics who complained that his Maple Leafs spilled too much blood on the ice, "we've got to stamp out this sort of thing—or people are going to keep on buying tickets!"

Their control of sports arenas led the NHL powerbrokers into staging attractions to fill those arenas. Wirtz/Norris' first venture into promoting was in the mid-1930's, when Wirtz booked a troupe of European ice skaters into Chicago Stadium. The promotion proved so successful that Wirtz signed Olympic gold medalist Sonja Henie to a contract, then featured her in a "Hollywood Ice Revue" that toured for years. From ice-skating, Wirtz/Norris moved into big-time professional boxing, in 1949 when heavyweight champion Joe Louis revealed that he was thinking of ending his career. "Joe wanted to take something out with him, so we got the idea of his promoting an elimination tournament between the four leading contenders to succeed him," says Truman Gibson, who was Louis' lawyer at the time. "We went looking for someone who would bankroll the deal and give us a slice. Harry Mendel, who was Joe's PR man, knew Jim Norris and suggested we try him. We did, and he checked with Wirtz. Arthur didn't know one fighter from another, but he knew that home television could make boxing pay even if no one showed up to see the fights in person. He gave the go-ahead."

Jim Norris, Jim Jr. and Wirtz formed the IBC (International Boxing Club). Owning 40 percent of the Madison Square Garden stock, they had no trouble convincing that organization to give them exclusive rights to stage boxing shows there. They also got the boxing rights to the Polo Grounds, Yankee Stadium and St. Nicholas Arena. Between June, 1949, and January, 1955, the IBC promoted forty-seven of the fifty-one championship boxing bouts held in the United States. Somehow, federal trust-busters got the idea that the trio had formed a monopoly over professional boxing. Both New York State and the federal government (the Kefauver Committee) launched separate probes of the IBC. They uncovered ties between the IBC and a number of hoodlums—in particular one Frankie Carbo, whose record included five arrests for murder. In 1957, the IBC was ordered to dissolve. Frankie Carbo received a twenty-five-year sentence for "conspiracy" and "extortion" in a plot to wrest control of a West Coast fighter from the two men who "owned" the fighter's contract. Truman Gibson received a suspended sentence. The elder Norris had died in 1952. Jim Jr. admitted only to associating with mobster Carbo. Wirtz had been his full partner in the IBC, but a silent one, and never an officer of the company. The Norrises had handled the promotional end of the business; there was no evidence to show that Wirtz had ever had any dealings with Carbo or any other criminal element.

Wirtz had always cultivated a low profile. He shunned the limelight. He took his pleasure in profits, not in publicity. "I don't know why anyone would be interested in me," he once told a newspaper reporter. "I'm just a real-estate man trying to make a living. I make a good deal once in a while, but I made two bad ones for every one of those."

Color the ledger entries for the arenas in black. Control of his arenas gave Arthur Wirtz a virtual lock on indoor professional sports. Arena owners such as Wirtz were, after World War II, the natural candidates to own—and develop—franchises in the professional leagues of hockey and basketball. To apply pressure against would-be competitors, the arena owners had only to refuse them permission to use their arenas, often the only suitable facilities in town. Or else, the arena owners could charge such exorbitant rentals that only their own franchises—effectively paying rent to themselves—could afford the facility. (Critics argue that one of the reasons the Chicago Bulls have for so long proved unprofitable is that part-owner Wirtz charged them a stadium rental of up to 33 percent of their receipts. Roy Boe of the New York Nets, by comparison, pays only 11 percent of gross receipts as rental in the muncipally owned Nassau Coliseum.) And no one came to own more indoor franchises than Wirtz and Norris. In hockey, for instance, they owned, though not on record, at the same time the Chicago Black Hawks, the New York Rangers and the Detroit Red Wings—three of the six teams in the old NHL—plus, of course, the arenas where these clubs played their home games. Add a pinch of ice-skating, spice with prizefights—and they had concocted a recipe for monopoly profit unsurpassed since. Eventually, in the face of accusations of antitrust violations, the combine sold the Rangers. They divested themselves of the Red Wings by "selling" the franchise to the younger Norris, half-brother Bruce. (Wirtz still has a controlling interest in the NBA Bulls and, through his son, the NHL Black Hawks.)

But they made money on their way out. In 1959, they sold their interest in Madison Square Garden for $4 million—more than they had paid for it. They made a substantial profit from the sale of their St. Louis holdings (purchased in 1949). Part of their St. Louis properties they sold for commercial use, for $900,000. They sold another portion for $1.8 million, for use as a community college, and they sold the arena to the present owners of the St. Louis Blues, for $3,750,000. (The St. Louis owners weren't in much of a bargaining position; it was only through Wirtz's influence that they had been awarded their franchise in the first place.) In total, Wirtz accumulated $6.45 million from the sale of his St. Louis holdings—more than three times the purchase price a decade before.

Today, Wirtz is worth over nine figures, but even at seventy-five, according to his friends, age hasn't blunted his sharp instinct or squelched his enormous energy. "He has slowed down a bit over the years, of course," says a close friend, "but then, he used to be inexhaustible. We kidded him that his initials, A.M., stood for 'After Midnight,' because he'd wake guys up at three in the morning to talk business. He never really had any goals besides making a lot of money. Other rich guys with pro sports teams love to fraternize with their players and that sort of thing, but not him. He doesn't even especially care for sports. He gets his jollies from seeing a good bottom line."

Wirtz now takes little interest in the day-to-day business of his sports enterprises, leaving those decisions—at least some of them —to his son Bill, who, along with Bruce Norris, is one of the powerbrokers of the NHL. Periodically, though, his ire is aroused sufficiently to make his presence felt in the Bulls' head office. Early in the 1975–76 season, for instance, the troubled Bulls staged a "hunger strike" in protest over their $19-per-day meal money.

The Rich Who Own Sports

"You'd think," Big Daddy Wirtz boomed, "that a guy earning a hundred and fifty thousand a year could buy his *own* lunch!"

While Wirtz and the Norrises prospered, not every arena owner was so lucky—or so shrewd. In 1950, Walter Brown, owner of the Boston Gardens, took over the Celtics franchise that was a tenant in his arena, paying for the privilage a token $2,500. Four years later, Brown had lost $462,000. He had mortgaged his home. Eventually, super-center Bill Russell would turn the Celtics into perennial winners, and profit-makers, but Brown's early years of struggle were typical in that postwar era of indoor expansion. "We used to have to spend all of the withholding tax," Brown's then–assistant treasurer, Eddie Powers, later told a reporter from *Sports Illustrated*. "One day the Internal Revenue Service man finally gave up and came to my office and said that the government had taken enough from us and had to take over. I stood up from behind my desk and spread out my hands—you have to be an actor sometimes—and said, 'Okay, you're going to have an auction sale of the Boston Celtics. How much do you think the government can get for a dozen T-shirts, some used jockstraps and a few beat-up basketballs?' He left shaking his head."

It wasn't till 1963 that a millionaire came on the scene who would help pro basketball become an attractive investment. In that year, Jack Kent Cooke bid for an NHL franchise in Los Angeles; competing for that same franchise was Dan Reeves, owner of the Los Angeles Rams in pro football. Reeves's trump card was his pull with the Los Angeles Coliseum Commission, which controlled the only viable indoor arena—the Los Angeles Sports Arena. At his prodding, the Coliseum Commission attempted to frustrate Cooke's bid by offering him only a two-year contract. Without the guarantee of a long-term rental, Cooke's NHL franchise right was worthless.

Cooke didn't have Reeves's leverage with the California sports establishment, but he had a higher leverage with the California financial establishment. He stunned his opponents by going out and building his own arena, the Los Angeles Forum. Today, Cooke still owns the Forum, in which his NBA Lakers and his NHL Kings play. Since Cooke is also a principal owner, along with attorney

The Emperors

Edward Bennet Williams, of the NFL Washington Redskins and Teleprompter, Inc. (the largest cable TV operation in the world and promoter of the first Ali-Frazier fight), he is one of the most influential owners in all of professional sports. Indoors, his power is equaled only by the monolithic Madison Square Garden Corporation, which owns the NHL Rangers and the NBA Knicks. Between them, Cooke and Madison Square Garden control the two most lucrative TV markets in the United States.

Professional sports offer great scope for the exercise of power. Imagine holding your employees—glamorous enough to be sought after for their autographs and bodies, and valuable enough to be accorded special treatment by the IRS—in the bondage that, until recently, the various forms of "reserve" and "option" clauses guaranteed. Jack Kent Cooke is not necessarily the only owner to exhibit a lust for power, but none has pursued that goal more avidly, obtained it more completely, or verbalized its significance more succinctly. "For the man whose horse wins the Kentucky Derby, it is *his* horse," Cooke once said. "In pro sports, it will be *my* team."

In September, 1971, newspapers announced that Jack Kent Cooke had purchased the Los Angeles Lakers from Robert Short, for the then-staggering sum of $5,175,000. The event was heralded as a new era of new money in professional basketball. Only three years before, the Philadelphia Warriors had been sold for a paltry $800,000.

Cooke was a former Canadian broadcasting and publishing magnate. Eventually, he would also become a former Canadian—powerful enough to get a legislator to push through a private bill making him a U.S. citizen. He had begun by selling soap, then encyclopedias door-to-door at $39.50 a set. When he wasn't playing baseball or hockey, and when people weren't buying his soap or encyclopedias, he was studying the saxophone. Piano lessons had helped Ray Kroc survive the land bust in Florida. Jack Kent Cooke paid for his college books and tuition by leading a band, the name of which spoke more for his future ambitions than his current status—"Oley and His Bourgeois Canadians." When he wasn't playing the saxophone, he was crooning through a megaphone, like Rudy Vallee. Barbara Jean Carnegie heard him sing a love song at the Lakeview Pavilion in Oshawa, Ontario—first on stage, then later that evening into her ear. "He came on so strong, I didn't much like him at first," she says, "but he was so strong he beat back my objections." On April 21, 1934, when Cooke was just twenty-one years old, "Jeannie" eloped with him. Today, they live in a Mediterranean-style mansion in posh Bel Air; their two sons, John and Ralph, are officers in Cooke's varied corporate enterprises. Cooke drives a Bentley, and prides himself on being a connoisseur of vintage wines and exotic cuisine. He surrounds himself with a menagerie of show-biz "names" and captains of industry. But back in the Thirties, all he had was a single obsessive dream: to become a millionaire by the age of twenty-nine.

That's why, in 1934, Cooke left college and traded in his saxophone for a courier's satchel. He became a "runner" in the Toronto stock exchange, earning $11 a week. After he got married, he asked for a promotion from "runner" to "trader," at the exalted salary of $25 per week. His bosses said no. Cooke quit and resumed selling encyclopedias, this time in the boondocks of western Canada. In 1935, he took a job with Colgate-Palmolive as a soap salesman. Then, in 1936, at twenty-four, he met Roy Thomson, who owned a few radio stations and a small newspaper. Thomson hired him to manage a nearly bankrupt station in Stratford—for $25 a week. Cooke's prospects didn't look particularly promising, but he held on, putting the station in the black. Six months after he had hired Cooke, Thomson was able to sell the station at a profit.

As Thomson increased his holdings, he also enlarged Cooke's share of the operation. Cooke became first a one-third, then a one-half partner in Thomson's burgeoning empire, which now included TV stations and newspapers, along with radio transmitters. Then, in 1949, Cooke and Thomson parted ways. "Roy's ambitions were toward the East, while mine lay to the South," Cooke said, and if his tone had the ring of a general preparing for a campaign, that was exactly his intention. In 1952, at the age of forty, he began his conquest of pro sports by purchasing, for $200,000, the Toronto Maple Leaf baseball club of the International League. He turned the team into one of the most profitable minor league franchises ever, then joined Branch Rickey's short-lived Continental League, which, in 1959, pressured the establishment owners into opening the doors of organized baseball to new members.

By 1961, at age forty-nine, Cooke had achieved his lifelong ambition: he was a millionaire many times over. He retired, awarding himself—instead of a gold watch—a $100,000 château beside a golf course in Pebble Beach, California. But his retirement was tactical, rather than permanent. An avid fan of Napoleon, Cooke's favorite quote is: "The combative urge is within all of us." Cooke was, in fact, only doing what Napoleon did in Elba; he might be forty-nine, but there were continents left to conquer.

"It was fun for a while," he recalls, "but oh God, it was dull."

To tranquilize that boredom, in 1963 he invested $23 million in the budding cable TV industry (American Cablevision Co.); he purchased a 25 percent share of the Washington Redskins. (He first tried to buy the team outright, but George Preston Marshall turned down his $4.5 million bid. Marshall later agreed to give Cooke 25 percent of the franchise, when Harry Wismer had to sell his one-quarter share to finance his New York franchise in the AFL.) According to the agreement between Cooke and Marshall, Cooke had the right to purchase majority control if Marshall sold the franchise or if he died. Cooke eventually wound up with about 71 percent. It was he who convinced the Redskins' board of directors to hire head coach George Allen. "Money ceases to be the object after a while," Cooke says, echoing Ray Kroc. "It starts out to be the object, but becomes less the object as you go along. Fun, excitement, satisfaction soon displace it as the object, and you find that doing things, like running a basketball team, transcends in importance merely having money."

Fun, excitement, satisfaction—and power. From the beginning, Cooke was interested only in acquiring majority control of any franchise he bid for. Dan Reeves once offered him 49 percent of the L.A. Rams for $7 million. Cooke rejected the offer. He wanted all of the franchise or none of it. Reeves also offered Cooke 57 percent of the minor league L.A. Blades hockey team, on the assumption that the NHL would grant a franchise in Los Angeles. Again Cooke said no—although this time Reeves's offer was harder to refuse, since a hockey franchise was what Cooke longed for above anything. As a Canadian, he wanted a team in the

Canadian sport. The only reason he bought into the Redskins, and bought the L.A. Lakers, was to enhance his image. Owning a franchise in basketball or football, he felt, would make him more attractive in the eyes of the National Hockey League.

Reeves's control of the only viable arena in Los Angeles was a stumbling block, hurdled only when Cooke promised to build a new arena on his own. On the strength of this promise—and his reputation in the local banking community—Cooke was allowed to buy the Los Angeles Lakers from Bob Short in 1965, and was awarded the NHL franchise right in Los Angeles in 1966. Reeves still refused to relax his stranglehold on the Los Angeles Coliseum Commission, so Cooke went out and did what few thought he could: he built, for $16.5 million, the Los Angeles Forum, inaugurated in late 1967, during the Kings' first season.

Ironically, the hockey franchise soon became secondary in Cooke's affections to the basketball franchise. The Kings, after some early success, became perennial losers. The Lakers became an NBA power, and Cooke—or the Napoleon in Jack Kent Cooke—found more satisfaction in identifying himself with a winner. Like Bonaparte, he tolerated no interference, from either the brigadiers of the board rooms or the corporals on court.

Cooke installed himself, along with a coterie of friends, in a special row of seats near midcourt at the Forum. Every time one of his Laker players made a mistake—and that first season, 1966, making mental errors was the only category in which the Lakers led the league—Cooke would inform him of the fact in a voice that thundered to the Forum rafters. Jack Kent Cooke's antics at midcourt made him unpopular with his players.

After a hapless exhibition season, the Lakers opened their campaign at Madison Square Garden, against the New York Knickerbockers. Laker forward Rudy LaRusso was pitted against Willis Reed, then playing a forward position. Halfway through the first period, the two big men, who had been pounding each other from the opening tap, ended up on one side of the lane, lined up as Elgin Baylor shot a Laker free throw. According to LaRusso, Reed whacked him with an elbow. "I just took a swing at him," LaRusso said. "I caught him in the head first. I wouldn't have started anything."

The Emperors

It was the last time anyone ever started anything with Willis Reed. Reed only lost his temper; many Lakers lost their teeth. Reed pummeled LaRusso, then rookie John Block, then Laker center Darrel Imhoff. But LaRusso suffered the worst damage of all—to his pride. Coach Fred Schaus dropped him from the starting line-up, replacing him with Connie Hawkins. Benched for the first time in his career, LaRusso sat and stared across court, where Jack Kent Cooke shouted endless instructions. Eight days after the Reed Massacre, the Lakers announced that LaRusso had been traded to the Baltimore Bullets; the Bullets immediately announced that LaRusso had been traded to the Detroit Pistons.

Instead, LaRusso retired. And the first thing he did after retiring was to blast owner Jack Kent Cooke. "A figure like Mr. Cooke in the background meant extra pressure on Fred Schaus and on the players," he said. "When the owner is at courtside, watching every move you make, it's difficult. The whole thing was not conducive to good basketball. We got frantic about winning every game. There was a mountain of pressure. We were never in a position to just go out and *play.*"

LaRusso went on to remind his listeners that the previous owner, Bob Short, had been criticized for spending too much time with his trucking firm in Minneapolis, and too little time sorting out the affairs of the Lakers. "Maybe," he added pointedly, "absentee ownership wasn't that bad at all."

LaRusso's words sound antiseptic enough today, so conditioned have we become to hearing athletes like Reggie Jackson say, when he was an Oakland A: "All owners are shit. Charlie Finley's just *bad* shit!" But in the early Sixties, and especially in pro basketball, even mild criticism like LaRusso's carried a sting.

The night after LaRusso's diatribe, the Lakers were in St. Louis to play the Hawks. The crowd recognized LaRusso as he returned to his seat after visiting with his ex-teammates. He was showered with applause. Then, at half-time, two sisters who were among the Lakers' most ardent fans passed around a petition in favor of rehiring him. It concluded with a bitter jibe at Jack Kent Cooke:

"We realize that the purchase of a ticket neither assumes a victory in a game nor gives us any managerial role.

The Rich Who Own Sports

"But please, if you cannot find a trader who is *shrewd,* could you at least try to find one who is *lucky?*"

The Lakers lost again that night, 123–121. At the end of that week, the petition bore hundreds of signatures. By beating out Dan Reeves for his NHL franchise, Cooke had offended the Southern California sports *establishment.* Now, by his cavalier treatment of Rudy LaRusso, he had managed to alienate most of the Southern California *fans.* Cooke dispatched his chief of staff, Eddie Coil, to LaRusso with the terms of his surrender.

Five days after the trade, the Lakers called a press conference at the Beverly Hilton Hotel. LaRusso was being reinstated to the team. "Upon returning from Toronto last night," said Cooke, who had been at the NHL All-Star game, "I have learned of the extenuating and unique circumstances from Rudy's standpoint. I agree with Rudy on this score. In light of that and the pleasant things Rudy has said to me this morning, I accept his apology."

It didn't matter that LaRusso then issued his apology publicly. History would record that Cooke, in the words of his Corsican idol, had "lost the favorable moment which in war decides everything."

Just as Arthur Wirtz controls the indoor sports scene in Chicago, and Jack Kent Cooke in Los Angeles, the monopolist in Cleveland is a young man named Nick Mileti, a fiery Sicilian who emerged as a sports baron as late as 1969 with ownership interests in the American League Cleveland Indians, the NBA Cleveland Cavaliers and the WHA Crusaders—plus the old Cleveland Arena and a new 20,600-seat arena halfway between Cleveland and Akron. Mileti also owned a franchise right in the original WFL, and still has the controlling interest in Cleveland's 50,000-watt NBC TV outlet as well as in WWWE, the radio station that carries play-by-play broadcasts of all three Cleveland teams.

Mileti legitimizes his multi-ownership by calling it his "synergistic concept"—the three teams working together to lure the public, permitting him to employ a single sales force selling tickets for all three franchises. In fact, his situation is rather unique among owners. Mileti put together syndicates of private investors to purchase the franchises, then set himself up as the titular head in each.

The Emperors

Unlike most of the other owners, Mileti has had to endure pressure from majority stockholders and not-silent-enough partners. And, most pressing of all, from bankers.

Mileti avoids the petty squabbles and locker room interference that have brought some of his colleagues—including Jack Kent Cooke—notoriety. His Mr. Nice Guy image and his knack at convincing people that whatever is good for Nick Mileti is also good for Cleveland have made Mileti admired by sports fans in his native city. However, the bankers of Cleveland do not regard the forty-three-year-old Mileti so highly. In their first five seasons, the Cavaliers alone lost $4.6 million, in addition to the $3.7 million it cost to join the NBA. Although president of the Indians and the Cavaliers, Mileti has never actually owned more than 10 percent of either franchise's stock. Moreover, his personal stake in his $45 million Ohio Coliseum never exceeded $1 million, and most of *that* is borrowed. The bankers perceive this financial underpinning as a flimsy structure, liable to be blown away by the first adverse wind. And Mileti's character contributes little to their peace of mind.

If any one facet of his personality arouses distrust among the businessmen who deal with him, it is an uncontrollable enthusiasm that sometimes blurs his vision. One morning, for example, Indian executive vice-president Ted Bonda (a former board chairman of Avis Rent-A-Car who once called Mileti's operations an "empire built on marshmallows") telephoned Nick to talk about the most significant prop in any club's profitability—a new television contract. "Tomorrow's a historic day at the Coliseum," he heard Mileti shout into the phone. "We're pouring cement on the main floor. Think of it!" Try as he might, Bonda was unable to get Mileti to concentrate on that crucial TV contract.

It was this fundamental suspicion of Mileti that led NHL owners to reject his bid for an expansion franchise, forcing Nick to satisfy his urge for a hockey club in the World Hockey Association. It was this same skepticism that led his colleagues in the American League to insist that Mileti sell $300,000 worth of his stock in the Cleveland Indians. And in March, 1975, he sold off a huge chunk of his personal holdings in the Crusaders hockey club —turning over control to Jay P. Moore, a businessman who was also associated with the Indians. Rumor had it that Mileti was even thinking of reducing his holdings in the Cavaliers—under pressure from the banks.

Mileti stumbled into sports back in 1967, when, in order to raise money for his alma mater, Bowling Green University, the young lawyer promoted one of Bowling Green's basketball games at the Cleveland Arena. "It drew eleven thousand," he says. "I figured if I could get eleven thousand one night, I could get eight thousand every night."

To get into big-time promoting, Mileti turned to an old army pal, Leo McKenna, a Wall Street banker who managed investments for the heirs of Charles F. Kettering. McKenna, in behalf of Kettering, gave Mileti the $1.9 million he needed to purchase the Cleveland Arena and the Cleveland Barons, a minor league hockey team. When the NBA awarded him its expansion franchise in Cleveland in 1970, Mileti obtained most of the required $3.7 million from his backers, but a proportion was contributed by fans who paid $5 per share for the privilege of becoming the most minor of minority owners.

Then somehow, between 1970 and 1972, Nick Mileti got his hands on an awful lot of money. In 1972 alone, he purchased NBC's local AM and FM radio outlet for $5.5 million; he purchased the Indians for $10 million; he bought 39 percent of the WHA Crusaders for $250,000. But Mileti has found making money harder than borrowing money.

Part of the problem is his life style. He is a *bon vivant* whose hobbies transcend jockstraps and linament and Ace bandages. Recently, he purchased for his wife, Gretchen, and his ten-year-old son, Jimmy, a forty-six-acre estate with a Tudor house surrounded by stables, orchards and fountains, in the Cleveland suburb of Gates Mills. Bankers felt that the $500,000 purchase money might have been better spent paying off business debts. Mileti disagrees. "Since I'm not home very much," he says, "the next best thing is to make life easy for my family."

Mileti is as familiar a face in the dim light of cocktail lounges and restaurants and night clubs as in locker rooms and executive suites. It was Mileti who introduced jump suits and $300 "Ultrasuede" shirts to the shores of Lake Erie. As a native, in an era when many owners of pro franchises are carpetbaggers, Mileti is a staunch defender of the city of Cleveland. "There's an old Sicilian saying," he says. " 'Don't curse the bridge that carried you across.' "

This attitude has contributed to his popularity among the fans of his franchises, but his ethics have turned off his rival for control of pro sports in Cleveland, Browns owner Art Modell. Modell had been the kingpin till Mileti became, almost overnight, a three-team owner. Modell and Mileti agreed to an informal truce: Mileti would stay out of football, Modell would stay away from basketball, baseball, and hockey. Then, in 1973, Modell learned that Mileti had been an early investor in Gary Davidson's World Football League, and was the owner of one of that league's original franchise rights. Mileti went out of his way to assure Modell that he definitely did not intend to bring a WFL franchise into Cleveland to compete with the NFL Browns. True to his word, he sold the franchise right; it was purchased by Tom Origer, a wealthy builder, and became the WFL Chicago Fire. According to local newspaper reports, however, there was something Mileti didn't tell Modell. At the same time as he was selling his WFL franchise right, he was trying to convince another WFL owner to shift his franchise to Akron, only sixty miles away from Modell's Cleveland Browns—and about twenty miles from Mileti's new Ohio Coliseum indoor arena.

Apart from the ethical questions raised by owners' machinations in slicing up a particular territory, multi-ownership often raises questions about other conflicts of interest. Take Jack Kent Cooke as an example.

• When the trustees of the Washington Redskins Foundation sold a 43 percent interest (representing the legacy of the late George Preston Marshall) to former minority owners Cooke, attorney Edward Bennett Williams and businessman Milton King, for between $5 and $6 million, that transaction brought the trio's combined stock interests to a total of roughly 56 percent, with Cooke holding 40 percent of the team stock, and Williams and King 8 percent apiece. Cooke, then, had become the single largest stockholder. Cooke owned the Lakers of the NBA and the Kings of the NHL, as well. An NFL rule stipulated that no majority stockholder of a National Football League team could be the majority stockholder in any other professional franchise. Publicly, the transaction had to be cloaked in the form of a "trust" purchase, while privately the NFL obtained from its member owners special permission for Cooke to bend the rule.

• As the owner of Teleprompter cable TV, Cooke is a party to a conflict with the major commercial networks as to whether cable TV networks have the right to broadcast, for a fee, sporting events that the commercial networks are willing to televise on a sponsored basis. Meanwhile, in his role as football, basketball and hockey owner, he is sharing in the profits of the NFL's, the NBA's and the NHL's commercial network revenues.

• As an NBA owner, Cooke has agreed to certain changes in the "option reserve" system. Meanwhile, as an owner in the NFL, he was involved, in 1974, in a players' strike in which similar changes to an "option reserve" rule—the Rozelle Rule—were a crucial issue.

• As owner of the Los Angeles Lakers, Cooke was sued by the American Basketball Association, and has also had to decide whether to merge with it. As owner of the Los Angeles Kings of the NHL, he has been sued by the World Hockey Association, and was party to the settlement between those two leagues. Meanwhile, one of his colleagues in the NHL, Roy Boe, also owned a franchise in the ABA, while one of his colleagues in the NBA, Nick Mileti, owned a franchise in the WHA, etc.

This pervasive incest between different teams—in different sports, sharing the same arenas or stadiums, and all depending on cable or commercial television for their survival—creates, for the owner with a finger stuck in several of those pies, the advantages usually associated with a monopoly. On the positive side, this "interlock" makes investing in indoor sports more attractive; an owner who controls an arena, say, and both the teams that play in it, has a better chance to make a profit. He can write off the losses from one franchise against the profits of another. He can devise a sensible schedule, one that benefits both teams equally.

On the negative side, this monopoly can prevent fans from checking the power of an owner at the box office. If, say, the Kansas City Royals' fans don't like what they see when the Royals take the field, they can stay at home, forcing owner Ewing Kauff-man (or at least pressuring him) to make changes to win their approval, and their dollars. When there's an interlock in a particu-lar city, however, that pressure from below becomes much less effective. Control of one privately owned arena, plus the Knicks and the Rangers, gives the Madison Square Garden Corp. a virtual lock on indoor entertainment in New York City—the number one TV market in the United States. If the Knicks became perennial also-rans, the Garden Corp. might decide that a decline in Knick attendance could be compensated for by a rise in Ranger attend-ance—that the corporation's overall interests might be better served by not investing the cash it would take to make the Knicks competitive again.

If there is anyone left who doubts that the Garden Corp. regards the Knicks and Rangers from a different perspective than the fans who support those two franchises, the doubters have only to consult Alan Cohen, the operating head of Madison Square Garden. "If you ask me whether I'd rather have a Stanley Cup and a basketball championship at the expense of a profit," Cohen says, "I say no."

No one has ever stated the bottom line of the multifranchise owner with more candor.

◄ 11 ►
The Cut-Rate Emperor

One day in 1973, five-foot-two-inch Fran Monaco was sitting in the office of his new Jacksonville franchise in the World Football League and speaking by phone to the League's founder, Gary Davidson. The topic was a name for the team. Florida legislators were complaining that the one Monaco and Davidson had selected would hurt the state's image.

"Isn't it true Florida is loaded with sports teams named after vicious animals?" Davidson asked.

"Right," said Monaco. "We've got Barracudas, Tigers, Rattlers, Panthers, Moccasins and 'Gators."

"That's what I thought," said Davidson. "Okay, tell them we're going to switch names."

"To what?" asked Monaco.

"From Jacksonville Sharks to Jacksonville *Killer* Sharks."

A year later, Monaco was describing to the world how he himself had been devoured—by his Jacksonville Sharks football team, and by the predators who had sold him that WFL franchise in the first place. After a single season, the forty-eight-year-old Floridian had lost everything he had earned in the last twenty-two years from his medical laboratory business and the restaurant he co-owned with ex-Chicago Bear Dick Butkus. The Jacksonville

Sharks, for which he had paid the World Football League $650,000 only a year before, had eaten up all of his capital, leaving only $1.8 million in liabilities. "Before, I had a good reputation," he said sadly. "I paid my debts. This is like a nightmare." During his first and only season as an owner, Monaco had been so hard-pressed that he'd had to borrow $27,000 from his head coach, whom he subsequently fired. His only consolation, in his misery, was that he had plenty of company.

In 1974, their first year of operation, the WFL owners had lost a total of at least $22 million. Worse, some of them had even lost their credibility. The Philadelphia Bell had bragged about the 55,534 spectators who purchased tickets for its opener on July 10 and the 64,719 who attended a nationally televised game on July 25—a total of about 120,000. Then, when newsmen learned the team had reported, for tax purposes, the sale of only 20,000 tickets for those same two games, the club's executive vice-president, Barry Lieb, had to admit that the announced paid-attendance figures were a complete fabrication. "We just had to do it, or we would have been a joke," he said. "I never thought the figures would come out."

As he stepped off a plane from New York, Rommie Loud, the managing general partner of the Florida Blazers, was taken into custody on an embezzlement charge in Orlando. Loud was accused of stealing state tax money from the sale of football game tickets. At the other end of the "Sunshine Belt," the owner of the Southern California Sun, Larry Hatfield, was pleading guilty to a federal charge of submitting false statements while negotiating a $365,000 loan. As collateral for the loan, the indictment charged, Hatfield had used a forged debenture.

The Houston Texans were ranked sixteenth in a listing of the nation's worst *college* football teams; the Florida Blazers were so broke that their players went without pay for the last ten weeks of the season, and their head coach had to supply the toilet paper for their locker room. And the day after the Birmingham Americans defeated the Florida Blazers to win the first World Bowl, they literally lost their shirts—and their pants and their helmets and their shoes. While the league was celebrating the end of its first season, sheriff's deputies were confiscating the Americans' uniforms. Bill Putnam, owner of the Birmingham club, had known better days as an executive vice-president of Jack Kent Cooke Enterprises, then as full owner of the Philadelphia Flyers and part-owner of the Atlanta Hawks and the Atlanta Flames. "So what?" he told reporters who questioned him about losing his team's uniforms because the supplier was owed $30,000. "The IRS and everybody else has liens against us; what's the big deal about losing our uniforms?"

At the end of that first season, 75 percent of the league's players were owed back salary—and Fran Monaco thought *he* had problems. He was, in fact, lucky he didn't survive into the WFL's second year, when, before calling it quits during the twelfth week of its twenty-game season, the league managed to lose an additional $20 million or so.

The Jacksonville Sharks were only one of many franchises sold since 1967 by Gary Davidson. Unlike more conventional owners, Davidson didn't *operate* pro sports franchises, he *invented* them. Unlike other multifranchise owners, Davidson didn't *buy* a sports empire, he *created* one out of whole cloth. Not just teams, but entire leagues spilled ready-made from his fertile imagination —and he sold these paper tigers for hard cash.

Davidson watched pro sports become a big business, hooked on expansion as a way to make profits: once professional leagues decreed that new members would have to pay multimillion-dollar entry fees, their owners campaigned for additional franchises with the fervor of a junkie lobbying for the legalization of heroin. And he had been struck by one singular fact: original AFL franchises that cost $25,000 in 1959 were worth, by the late 1960's, many many millions, whether or not they had ever turned a profit. Davidson added a new twist to the franchising game. He invented a whole new series of professional leagues, merely for the purpose of selling franchises. Like the fried chicken barons, he had discovered that selling franchises was an easy way to make money. In 1967, Davidson started a new basketball league, the American Basketball Association, with eleven teams. In 1972, he started a brand new hockey league, the World Hockey Association, with ten teams. In 1974, he started a new football league, the World Football League, with twelve teams. In his spare time, he became a consultant to the

The Rich Who Own Sports

International Track Association, the World Team Tennis league, the Grand Prix Bicycle Circuit. Overall, he has sold—or helped to manufacture—pro franchises in fifty-six different localities, from Houston to Winnipeg, from New York to Honolulu, from Cherry Hill, New Jersey, to beautiful downtown Edmonton, Canada.

"Lots of older men with super wealth have no idea how to enjoy it," he says. "I try to help them out. No one has the ego of a millionaire, and by owning a big league team a man becomes a celebrity. I've been cultivating important people since I was in college—on tennis and handball courts, at golf and socially. I've had to turn down buyers. More than forty groups wanted in on World Football, and I could only accept twelve."

Gary Davidson was born in Missoula, Montana, on August 13, 1934. His parents separated, then divorced, when he was only an infant. Gary's father, Truman Ross Davidson, wandered west, to take up farming in southern Idaho. His mother, Estella, remarried—again and again. Each time, Gary and his half-brother were uprooted and transplanted in a different state, torn loose from familiar friends. Eventually, Estella's odyssey in search of love led her and her two children to California. After living in towns like Compton and Corona and Santa Ana, Estella finally settled in Garden Grove, where Gary attended high school.

He was a tough kid, restless and rebellious. More than once, he had scrapes with the local juvenile authorities. His mother was trapped between her drab life as a grocery clerk and her dreary love affairs. He had no father. Somehow, though, at Garden Grove High School, Gary began to find a sense of purpose in life. He stopped getting in trouble; he spent his time improving his academic grades, and, in his senior year, was accepted at Redlands College. But he wasn't done drifting yet. He lasted only one semester at Redlands, transferred to Orange Coast Junior College, then dropped out again. The following year, he enrolled at Long Beach State, supporting himself with odd jobs—laying pipe, digging ditches. Then he met a girl who attended UCLA. She took him to the campus, and for the first time in his life Gary Davidson felt at home. He applied for admission, and was accepted.

What made UCLA different and exciting was its diversity of

students. There were kids from broken homes, with no money. And there were kids who actually lived out his fantasies: the middle-class students in varsity sweaters who sat munching Cheerios in TV commercials; the affluent Americans who drove gleaming sports cars; the ones who got the cushy job, and the boss's daughter. Gary joined a fraternity. He dated a beautiful and vivacious cheerleader named Barbara Jane Dapper. Barbie was an education major, specializing in speech; she chipped away at Gary's flawed ghetto diction, and soon she had him talking with the ease and polish of a banker's son. In 1958, two years after Gary graduated, they were married.

Gary's first job was with an insurance company. But he grew bored with the routine, and depressed by his limited earning potential. He decided to attend law school at UCLA, financing his studies with a job both morbid and ironic: by day, he absorbed the nuances of torts and technicalities; by night, he worked for the Armstrong Mortuary, speeding around Los Angeles in an undertaker's truck, picking up the still-warm bodies of murder and accident victims. A few years later, he would begin collecting the warm bodies of another set of victims—prospective owners for his pro sports franchises.

In 1967, after practicing law for a few years with only modest success, Davidson, in league with Don Reagan and Pat Nagel, stumbled onto his sports franchising scheme. At the time, he was worth less than $50,000. Seven years later, he would be worth several millions. "Much of what he touches breaks down financially, and you don't see Davidson getting hurt," says L.A. Rams owner Carroll Rosenbloom. "He comes out of his deals with more money than he put in. Much more."

In starting his new leagues, Davidson was always careful to collect a share of the dollar bonanza up front. To join the WFL, for instance, each of the twelve franchise owners had to pay him a $600,000 fee, as "founders' shares." Before any of its teams had played a single game, the WFL had put over $7 million in Davidson's pocket. Furthermore, both the World Football League and the World Hockey Association were represented by Davidson's legal firm—Nagel, Reagan and Davidson. In 1973, that firm won

211

an antitrust suit which the WHA had filed against the National Hockey League. The bulk of the $1.7 million settlement went for lawyers' fees.

Besides his Midas-like knack for turning paper franchises into gold, Davidson displayed an ingenuity for recruiting surpassed only by Al Davis'. In the winter of 1973, Davidson and a partner, Steve Arnold, were faced with a dilemma. They wanted to tell 500 or so NFL players how much better off they'd be in the WFL. The problem was, Davidson and Arnold didn't know the players' addresses—and did know that the NFL head office, and the NFL team publicity directors, would be less than eager to supply that information. Then Davidson thought up a strategem—awesome in its utter simplicity. He and Arnold inserted the recruiting letters into 500 plain white envelopes. They stamped each envelope "Please Forward" and sent it to the NFL headquarters in New York City. They were counting on both the efficiency and bureaucracy of the NFL; on both counts their gamble paid off. Secretaries at the NFL's home office forwarded, without delay, the 500 envelopes to the 500 players. More than 250 of those players wrote to Davidson, expressing their interest in the World Football League.

Davidson, in turn, claims that he learned all about "dirty tricks" from the NFL itself, and was, in effect, only doing unto others what had been done unto him—or a colleague of his, the same Steve Arnold who had conspired in the "plain white envelope" caper. "I'll give you an example of what we were up against," Davidson says. "Before Steve got into this thing [he was Gary's partner, and he was also president of the Houston Texans], he was the manager of top athletes in the San Francisco area. Well, somebody—you can use your imagination—*somebody* approached him and threatened blackmail if he let his clients sign with the WFL. The blackmail concerned shack-ups with women—girls Arnold never heard of in his life. When it gets that dirty, you start looking over your shoulder. You stay out of alleys."

One reason the NFL was after Gary was that (just as Davidson's ABA had signed Billy Cunningham and Rick Barry and Joe Caldwell away from the NBA, and his WHA had stolen superstar Bobby Hull from the NHL) his WFL owners had signed NFL stars like Ted Kwalick, John Gilliam, Larry Csonka, Jim Kiick, Paul Warfield, Bill Bergey, Calvin Hill, Daryle Lamonica and Ken Stabler to contracts. Another reason the NFL was so antagonistic was that the WFL, like the WHA, had only a loosely structured option system, in which a player could fulfill his contract and then move on to the highest bidder. By offering an alternative to the NFL's ironclad "Rozelle Rule," the WFL gave players the chance to opt out of the "option system" altogether. The existence of the WFL gave NFL players bargaining leverage during the 1974 strike, in which "freedom issues" were paramount.

But it was to financiers, rather than players, that Davidson's new league had an almost irresistible appeal. "I give potential backers a detailed plan for starting a franchise for a fraction of what one costs in the older leagues," Davidson explains. "The new franchise could be worth three to five million dollars in the next few years, even if it loses at the box office. You can't get that kind of tax write-off and capital appreciation in any other existing business."

The Anaheim Amigos were a classic illustration of how valuable a losing franchise could be. An ABA charter franchise, in 1967 the Amigos cost its original owners $1.7 million and never made a profit. Later, in 1971, as the Utah Stars, the Amigo franchise won the ABA championship and was still operating in the red. Nevertheless, in spite of the franchise's inability to make money, its market value had swelled to $5 million—$3.3 million more than the original owners had paid for it.

What, in fact, Davidson was selling was the special tax benefits that went along with owning a franchise. The new owners in his leagues were anxious to make a profit, but they were also anxious to write off any losses incurred against their other businesses. The same motivation had accounted for big businessmen getting involved in the established leagues in the late 1950's. Tax breaks were the catalyst that kept pro franchises increasing in value, even though most of them operated at a net loss. In the 1973–74 season, for example, out of twenty-four major league baseball teams, only half made money or broke even (the three largest dollar earners were the Dodgers, the Mets and the Reds); ten of twenty-eight major league hockey teams lost money (the most profitable club was the Rangers, with a net profit of $3 million); and twenty-two of twenty-seven major league basketball teams lost money (with the Knicks, Lakers, Braves, SuperSonics and Celtics the only clubs operating at a profit). Only NFL football was a decidedly good investment, with twenty-four of the twenty-six teams turning an average $945,000 pre-tax—and $472,500 post-tax—profit. By 1975, however, due mostly to increased player salaries caused by the bidding war between the NFL and WFL, eight NFL clubs were losing money—the Giants, Dolphins, Cowboys, Redskins, Packers, Chargers, Eagles and Oilers—while three others showed a profit of less than $100,000. And the average after-tax operating profit was $256,000, down 45 percent from the previous season.

The tax breaks explain why Davidson was able to start leagues in basketball and hockey and football, and why, since 1966, the unprofitable NBA has sold nine franchises and the marginally profitable NHL has sold twelve. It was, in part, to take advantage of tax benefits that groups of investors in eleven different cities started baseball franchises in the last decade, with New Orleans, Denver, Buffalo and Honolulu waiting in the wings; why World Team Tennis could field sixteen teams; why the North American Soccer League could field twenty-two by 1976. The fact is, sports franchises, for the very rich who own them, are tax shelters.

The key to the tax law concerning sports franchises is "depreciation." Depreciation allows a team to treat its players—who comprise the bulk of any franchise's value, according to the Internal Revenue Service—as an asset that gets "used up" over a period of time. Players get older, they get injured. An owner can regard them, for tax purposes, the way he would regard the typewriter in his secretary's office—depreciating the value of their contracts over, say, five years. Then he applies these deductions against the profits he's making from his other enterprises. If, say, his total deductions from all his businesses combined are more than his total profits, he pays no taxes at all.

A few years ago, for instance, a group in the NBA bought a franchise for $3 million. The owners were able to take advantage of tax laws and write off $2.5 million in depreciation in the first eighteen months of the team's operation. In its first year, however, the owners actually collected $300,000 more in revenues than they paid out. But when depreciation was figured in, the team was able to declare a loss of $1.6 million to the IRS. Each member of the ownership group could then subtract his share of the loss from his profits in his other enterprises, reducing his taxable income substantially. Yet the "losses" were only on paper.

The effect of these tax laws is that owners tend to sell teams, at a higher price than they originally paid, as soon as the tax benefits have been exhausted—five years, or however long the owners agreed to depreciate their players. In the first seven years of the ABA, only one team— the Indiana Pacers—did not change owners. Most other teams had two or three different owners. Each new owner, of course, can start the tax write-off syndrome all over again, depreciating the player contracts . . . and so on.

Often, an owner can claim that 90 percent of his purchase price was for players—and then write off that 90 percent. Sometimes, however, the Internal Revenue Service isn't so cooperative. In 1966, when the baseball Braves moved to Atlanta, the owners claimed that 99 percent of the purchase price ($5.5 million) was for depreciable player contracts. Four years later, the IRS audited the franchise's returns, and reduced the proportion allowable for player contracts by $450,000, to 90 percent of the total cost.

More recently, an IRS decision shook the pro sports establishment. It began when the owners of the NFL Atlanta Falcons bought their expansion team for approximately $8.5 million. In line with long-time practice, the owners (headed by Rankin Smith, of Life Insurance of Georgia) assigned for the IRS a value of 8 percent to the franchise itself, and the remaining 92 percent— about $7.8 million—to the value of the player contracts. The new owners, Smith and his partners, anticipated that the IRS might lower that depreciable portion of the purchase price to about 80 or 85 percent. What they did not expect, however, was what the IRS did: it assigned all the value to the *franchise* (the team name, office equipment, etc.) and *none* to the player contracts. Thus, the new owners had almost nothing to depreciate, nothing to subtract from their profits in other businesses. The Atlanta owners went to court, and in a landmark decision the federal court voted to uphold the right of a team to depreciate the value of its player contracts. The commissioners of the pro leagues were happy that the main bait to ownership had been not only preserved but codified by the court. But some details of that decision threatened to make ownership less attractive in the future, particularly to men without the enormous financial resources of a Kroc, a Cooke or a Hunt.

Along with swollen payrolls, new owners might have to contend with a lower rate of depreciation than the IRS had permitted in the past. In the precedent-setting Falcons' decision, the court ruled that the true value that could be depreciated over a period of five years was $3 million—58 percent less than the sum the Falcons had been trying to depreciate. Most observers felt that the days when the IRS would allow new owners to assign 80 or more percent of the price of a franchise to depreciable player contracts were over.

It's doubtful, however, that the tax breaks will ever disappear completely. Pro franchises today are so costly to run that without the tax benefits few investors would be willing to commit large amounts of capital to pro sports.

Aside from turning pro franchises into tax shelters, the tax laws have, if indirectly, contributed to the bad blood between the owners and their players. Ballplayers base their salary demands in part on their team's profitability; the owners often reject those demands on the basis of a team's unprofitability. But whether a team registers a profit or a loss has come to depend more on who does the accounting than on how much revenue a club takes in during any given season. The owners' tendency to juggle their books for tax purposes has generated a great deal of distrust among their players.

However, the players in Gary Davidson's WFL never reached the stage where the profitability of their franchises was in doubt. Heavy and obvious losers from day one, the WFL owners learned that the franchise con has a Catch-22. "Normally, when a new league is formed, the first guys in never lose money," says Lee Meade, a former sports editor and publicist who helped set up the ABA and was later part-owner of the Minnesota Buckskins of World Team Tennis. "Typically, an owner says, and he's right, 'I may have been a great fool to buy this thing, but there's a bigger fool around the corner who'll buy it from me.' "

Almost without exception, the WFL owners played the fool

to Gary Davidson. In order to participate successfully in the franchise game, an investor has to be very, very rich—Lamar Hunt rich. Especially during the first year or two of operation, the costs of any pro franchise can be astronomical. As owners of the ABA and WHA and WFL soon found out, it doesn't do any good to sustain enormous tax-deductible losses, if those losses exceed the total profit from all your other investments combined—or if, faced with a cash shortage, you lack the collateral to float loans with the ease of a Lamar Hunt. Unlike Hunt, many of the owners in Davidson's leagues couldn't afford to lose a million dollars a year for 120 years before going broke. The comparative paupers among them couldn't even afford to lose a million dollars in *one* year. In fact, too many of them resembled Harry Wismer more than Lamar Hunt. Wismer had owned the New York Titans in Hunt's original AFL. A radio announcer whose claim to fame was that he had married first the niece of Henry Ford and later the widow of Abner "Longy" Zwillman, a notorious New Jersey mobster, Wismer ran his franchise from an apartment on Park Avenue—with an incompetence unequaled till Gary Davidson collared a crew of unwitting imitators.

Once, Wismer demoted Sammy Baugh from head coach to "kicking consultant." Another time, he assigned his general manager, George Sauer, to the additional duty of backfield coach. Like some WFL owners, Wismer had an incurable habit of seeing spectators when everyone else saw only empty seats. He let neighborhood children into his stadium free, then multiplied their number by a factor of 100 to get a respectable attendance figure. His accounting methods would have seemed perfectly rational to Lewis Carroll's Mad Hatter. His players once had to inform him that the payroll was "194 hours late."

Nor was he averse to telling little white lies. Before a game against San Diego, his players were led to understand that every touchdown would be worth a $100 bonus. The Titans beat the Chargers, 23–3. Not only did they not get bonuses, they didn't even get their pay checks that week. Even if they had gotten paid, only one teller at the team's bank would have been authorized to cash their checks. The teller would deduct the amount from Wismer's bank balance, then hand over the money. Overall, Wismer would probably have felt very comfortable in the company of Davidson's merry band of owners.

In Davidson's ABA, there were men of real financial substance like Roy Boe of the New York Nets—and a woman of not only substance but beauty: Ellie Brown, wife of John Y. Brown, who owned the Kentucky Fried Chicken chain. But while the Nets and Kentucky Colonels rested on a firm financial footing, too many other ABA operations were fly-by-night—and fold-by-night. Among the early ABA flops were the Anaheim Amigos, the Houston Mavericks, the Miami Floridians, the Minnesota Pipers, the New Orleans Bucks, the Oakland Oaks and the Pittsburgh Condors. All folded after a year or so. Too many of the men queuing to play musical franchises resembled Dr. Leonard Bloom, the orthodontist who owned both the San Diego Conquistadors of the ABA and the Los Angeles Sharks of the WHA.

"An awful lot of people with money are being seduced into sports," says Mike Burke, the Garden executive in charge of the New York Knickerbockers. "The rich jocks are being drawn into doubtful investments. They think life in the new leagues is going to be like life with the Knicks. The investors are clamoring to get in because they think every sports franchise is a bonanza. Well, it isn't. A number of them are going to get burned."

Dr. Leonard Bloom was one of those "rich jocks" who got "burned." In college, Bloom was clocked over 100 yards in 9.7, and over 400 yards in 46.9. He still works out at his alma mater, San Diego State, where he once outraced Speedy Duncan, then one of the best kick-returners in pro football. Bloom lives ostentatiously, in a hillside home surrounded by a swimming pool, a tennis court equipped with a Coca-Cola vending machine, a basketball court and a landing pad for his private helicopter. He didn't have experience in administering a franchise, nor the financial muscle to withstand the financial battering his two franchises took in the early years. An owner who straightened teeth one day a week, and spent the remaining time running around a tartan track or playing guests at basketball, one-on-one, full-court, was not likely to inspire overwhelming confidence in local bankers. Ultimately, the ABA and WHA were forced to assume control of his franchises.

Besides having fewer multimillionaires who could afford to

lose vast amounts in order to gain vast tax advantages, the leagues Davidson and his partners started had the added impediment of poor team locations. There's an axiom in pro sports that no league can succeed without a healthy franchise in New York City—the country's number one TV market. The WFL began its first season with a New York franchise, but for only eight games. The New York Stars then closed up shop, declaring assets of $94,750 and liabilities of $2.5 million. Without a franchise in New York, the WFL couldn't get the kind of TV contract that sustained the AFL in its bidding war with the NFL.

The ABA, by contrast, did have a franchise on the fringe of the New York market—the Nets—but only a short-lived one in Los Angeles and none at all in Chicago, the second and third largest TV markets. Cities like San Antonio and Denver didn't have the population base to justify a large-scale network commitment. Nor was the World Hockey Association much better off. It started with a franchise in New York, which was quickly transferred to that metropolis known as Cherry Hill, New Jersey. The NHL had New York, Los Angeles and Chicago; the WHA had Edmonton, Calgary and Quebec. No contest.

The WHA franchise in Quebec (a city of 425,000) is a symbol of both the impotence of Davidson's leagues and the flimflammery of his salesmanship. In 1971, when Davidson concocted the WHA, he awarded himself, as was his practice, one of its franchises, free, in San Francisco. This so-called "franchise," of course, existed only on paper. It had no players, no arena—not even jockstraps. Once he had sparked sufficient interest in the new league, Davidson went hunting for buyers for his invisible hockey team, finally selling it to a group in Quebec for $215,000. Up to the summer of 1974, Le Club de Hockey des Québec Nordiques had lost a cool $900,000.

As each new league was manufactured, the new owners tried to outdo the established leagues, tossing money around like kids playing Monopoly in the midst of a hurricane. Player salaries and operating expenses soared, and so did the potential for losses. Construction man James J. Kirst bought the ABA Los Angeles Stars from an original franchise owner for $250,000, and then dropped about $1.7 million before he sold out to a buyer from Salt Lake City, for $345,000. In the first seven years after Davidson conjured up the ABA, the league lost some $70 million, while wobbling among twenty-four different locations.

The World Hockey Association opened up with a reckless plunge toward financial suicide. After only two years, it had lost $25 million in twenty different meccas. Although, as of 1976, it boasted twelve franchises (two more than when it began in 1972), every time the league clashed head-to-head with the NHL the older league scored an early kayo. The New York Golden Blades were booked into Madison Square Garden alongside the New York Rangers—and shortly were transformed into the Jersey Knights. While the Jersey Knights were wandering off to San Diego, the Philadelphia Flyers were forechecking the Philadelphia Blazers all the way to Vancouver, British Columbia. And in cities the NHL deemed too insignificant to warrant a franchise, the WHA was defeated by apathy. The Alberta Oilers lasted only a couple of months. The Ottawa Nationals soon became the Toronto Toros. Leonard Bloom's Los Angeles Sharks swam off to Detroit, leaving debts of $2 million in their wake.

Some critics suggested that the WHA's inadequacy may have had something to do with the fact that Gary Davidson, the Creator, had never seen a hockey game when he and Dennis Murphy, who promoted a girls' softball team, drew up the WHA constitution. "As a game," Davidson says blithely, "hockey meant absolutely nothing to me."

Doug Michel once owned the Ottawa Nationals. In *Left Wing and a Prayer,* Michel wrote that, in 1971, he and a partner offered Davidson $25,000 for a WHA franchise. "That's what they quoted as the price," Michel says, "along with a ten-thousand-dollar contribution to the league office to be paid later." Then, alleges Michel, Davidson suddenly upped the ante, from $25,000 to $200,000, plus immediate payment of a $100,000 bond. "We figured then that he might be a con man," Michel says, "but we raised the money anyway, because we were hockey enthusiasts." Michel's franchise failed. He lost almost all his money; he almost lost his sanity.

Davidson eventually surrendered control of every league he founded, but it's doubtful if he cared. The owners in his leagues might delude themselves that they were buying franchises for the tax benefits, when what they really craved was the instant celebrity.

The Cut-Rate Emperor

Davidson yearned for only one thing—money—and managed to walk away from his tottering, knock-kneed leagues with millions. At forty-two, he can give his four children all the amenities he lacked at their age. He, Barbie and the kids live in a $200,000 house on the beach in Southern California's exclusive Emerald Bay. If he gets bored driving his E-type Jaguar, or his Jaguar sedan, he can pack his brood into his golden-bronze Mercedes 450 SEL. And while he fashions his sports leagues to mirror his vagabond childhood, he has strived to provide for his own children the sense of place, identity and stability he did without. "He never plays around on his wife," says one acquaintance. "He's a family man, to the core."

Like Al Davis, football's other super-recruiter, Davidson doesn't drink or smoke. "He's a health nut," reports a woman who used to work for him. "He made us run, not walk, up five flights of stairs, 'to keep us in shape.' It wore out a lot of gals. Some got broken leg veins. After a while, we went on strike and refused to run."

Davidson works out regularly, to keep his five-foot-ten frame trim at 165 pounds. He plays basketball in a local industrial league, more to get off steam, though, than excess poundage. "One night a guy ran off our opponent's bench and began slugging me," Tim Grandi, once the executive chief officer of the WFL told *True* magazine writer Al Stump. "Gary leaped at this guy, who was about six-foot-five, and began to punch him back. He kept swinging, and was beating up on him when they broke it up, although he was giving away seven inches and fifty pounds."

Davidson admits he has a short fuse. "Like Tim Grandi says, I get into brawls," he confided to writer Stump. "Once I was in a fight with a sailor in an L.A. bar—I forget why we were fighting. This big bartender took me by the pants and threw me into the street. God, it was embarrassing."

Not as embarrassing as the WFL debacle. At first, the WFL seemed promising—especially for Davidson and his six partners, each of whom got a free franchise right, plus a percentage of other franchises. Davidson also took home a share of the league's $1 million television contract. He sold his franchise right to a group from Philadelphia for $690,000. Nick Mileti of Cleveland, another

221

insider, sold his franchise right to Tom Origer, a wealthy constructor from Chicago, for about $500,000.

The WFL signed their million-dollar contract with TVS, an
independent network owned by Dun & Bradstreet. Then the rival
NFL players went out on strike, and suddenly the WFL had the
field to itself. Deprived of NFL summer exhibition games, fans
turned out in sometimes substantial (sometimes fanciful) numbers
to watch the WFL. But once the NFL strike was settled, the WFL
began to slip quietly toward oblivion. Part of the problem was that
WFL owners had invested too much money in too many NFL
players—for too little return. Bill Putnam, the Birmingham owner,
for example, had signed up Tim Foley and Bob Kuechenberg of the
Dolphins, and L.C. Greenwood of the Steelers, besides quarterback
Ken Stabler of the Raiders. Neither Foley nor Kuechenberg nor
Greenwood had the Namath-like charisma to justify their Namath-
like bonuses and salaries. Burdened with impossible debts, the
league started to stagger. Houston moved to Shreveport, and not
one of the five teams that came to Shreveport to play was able to
pay its hotel bill. New York moved to Charlotte. Detroit filed for
bankruptcy. Jacksonville quit, and a check for $1.5 million dis-
played on TV to prove the Florida Blazers' solvency bounced a few
days later. The Portland Storm players became so desperate after
weeks of no pay checks that local citizens raised $2,500 for them.
John Bassett, owner of the Northmen, laid out almost $5 million
to sign Larry Csonka, Jim Kiick and Paul Warfield away from the
Dolphins, then got booted as far south as Memphis by the Canadian Football League, supported by the Canadian federal government. At the end of the league's first season, Alan R. Miller,
executive director of the WFL Players' Association, estimated that
somewhere between $4 and $7 million in compensation was still
owned by the various franchises to their players. The WFL was
supposed to present a $10,000 purse to the league MVP at half-time
of the World Bowl. Three rookies tied for the award, and got
$3,333.33 each. One writer said the winners would have a choice
of taking a WFL check in that amount, or a WFL franchise.

By season's end, the owners had kicked out Davidson, replacing him with a Hawaiian business tycoon named Chris Hemmeter.
Davidson's exit was as casual as his entrance had been energetic.

The Cut-Rate Emperor

"I never was much of a sports spectator, anyway," he commented. "I'd rather play tennis and basketball myself." The next season, 1975, a "new, revitalized" WFL took the field, led by Hemmeter. Then, on October 22, Hemmeter announced that the league was dead, citing the causes of death as backlash from the chaotic first season, the league's inability to draw customers in its franchise cities, and its lack of a lucrative TV contract. The total loss, over two seasons, was estimated at about $45 million—a windfall for someone like Lamar Hunt, but far too much of a good thing for Fran Monaco.

◀ 12 ▶
The Entertainers

In 1950, almost overlooked, an event occurred that was to have profound implications for the future of pro sports. In 1946, Dan Reeves had shifted his Cleveland Rams of the AAFC to Los Angeles. Four years later, Reeves tried a revolutionary experiment. He put the Rams' games on home television. The innovation was only a partial success; fans watched the Rams on television, but avoided Reeves's ball park. Still, Reeves had faith in the exploitative power of this new medium. Together with the influential Bert Bell, owner of the Philadelphia Eagles and one of pro football's founding fathers, he devised a plan that would generate TV revenues while luring customers through his turnstiles. A seventy-five-mile blackout was imposed, in a circle whose midpoint lay approximately at the 50-yard line of each owner's stadium. Fans outside that magic circle would be allowed to watch a team's games on home TV, free, except for the psychic cost of having to listen to scores of sponsors' commercials. Fans within that circle would have to pay in person to see their heroes play.

The blackout was put into effect for the league's playoff game in 1951, and everyone seemed content. It took only a soft sell to convince fans within driving distance to keep on attending home games. Fans outside the seventy-five-mile radius were getting the chance to watch football "free." And the players received almost $1,000 more per man than they had the year before. After that first season, the Justice Department filed a suit in Federal Court, alleging that the blackout of home games was a violation of the Sherman Anti-Trust Act, and thus illegal. But on November 12, 1953, Judge Alan K. Grim delivered a verdict that found the owners innocent of any violation. TV as a factor in promoting professional sports had come to stay. (Since the 1974 season, a federal law has been in effect that permits local broadcast of games sold out seventy-two hours in advance.)

From TV revenues came the large bonuses clubs started offering college superstars. The stars drew fans, generating a new demand for more sports on TV, at higher revenues than ever. In 1963, the two major football leagues, the AFL and the NFL, collected $6.5 million for rights to televise their games—$4.7 million to the NFL and $1.8 million to the AFL. By 1969, with sixty million viewers watching the Super Bowl in which the Jets beat the Colts, networks were paying nearly $28 million to telecast the regular-season games alone—nearly $19 million to the NFL and $9 million to the AFL, with an additional $8 million earmarked for post-season games. In August, 1974, *U.S. News & World Report* would estimate that, in their latest full seasons, pro football had collected $45 million in gross revenues from TV, and major league baseball another $46 million. By 1975, the networks were devoting roughly 1,000 hours of TV time a year to pro sports, double the number in 1969. In 1975, pro football received about $59 million from network and TV revenues. In 1976, that figure would swell to approximately $60 million.

Nowhere did TV have a greater impact than in indoor sports. By their very nature, basketball and hockey could accommodate fewer spectators than football or baseball. With their teams playing in arenas whose capacities rarely exceeded 20,000, and faced with spiraling salaries created by interleague bidding wars, indoor owners were even more dependent on TV revenues to turn a profit than their colleagues outdoors. In 1969, the Milwaukee Bucks had a total revenue of $863,000. In 1970, the year after they signed Kareem Abdul-Jabbar at an estimated salary of $400,000 per year, the Bucks' revenues leaped to $2,166,000—a tribute to Jabbar's appeal at the box office and on TV screens. It was the assurance of TV revenues—an equal share of the league's $10 million television gross—that had permitted the Bucks to sign Jabbar in the first place.

TV caused a subtle shift of emphasis in pro sports. The producers and packagers of televised sports began to regard athletes as showmen; soon arenas and stadiums around the country began to resemble three-ring circuses.

In 1968, the new Madison Square Garden opened—a $133 million complex of office buildings, surrounding an arena shaped like a snare drum. In fact, that's what the 20,234-seat facility was: a drum beating out the rhythm of basketballs on a hardwood floor, the music of skates squeaking on ice. Customers were enticed into a slew of new auditoriums and skating rinks and cafeterias and restaurants. Internally, the corporation was organized into departments, whose heads held a status similar to that enjoyed by cabinet members in the federal government—one "minister" for basketball, one for hockey, one for boxing. And, of course, one for TV.

Meanwhile, the Garden Corporation, with its arena, its string of hotels, its several race tracks, its cable TV interests and its pro franchises, was itself merely one "department" of a much more formidable entity, Gulf & Western Corp. Gulf & Western owned the Kayser-Roth Corp., the Bulova Watch Co., Seeburgh Industries, Simon & Schuster Publishing Co., most of the sugar plantations in the Dominican Republic, the biggest sugar mill in Mexico, the New Jersey Zinc Co., the Quebec Iron and Titanium Corp., Paramount Pictures, the Schrafft Candy Co., Dutch Masters and Muriel Cigars—plus 37 percent of Madison Square Garden. Gulf & Western's chairman, Charles Bludhorn, and its president, David Judelson, were directors of the Garden Corporation.

In the business of sports, as in its other areas of commerce, Gulf & Western was aiming at diversity. In the hearts of New York's basketball and hockey fans, the old Garden was simply the home of the Knicks and Rangers; Gulf & Western conceived of the new Garden as something more. Instead of being simply an arena where plain folks traveled to watch their heroes compete, Madison Square Garden would become a massive amusement park. It had the Felt Forum, an auditorium that could accommodate 5,227. It contained a cinema, with 501 seats. The new Garden also had a sports gallery, an exposition rotunda and four bowling alleys. Meanwhile, a satellite company called Madison Square Garden Attractions, Inc., arranged for acts and entertainment to travel to places like Poughkeepsie and Podunk. A subsidiary called Madison Square Garden–ABC Productions, Inc., was set up to specialize in TV—commercial and pay. For a while, the Garden operated the Skyliners soccer team, and even considered purchasing the New York Jets.

"The existing Garden wasn't obsolete in 1960," says Irving Felt, who took over control of the Garden that year, "but we believed it would be by 1970. And we figured that, by then, good available property in Manhattan would be nonexistent. Madison Square Garden had become a household name over the years, and we intended to keep it that way."

The inaugural ceremony, on February 11, 1968, had all the pomp of a coronation. The royalty of show business, including Bob Hope, Bing Crosby and Pearl Bailey, strolled across a stage to emphasize that the new complex would be as much oriented toward *entertainment* as toward that peculiar brand of entertainment called professional sports. And soon the Rolling Stones and Bob Dylan were luring in customers whose sweet pot-smells mingled with the still-fresh scent of spilled beer deposited by Knick fans. Russian bears from the Moscow Ice Show were skating in clumsy parody of the hapless, eternally Stanley Cup-less New York Rangers. Fans got a Clyde Frazier one night and a Mrs. Black America the next. Boxing vied for their attention with the annual Disney Carnival: Muhammad Ali vs. Donald Duck.

Not only had Felt and company introduced a new kind of sports/entertainment complex, they had devised a new way of marketing their attractions—a series of monster packages designated "Plan I," "Plan II," etc. A customer who elected Plan I, for instance, received tickets for ninety-seven events, including forty-one Ranger hockey games, forty-three Knick basketball games and thirteen "special sports and entertainment events," all for the price of $985 down front, $815 a little further back and $705 beyond that. Every one of the seats in Plan I was annually sold out, leaving some $560 or $440 bargains for the people who, as one writer put it, "had eyes like the telescope on Mt. Palomar."

Later, the Garden Corporation would devise a new strategy for supporting their fabulous indoor amusement park—one involving the already-overburdened taxpayers of New York City.

TV turned pro sports into an entertainment, no different really from circuses or sit-coms. It was only a matter of time before franchise owners began wearing two hats: one labeled SPORTS; the other, BROADCASTING. Jack Kent Cooke and Madison Square Garden and Arthur Wirtz all have cable-TV interests. Other owners, like Ted Turner of the Atlanta Braves, Nick Mileti of the Cavaliers and Indians, and John Fetzer of the Detroit Tigers, own either radio or TV stations, or both. But no owner exemplifies the incestuous triangle formed by pro sports and entertainment and TV better than Gene Autry of the California Angels. A real cowboy, offspring of a Wild West now tamed everywhere except in our dreams, Autry was once America's Singing Cowboy, from 1936 one of the world's highest-paid entertainers, earning $500,000 to $750,000 per year. He made movies for Republic. He made records for Columbia. His weekly radio show on CBS, *Melody Ranch,* ran for eighteen years under a single sponsor—Phil Wrigley's Doublemint gum.

Now the Singing Cowboy is sixty-eight years old, his fleshy body flowering into fat, his nasal tenor voice pitched a few halftones lower, a few decibels softer. Instead of sitting astride his horse Champion, Autry straddles a $70 million business empire. His company, Golden West Broadcasters, owns four radio stations, Los Angeles TV station KTLA, a national radio-time sales firm, a ten-acre movie and TV production center, and the Angels baseball team. In addition to what his company owns, Autry himself owns a 118-room hotel in Palm Springs, California, a 20,000-acre cattle ranch in Colorado, a valuable collection of antique cars and locomotives, the 100-acre movie ranch where he made his first movies forty years ago, and a library of eighty-eight cowboy films and one hundred half-hour TV episodes, all starring the good guy in the white hat, Gene Autry. Taking into account minority interests in radio and TV stations, and a cattle ranch in Arizona, Autry's personal fortune is approximately $30 million.

The Rich Who Own Sports

"I would say that KTLA in Los Angeles is worth twenty-five million dollars," he told an interviewer recently, sitting on a lawn chair outside his Gene Autry Hotel in Palm Springs. He was dressed in dark slacks and a red-and-black plaid wool shirt, and his life style nowadays is as casual as his clothes. He owns a ten-room Colonial-style home in the Hollywood Hills, where he lives with his wife of forty-three years, Ina Mae. He wakes up at 7 A.M. every morning of the week, and follows the same ritual. First he reads the newspapers. Then he drives to the Lakeside Golf Club for a game with his close adviser and attorney, Clair Stout. From 11 A.M. to 5 P.M., he locks himself in his offices at Golden West Broadcasters. When his California Angels are in spring training, he lives at his hotel in Palm Springs and spends hours on the telephone conferring with his executives at Golden West. "The radio stations are worth another twenty-five million dollars. This hotel is worth about five million. I would say the cattle ranch is worth three million. I don't know what the livestock we have there is now worth; that goes according to the market. We feel that the Angels baseball club is worth at least ten million, because the San Diego club was sold for twelve million and Finley in Oakland wants fifteen million for his club."

Autry's impact on professional sport has been less publicized than some of his fellow Texans', but has been no less crucial. Without Gene Autry, the major baseball leagues might not have expanded from ten to twelve teams and the major leagues might never awarded, as they did in January, 1976, a pro franchise to Seattle.

Unlike the Hopalong Cassidys and Clint Eastwoods, celluloid superstars who couldn't tell a bull from a heifer without a diagram, Gene Autry was a real cowpoke. He was born in Tioga, Texas. He was raised on a ranch in Oklahoma. His father was a farmer and a livestock breeder, and young Orvon Gene Autry could ride and rope before he could read. When he was ten, his mother bought him a guitar and taught him how to play. Ten years later, he was working at a railroad station in Chelsea, Oklahoma, when cowboy humorist Will Rogers stepped off a train and noticed him strumming his guitar. "Boy," said Rogers, "you pick good. You should be a professional."

Autry took Rogers' advice. Soon he was "Oklahoma's Yodeling Cowboy" on station KVOO in Tulsa. In 1930, he was yodeling for station WLS in Chicago, owned by Sears, Roebuck. That year he composed his first hit, "That Silver-Haired Daddy of Mine." Four years later, in 1934, he was in Hollywood, a movie star.

Autry kept making movies—and churning out hit records. He composed hundreds of songs, some of which, like "Back in the Saddle Again," eventually gained the timeless status of folk ballads. "Autry was a kingpin artist," says John Sipple, marketing editor of *Billboard* in Los Angeles. "He was head and shoulders above everybody else in Western music at the time." His fame spilled over the borders of America. In 1939, he toured Great Britain and drew more hordes of screaming fans than Elvis Presley and the Beatles, three decades later. His movies, strictly grade B, were never taken seriously by the critics. But the paying public loved their black-and-white simplicity, their sharply drawn distinctions between the good guys, who got the girls, and the bad guys in black, who got the hangman's noose.

Throughout his career, Autry showed a business sense uncommon among the performers of his day, unanticipated from a humble cowboy out of Texas and Oklahoma. "I've had two or three different careers," he explains. "During my last year in high school, I learned to be a telegraph operator. Then I took a correspondence course and became a CPA. I put in about five years on the 'Frisco Railroad and learned an awful lot about responsibility and business. This helped me out later, when I first started out in show business. I used to have to check the box office myself because I didn't have a manager."

When Autry made personal appearances in theaters across the country, he took a percentage of the gross rather than a flat fee. He was also one of the first movie stars to merchandise his name. His Gene Autry Guitar was the first of many products that he endorsed and Sears, Roebuck retailed.

Then, as it would with Ewing Kauffman and Charlie Finley, World War II caused Autry to completely reevaluate his future. One day he was a movie star, earning $10,000 a week. The next, he was a technical sergeant in the Air Force, earning $135 per week. "I started kind of reviewing things," he recalls, "and I thought to myself, Well, as long as I can work, I know I can make money. But suppose something happens, suppose my voice goes haywire and I can't sing any more. So I thought, By golly, I'd better start looking for a business in case I'm incapacitated. And times change, too," he adds. "If you don't part your hair right, they go for somebody else."

After the war, Autry made two more movies for Republic, then reached a stalemate with the film company over how much percentage he would get from each picture. As a result of Autry's hard bargaining, Republic signed another country singer named Leonard Slye. Leonard Slye became Roy Rogers.

Gradually, Autry drifted out of show business and into finance. In 1952, he bought radio station KMPC and founded Golden West. He added stations in San Francisco, Seattle and Portland to his network. In 1964, he bought KTLA from Paramount Pictures for $12 million. Three years later, he purchased Golden West's production facilities—a two-block complex—from Paramount for another $6 million. The Golden West Production Center films commercials, pilots and specials for TV, and movies for industry. "Gene is considered in his judgment," says Robert O. Reynolds, who was Autry's partner for twenty-two years and one-time president of Golden West. "He's a good listener. He's an avid reader. He's a perceptive guy. He's got an inquisitive mind. He knows the bottom line. He's just got a lot of natural good business sense."

Autry got involved with baseball through his radio interests —and with hotels through his baseball interests. In 1960, his radio station in Los Angeles, KMPC, lost the right to broadcast the Los Angeles Dodgers' games, just when the American League was announcing plans for an expansion franchise in Los Angeles. Autry decided to persuade whoever won the franchise to broadcast on KMPC. He revealed his plan to a friend, Del Webb, then the New York Yankees' owner. Webb, in turn, suggested an alternative. "Buy the franchise yourself," he told Autry.

Once he became owner of the Angels (based in Anaheim), Autry decided to purchase a hotel for the Angels to stay in during spring training. Soon he owned a chain of hotels, including the Ocotillo Lodge in Palm Springs, the Continental in West Hollywood, the Mark Hopkins in San Francisco and the Sahara near Chicago's O'Hare Airport. But the hotels weren't profitable. "We were not hotel people," says Bob Reynolds, "and we should not have been in the business. We just had to take our loss and get out."

Autry sold the last of the hotels in 1967, then purchased another one in Palm Springs and renamed it the Gene Autry Hotel. This hotel, the home of the Angels in spring training, is turning a profit. But his Angels, over the fourteen years of their existence, have been even bigger losers than his hotel chain—on the field and at the box office. Still, Autry's impact has been awesome. From the beginning, Gene Autry's Golden West network made him a force to reckon with.

During the five years before he shifted his Kansas City Athletics franchise to Oakland, Charlie Finley kept badgering American League owners for permission to move. The owners, on the other hand, kept telling Finley that nothing would make them happier than to see him out of Kansas City—as long as that meant he was out of major league baseball altogether. They wanted him to sell the franchise, and Finley refused. It looked like a hopeless stalemate, until, in a scenario that evoked the faded frames of an old cowboy movie, he got last-minute help. As he had in so many films throughout the 1930's and 1940's, Gene Autry rode to the rescue. At the time, in 1967, Autry's Angels were the only one of the league's ten franchises located further west than Kansas City. Autry reasoned that if Finley moved to Oakland, the rivalry between the two California clubs would help his Angels' flagging attendance. Besides, he would save money on traveling expenses with the Athletics in nearby Oakland, instead of distant Kansas City.

Autry timed his cavalry charge for the American League meeting in Chicago, before the 1968 season, at which Finley again filibustered for permission to pick up bats and baggage and depart from Kansas City. A majority of the other owners was still unalterably opposed, but Autry soon altered that.

The owners rejected Finley's proposal by one vote. One of the teams that cast a negative was the New York Yankees, then owned by the Columbia Broadcasting System. Autry's Golden West Broadcasters network was enmeshed in deals with CBS. Autry told the Yankees' representatives that it might be in their interest to think over that negative vote, the implication being that if the Yankees persisted in their stubbornness, he might reconsider his mutually lucrative relationship with their parent company. Mike Burke, the head of the Yankees' delegation, talked over the situation with his bosses at CBS. The Yankees decided to change their vote to a yes. Finley moved to Oakland.

And the repercussions that followed shook the structure of organized baseball. Powerful Congressmen began putting pressure on the American League, demanding a new franchise in Kansas City to replace the one Finley had shifted. But adding an eleventh team to the league meant, for reasons of scheduling, etc., that the American League would have to add a twelfth team, too. The beneficiary—or, as it turned out, the victim—was the city of Seattle. The Pilots lasted one year before drifting off to Milwaukee, bequeathing to Seattle a monumental corporate mess and the memory of an artistic flop. (In January, 1976, the league would have to agree to expand again, putting a franchise in Seattle to satisfy that city's $32 million suit, charging the league with breach of contract for transferring the franchise to Milwaukee back in 1970).

But there was more. To keep pace with its partner, the National League also had to expand from ten teams to twelve. With the addition of San Diego and Montreal in the National League, and Oakland and Seattle in the American League, the leagues were forced to reorganize into divisions. From then on, a team could finish first in a feeble division, get lucky in a few playoff games and end up in a World Series.

Finally, Horace Stoneham, who had shifted his Giant franchise out of the Bronx in 1958 in order to mine the population lode in San Francisco, suddenly found Charlie Finley's Oakland A's camped right across the Bay, claiming squatters' rights. Finley's arrival killed any chance Stoneham had to make his Giants profitable. It was small solace for Stoneham that Finley wouldn't fill his ball park, either. All this, because a lonesome cowboy had doffed his baseball cap for one that read BROADCASTING EXECUTIVE, in order to pressure a baseball team to do something that might be profitable for the TV network that owned it.

●　　　●　　　●

The Entertainers

It was, of course, just this kind of embarrassing conflict of interest that eventually drove CBS out of baseball. At the time CBS purchased the Yankees in 1964 from Del Webb and Dan Topping, the network had been investing in a variety of prestige companies, all somehow related to entertainment. It had purchased Creative Playthings, the leader in the toy industry, and Steinway, Inc., the Stradivarius of mass-produced pianos, and now the Yankees—the winningest and most charismatic franchise in baseball. Says Mike Burke, then vice-president of CBS in charge of investments: "The Yankee purchase fit the CBS pattern. We wanted to be associated with first-class operations and the Yankees were certainly that." CBS wanted a warmer image; the network was after public good will it could translate into profits.

During the next eight years, however, CBS saw the Yankees change from a coveted bauble into a public-relations liability. The Yankees won a pennant the year CBS bought them. Then, gradually, as their superstars slipped into old age and retirement, the Yankees slid toward mediocrity. "I think CBS suffered some small embarrassment in buying a club at its peak and then having it fall from first place in the league to sixth, and then to tenth," says Mike Burke. "The bottom fell out. The Yankees no longer fit comfortably into CBS's plans.

"That huge shadowy emminence of CBS over the Yankees made people uneasy. The fact that CBS had a lot of tender public-relations surfaces—with the Federal Communications Commission and other places in Washington—was something we had to consider. All the Yankees' thinking had to be strained through CBS situations. As a ball club, we had to be alert not to bruise other surfaces."

Gene Autry—as a broadcasting executive as well as owner of the California Angels—knew how to raise a blister by threatening to take business away from CBS if it didn't approve Charlie Finley's move to Oakland. As early as 1964, amid cries of conflict of interest, Congress had started investigating CBS's purchase of the ball club. (In 1964 and 1965, the Yankees were the feature attraction in CBS's coverage of major league baseball. In 1964, however, NBC televised five of eight Saturday Yankee road games from four cities—the Yankees were, in fact, competing then with their parent company.) In 1972, the Yankees drew less than one million spectators for the first time in more than a decade. The next year, CBS decided to sell for $10 million—$3.2 million less than it had paid for the franchise. Herman Franks, former manager of the baseball Giants, who had been negotiating for a group that wanted to buy the Yankees, was surprised. "We were talking with CBS somewhere between thirteen and fourteen million dollars," he said at the time. "I thought we had a chance."

Exactly why, in January of 1973, CBS decided to sell at a $3.2 million loss still remains somewhat of a mystery. It was an era when expansion franchises, whose purchase price should have been much lower than the Yankees', sold for $10 to $12 million in TV backwaters such as Seattle and San Diego. In 1972, a National Football League franchise, the Los Angeles Rams, had changed hands for $19 million. One clue may be CBS's dealings with the Internal Revenue Service. According to Mike Burke, the name "Yankees" carried with it such glamour that the IRS assigned more value to it than to the depreciable player contracts. "We tried to write off eight million six hundred thousand dollars [of the $13.2 million purchase price] over six years. The IRS changed that to six million five hundred thousand." But CBS's difficulties with the IRS are only a small part of the explanation. CBS had bought the Yankees as an image builder, not as a tax shelter.

Perhaps the best answer is that pressure from Congress at the top, combined with pressure from the fans below, led CBS's own experts to take a pessimistic view of the future. "The Yankees were always a distraction to CBS's real business, and an expensive one in view of their weak profits," says one CBS analyst.

CBS's negative experience may have served as a deterrent to other corporations anxious to identify themselves with a pro sports franchise. "CBS came to the conclusion that perhaps it was not as viable for the network to own the Yankees as for some people," said CBS vice-president Arthur B. Taylor. "Fans get worked up over great men, not great corporations. We came to the realization, I think, that sports franchises really flourish better with *people* owning them."

The Entertainers

Only corporate eagles soaring high above the Himalayas of technocracy could mistake George Steinbrenner's "committee of fifteen," who purchased the Yankees from CBS in 1973, as just "people."

◀ 13 ▶
The Politicians

Apart from Mike Burke, the ex-CBS vice-president, and Gabe Paul, a career baseball executive scheduled to become the Yankees' "special projects director," George Steinbrenner's "committee of fifteen" was typical of the new breed of owners, with little in common except enormous wealth. Some wore mod haircuts and Cardin jump suits; others, Savile Row pin-stripes and crew cuts. More of them had pumped the hand of President Richard Nixon than of manager Ralph Houk. Some, like Cincinnati real-estate broker Marvin Warner, could not recall the last time they had seen the New York Yankees play. "I've always admired and respected the Yankees," Warner said, "but I haven't been a fan. I don't remember when I saw them play—in some World Series."

Besides the fifty-three-year-old Warner, there was Jess Bell, forty-eight, who headed the Bonne Bell cosmetics firm in Cleveland; Lester Crown, forty-seven, a constructor from Wilmette, Illinois; James Nederlander, fifty, who owned theaters and art centers in Baltimore, Chicago, Detroit, New York, Phoenix and Washington; Daniel R. McCarthy, forty-eight, and his partner, Edward M. Greenwald, thirty-eight, both Cleveland tax attorneys. The House That Ruth Built would now be superintended in part by Nelson Bunker Hunt, forty-seven, Lamar's brother. The managerial shenanigans of Huggins and McCarthy and Stengel would now become the property of Francis J. ("Steve") O'Neill, a retired transportation tycoon from Cleveland. Babe Ruth's 714 homers and Joe DiMaggio's fifty-six-game hitting streak and Don Larsen's perfect World Series game were now among the assets of forty-eight-year-old John DeLorean, a vice-president of General Motors. The Yankees' twenty-nine American League pennants and twenty World Series titles over the past fifty-two years now belonged to Sheldon Guren, forty-eight, a Cleveland real-estate lawyer, and to his partner, Edward Ginsberg, fifty-five, and to Thomas W. Evans, a partner in the Manhattan law firm of Mudge, Rose, Guthrie, Alexander and Mitchell—formerly the home office of Richard Nixon.

And then there was George Steinbrenner III. His partners could sum up their motive for owning the Yankees in dollars and cents. Steinbrenner was smitten by nostalgia. As a young boy, in Cleveland, he recalls, "Watching the Yankees come to town, it was like watching Barnum & Bailey. I don't mean that they were like a circus, but it was the excitement. They had these gray uniforms, but there was a blue hue to them. I'll never forget them. Watching them was as exciting as watching the game. Being in Cleveland, you couldn't root for them, but you would boo them in awe."

Steinbrenner was a born rooter and booer. Back in the 1960's, he owned a professional basketball team called the Cleveland Pipers. One night, he was sitting in the back of the Pipers' arena, watching his team in a close, hard-fought game. Steinbrenner grew more and more excited. Gradually, row by row, he began edging forward until he reached courtside. A referee made a controversial call that favored the Pipers' opponents; the enraged Steinbrenner couldn't contain himself. He started screaming at the referee—and so became the first owner in the history of professional basketball to be penalized with a technical foul.

A decade later, in 1974, Steinbrenner would be similarly penalized in another arena—the federal courts. On August 23, he pleaded guilty to making illegal contributions to the 1972 campaign of former President Richard Nixon, as well as to several Democratic candidates for Congress. Aware of the law against corporate campaign contributions, Steinbrenner had set up an elaborate system of phony bonuses for company employees, who then delivered the money to the political candidates. He got caught, and he lied (the indictment called it devising a "false and misleading explanation"), then tried to "influence and intimidate" some of his employees into committing perjury in his behalf. According to the indictment, the amount he was trying to conceal was $142,000. He was fined $15,000 and his firm was fined an additional $20,000.

It's possible that Steinbrenner wasn't the only owner to misuse campaign contributions. According to a speech delivered by Donald M. Fraser (Democrat, Minnesota) in the House on December 13, 1973, and reprinted in the *Congressional Record,* on May 31, 1972, the Price Commission ordered McDonald's to reduce the price of its Quarter Pounder Cheeseburger. Ray Kroc, McDonald's board chairman, and owner of the San Diego Padres, then contributed more than $200,000 to the Nixon reelection effort. Later, he contributed $55,000 more. The Price Commission reversed its earlier ruling.

But Steinbrenner was the only owner who got caught in this area. Everyone wondered how severely Commissioner Bowie Kuhn would punish a franchise owner who was also a convicted felon. In 1953, Commissioner Ford Frick had forced Cardinal owner Fred Saigh—fined $15,000 and sentenced to fifteen years in prison for income-tax evasion—to sell his franchise.

Kuhn dealt with Steinbrenner as leniently as he could, outside of not punishing him at all. He suspended Steinbrenner as owner of the Yankees, for two years, without making him sell his stock in the franchise. In a twelve-page ruling, Kuhn said that Steinbrenner was "ineligible and incompetent" to have "any association whatsoever with any major league club or its personnel."

After only a year or so, however, before the start of the 1976 baseball season, Kuhn reinstated the Yankee owner—despite strong evidence that Steinbrenner had ignored the Commissioner's injunction against mixing in the affairs of the Yankees. Most observers are convinced that Steinbrenner gave Gabe Paul the go-ahead to sign pitcher Catfish Hunter for $3.75 million, and made the decision to switch from Bill Virdon to Billy Martin as team manager. Cynics suggested that these instances of interference in Yankee affairs were canceled out, in Kuhn's mind, by one other:

the Yankees had played a crucial role in stopping Charlie Finley's "Dump Bowie Kuhn" effort, in the summer of 1975, by switching their vote from no to yes on the question of giving the Commissioner a new seven-year contract. George Steinbrenner could play politics at the intraleague as well as the federal level.

George Steinbrenner III was the son of a collegiate hurdler; he ran in that same event at Williams College, and was a halfback on the football team during his senior year. When he graduated, he went into the Air Force. He served with the Strategic Air Command. Afterwards, he became a high school football and basketball coach in Columbus, Ohio. He moved into college coaching, serving one year as assistant football coach at Northwestern, and a year as assistant coach at Purdue. Then, in 1959, he operated the Cleveland Pipers of the National Industrial League. Aside from winning two league titles, and losing about $250,000, the most memorable thing Steinbrenner did as owner of the Pipers was to sign superstar Jerry Lucas to a contract. Before Lucas had time to get fitted for a Piper uniform, however, the team folded.

George quit sports and devoted his attention to the family business. Kinsman, Inc., had a flotilla of five antique ships which carried iron ore down the Great Lakes to the steel mills of Pittsburgh. It was being forced out of business by competition from the giant steel mills themselves, which were building and sailing their own vessels. Steinbrenner bought Kinsman from his father. "He was down to zero financially, and nobody in Cleveland thought he could do it," says Tom Roulston, a close friend, and president of Roulston & Co., a Cleveland brokerage house. "But George is a tough-nosed S.O.B."

New methods of extracting iron ore soon made the fields around the Great Lakes more attractive, with profits aplenty for everyone. Kinsman began hauling grain as well, and when the hauling rate rose from three cents a bushel to twelve cents, Kinsman's profits leaped astronomically. Meanwhile, Steinbrenner, Roulston and a few partners had started buying up stock in the American Ship Building Co. In 1967, Steinbrenner led a successful proxy fight that put him in charge at AmShip.

When Steinbrenner took over, not only AmShip but the entire

The Politicians

Great Lakes shipbuilding industry was on the downgrade. No private corporation had ordered a new ship to be built on the Great Lakes since the late 1950's. Steinbrenner went to Washington. He put together a powerful Congressional lobby that succeeded in getting the Great Lakes included in the 1970 Maritime Act, which permitted businessmen to use pre-tax dollars for ship construction, and permitted the federal government to guarantee 87.5 percent of any loan used for shipbuilding. It was George's first venture into politics; it wouldn't be his last.

The impact of the Maritime Act on Great Lakes shipbuilding in general, and American Ship in particular, was dramatic. AmShip received a contract to build an iron-ore supercarrier, at a cost of more than $20 million. Revenues climbed from $45 million in 1968 to $95 million in 1974. AmShip went on to acquire a bridge and barge construction company in Nashville, and a shipbuilding and repair yard in Tampa. By the age of forty-three, when he purchased a controlling interest in the Yankees, Steinbrenner was the chief executive officer of the largest shipbuilder on the Great Lakes, the owner of the 860-acre Kinsman Stud Farm in Ocala, Florida, a general partner in Kinsman Stables (whose two-year-old, Kinsman Hope, won the Remsen Stakes at Aqueduct in November, 1972) and part-owner of a fleet of New York City limousines. In pro sports, apart from his holdings in the Yankees, he owned 10 percent of the NBA Chicago Bulls, and a Cleveland harness track. He also had extensive investments in show business, including a theater outfit that produced the musicals *Applause* and *Seesaw* on Broadway. When, with his wife and four children, he attended the opening of one of his musicals, he could stay at his apartment in New York City. When he wanted to watch his horses train, he could stay at his ranch in Ocala, or at his home in Tampa. When he wanted to supervise his shipping and shipbuilding interests, he could relax at his mansion in Lorain, Ohio.

"I won't be active in the day-to-day operations of the club at all," Steinbrenner promised when he bought the Yankees from CBS. "I'll stick to ships."

Those who knew Steinbrenner intimately treated this disclaimer with the skepticism it deserved. If ever two men were on a collision course, it was Steinbrenner and Yankee president Mike

Burke, who had run the team for CBS and was a member of the new ownership syndicate. Burke, at fifty-four, was elegant, sophisticated and slick, the paragon of radical chic. Born in Enfield, Connecticut, he had attended the University of Pennsylvania, and was so talented as a six-foot-one, 175-pound halfback that Bert Bell of the Philadelphia Eagles had offered him a pro contract. Burke declined Bell's generous offer—of $125 a game. During World War II, Burke achieved passing fame as a spy, parachuting behind enemy lines. His war career led him to Hollywood, as a film writer and producer. Cary Grant portrayed him in a film about his war exploits.

Burke blended New York sophisitication with a subtle sense of media diplomacy. He had old Yankee Stadium repainted, blue on the inside and white on the outside. To prove to New Yorkers that the new Yankee ownership was human, in contrast to CBS's arctic impersonality, he made himself very visible, sitting just beside the Yankee dugout in a box seat. He endeared himself to New York's culture vultures, too—by convincing poetess Marianne Moore to throw out the first ball one opening day, and keeping a copy of James Joyce's *Ulysses* on a bookshelf in his office.

Steinbrenner, on the other hand, was naturally inclined toward winning another constituency. Early on, for example, he kept getting letters from a saloon called Joe's Bar, in Astoria, Queens, always with the same complaints from the same irritated Yankee fans. One day, on his way into Manhattan from LaGuardia Airport, Steinbrenner told his cab driver to take him to Joe's Bar. "It was a typical neighborhood bar," Steinbrenner recalls. "These big, burly guys with their bellies flopping over their belts, sitting at the bar drinking quart bottles of beer. At first, they didn't believe who I was. But I convinced them, and I bought a few rounds and we had a good talk. When I left, they were my friends."

When the inevitable comparisons between Burke and Steinbrenner were drawn, George came off as desperately dull and incurably provincial. Both his self-image and his image of the Yankees were conditioned by the past; his favorite movie, he declared, was *Pride of the Yankees.* Burke wore his hair stylishly long; Steinbrenner hated sloppiness, and by his lights there was nothing sloppier than hair that crept surreptitiously past someone's

248

ears. Despite his promise to leave the management to others, Steinbrenner began to show up in the stands, as an unofficial spotter. Rumor was that he would write down the uniform numbers of players and turn them in to manager Ralph Houk. "Number 28's hair is too long . . . Number 38 doesn't wear his pants high enough . . . Number 19 had his hat off . . ."

"It's kind of true," Steinbrenner admits. "Houk had these rules—his rules, not mine. I don't care what a manager's rules are, but if he has a rule, it should be obeyed. I have nothing against long hair, provided that it's neat. But I do believe a rule should be enforced. Otherwise, why have rules?"

The players didn't appreciate his playing the informer. Their disgruntlement showed up in an incident that took place while the Yankees were playing a game with the Texas Rangers. "We were in a pennant race," Steinbrenner says, "and somebody put a hot dog in Gene Michael's glove. It disturbed him. He took the hot dog and threw it and it landed at my feet. I told Houk about it. I wanted him to do something about it. There is a time for levity. In the clubhouse, on the bus, but not on the field, in a pennant race.

"I watched Michael. All of the next inning, in the field, he was thinking more about who pulled the joke on him than he was about the game. Was I wrong to report the incident to Ralph Houk? I don't think so."

Many of his players did think so. They thought maybe Steinbrenner should have reported the individual who *put* the hot dog in Michael's glove—whoever, and however important, the culprit was. Maybe Ralph Houk agreed with those players. He left the Yankees a year later to manage Detroit. One of his first moves was to buy Gene Michael from the Yankees.

Within a few months, Steinbrenner had eased Mike Burke out of power. Burke had most of the sympathy on his side, but Steinbrenner had some of the logic. It was hard to refute him when he argued that Burke—the ex-CBS vice-president—had bungled in the one area he should have been expert: in making a decent deal for the Yankees' broadcasting rights. In the glory years, the Yankees had regularly collected more than $1 million a year in broadcast revenues. By the 1972 season, however, the Yankees' earnings had slipped to below $200,000, while that same season the Rheingold Brewery was paying the New York Mets $1.25 million. "The Yankees are in a major market," Steinbrenner complained, "and still they have one of the worst set-ups in baseball."

Yet, when Burke left the Yankees, Steinbrenner was reportedly very generous to him. One former associate of Burke's alleges that although Burke put in practically nothing, he retained stock worth as much as $1 million. Burke soon turned up as president of the Madison Square Garden Center, with 500 shares of Garden stock and a five-year contract that paid him $100,000 a year in salary, plus substantial fringe payments.

In Burke's place, Steinbrenner installed Gabe Paul, an ex-general manager of the Cleveland Indians and a minority shareholder in the Yankees. It was Paul whom the public thought was running the Yankees during Steinbrenner's suspension. Instead, in at least one crucial area of Yankee dealings, Steinbrenner's alter ego was a politician named Patrick J. Cunningham, the man responsible for getting the New York taxpayers to pay for the Yankee Stadium renovations.

The early 1970's were years of economic uncertainty. A leading London financier kept a "survival kit" in his office; it contained twelve days' rations of canned foods, 1,200 gold coins—and a Thompson submachine gun. In the United States, for the first time since the 1930's, unemployment skyrocketed, as energy resources dwindled and the Gross National Product ground toward zero growth. One of the industries hardest hit by the recession was the building trade. Mortgage money became scarce; interest rates, exorbitant. The construction of private dwellings slowed virtually to a standstill, while civic projects were also curtailed. But one sector of the industry didn't wither in the economic drought. The fever for building new sports stadiums that had driven Walter O'Malley from Brooklyn to Los Angeles, and Clint Murchison, Jr., from Dallas to Irving County, and Roy Hofheinz from solvency to near-bankruptcy, raged unabated.

The reason that pro franchise owners—and potential owners —could keep on building extravagant stadiums in the midst of a dismal economy is not hard to fathom. They didn't have to pay for them. Ancient Rome taxed its brothels to support its stadiums.

The Politicians

Modern America duns just about everyone else. The taxpaying public has financed every one of the sixteen major stadiums erected since 1960. More than 70 percent of all pro sports facilities in the United States are publicly owned, and scores more are on the drawing boards. The taxpaying public will spend close to $1 billion over the next twenty years to cover the new stadiums' financing costs and operating deficits.

Why do cities get into the stadium-building and stadium-renovating business in the first place? Advocates of municipal ownership argue that having a pro team in town is like having a Rolls-Royce in your driveway: it enhances a community's prestige. In order to obtain a pro franchise, you have to have a suitable stadium, preferably built at the public's expense. Besides, they insist, publicly owned stadiums directly benefit the public. Apart from giving a city an alluring image ("Podunk is a progressive town, they've got the Podunk Dodgers; let's put our next IBM plant there . . ."), stadiums—new and renewed—upgrade their local neighborhoods, provide more jobs, stimulate consumer sales, increase tax revenues for the local government and keep teenagers off the streets.

The critics, however, point out that rent payments are not keeping pace with rising construction and financing costs—in other words, franchise owners are getting their stadiums cheap. They insist, furthermore, that while a few people do get new jobs, all the people get new tax increases, to pay for the stadiums' upkeep and construction. And as for increasing tax revenues, the critics point out that the main reason owners lobby for municipally owned facilities is to *escape* paying the real-estate taxes levied on private property. In sum, the critics argue, the only "citizens" who benefit are the handful of millionaires who sign the bottom line of those lucrative leases.

San Diego's citizens have already paid an estimated $8 million to keep in operation their $28 million stadium, built in 1967. In 1966, the cost of building the municipally owned Louisiana Superdome was set at $35 million; by 1976, those costs had escalated to $163 million, not including tens of millions in interest, and millions of dollars more in future operating deficits. The 'Dome was being plagued by minor problems, such as the flock of pigeons nesting in its rafters who delighted in bombarding patrons below with bird droppings, and major ones, such as political scandals over how—and to whom—construction and servicing contracts had been dispensed. Meanwhile, taxpayers in Philadelphia were paying $1.5 million a year to cover debt and operating deficits in their four-year-old Veterans Memorial Stadium. The citizens of Seattle would be paying $2.5 million a year to cover debts and principal for their domed stadium.

Of course, none of this was news to the franchise owners. If operating an arena were good business, they would be building their own stadiums rather than conning local politicians into conning the public to pay, "for the good of the city." Nowhere has the public financing of privately controlled stadiums become more of an issue than in New York City. In late 1975, the city was haunted by the specter of imminent default; it was firing cops and closing schools and cutting essential services. Meanwhile, the New York Yankees were preparing to inaugurate their newly refurbished, municipally owned one-hundred-million-dollar stadium. And the football Giants were getting ready to take over their municipally owned three-hundred-and-two-million-dollar stadium complex, under construction in a swampy New Jersey dump opposite Manhattan. And the Madison Square Garden Corporation was simply trying to become municipally owned.

How franchise owners obtain the funds for their stadiums, and why cities acquiesce, even in times of trouble, is a charade whose theme is the incest between politics and money—a tragicomedy full of shady deals and stage whispers, inflated estimates and political puppetry. The financing of Yankee Stadium is a case in point, a tale even more convoluted—and full of more cunning—than Clint Murchison's deal for Irving Stadium.

In 1955, Yankee owners Dan Topping and Del Webb sold the stadium, and the land under it, to John M. Cox of Chicago, president of the General Packaging Corporation. Cox, in turn, sold the land to the Knights of Columbus and donated the stadium to Rice University, his alma mater. Rice then gave the Yankees a twenty-eight-year-lease, with an option for forty-two more years, at a rental of $180,000 a year.

The Politicians

CBS purchased the franchise in 1964, but not the stadium or the land under it. By the terms of the stadium lease, CBS had to pay for real-estate taxes and repairs and maintenance, both on the stadium and on the land. Even then, however, the Yankees had powerful friends in the city government. From 1965 through 1972, the city valued the property at $5 million for tax purposes each year, but the city tax commission lowered these assessments year by year on appeals from the Yankees. In 1971–72, for example, the final valuation for the stadium was $2,875,000, reducing the stadium taxes to $173,420.

It was clear, by the start of the 1970's, that the stadium was antiquated as a baseball facility, at the edge of one of the worst ghettoes in the United States—the South Bronx. Both the Yankees and the New York Giants, who shared the stadium, began to rumble about seeking a better neighborhood and a better home for their franchises, unless someone agreed to give the stadium a thorough face lift. In March, 1971, Mayor John V. Lindsay announced that New York City would buy the stadium in order to keep the Yankees and Giants from wandering off. But Giant owner Wellington Mara got an offer he couldn't refuse from ex-Jet owner Sonny Werblin—a home in a multimillion-dollar sports complex to be constructed in New Jersey's Hackensack Meadows. That left the Yankees as sole beneficiary of the City's planned renewal of the stadium.

Lindsay's plan was to lease the renovated stadium back to the Yankees on the same terms by which the City leased Shea Stadium to Mrs. Joan Payson's Mets. The Mayor estimated the cost of renovating the stadium at $24 million. Asked how he intended to finance the project ($3 million for land acquisition—now estimated at between $8 and $9 million—and $21 million for improvements —now estimated at anywhere up to $92 million), Lindsay said he wouldn't take the money from his beleaguered executive budget. Instead, he said in 1971, he would finance 25 percent of the costs with funds from the capital or constructions budgets, and the other 75 percent by the sale of bonds to the public.

It's hard to understand why the city of New York would spend such an awesome sum for a sports stadium while it was

253

effectively on the dole, or why the city should cling to a brutal set of priorities in which renovating a stadium was held to be more important than urban renewal in the bombed-out, blighted South Bronx. The answer is, of course, that the citizens of the South Bronx were not only destitute, they were powerless. George Steinbrenner III, by contrast, had both money and powerful political allies. Although he had gained his notoriety as a contributor to the campaign of a Republican president, he had, in fact, also been indicted for contributing illegally to the campaigns of several Democratic Congressmen. The fact is, Steinbrenner has been an influential fund-raiser for both political parties. Democrats have looked on him kindly since he raised $2 million for their Senatorial candidates after the 1968 Presidential campaign drained the party treasury. Steinbrenner had become a friend not only of Richard Nixon, but of Ted Kennedy, too; indeed, Kennedy flew to the 1972 Democratic Convention in Miami with Steinbrenner. At one time, Steinbrenner was being called Kennedy's "Bebe Rebozo"—after Nixon's multimillionaire backer. "I don't know that I'd want to be compared to Rebozo—not that there's anything wrong with him," Steinbrenner told a reporter in 1973. "Ted Kennedy and I are close personal friends. If he runs for the Presidency in 1976, I'll help out."

Steinbrenner's political muscle gave him more leverage in getting New York City to provide more and more money to meet the swelling costs of renovating his stadium. Despite the city's pitiful financial woes, according to the New York *Times,* several upper-echelon city officials said in December, 1975, that the Yankee Stadium project was viewed as being "politically blessed, and had the highest priority of any city project."

"It doesn't hurt that Pat Cunningham is involved," the *Times* quoted one official as saying.

Cunningham, the Democratic leader in the Bronx, and so one of New York's most powerful political brokers, first became involved with the Yankees in 1973. The year before, 1972, New York City had approved a lease that gave the Arol Development Corporation control of the Bronx Terminal Market, next-door to Yankee Stadium. That same year, the city had approved the Yankee Stadium renovation pact.

The Politicians

At the time the city signed the lease with Arol, both parties recognized that that agreement was in conflict with the Yankee pact since Arol was awarded part of the parking space promised to the Yankees. According to Ken Patton, the former Economic Development Administrator, the city reached an understanding with Arol—the lease would eventually be revised to satisfy the Yankees, but in such a way that Arol's interests would be protected.

In 1973, the city, the Yankees and the Arol Corporation met to iron out their conflict over the parking spaces. The City offered the Yankees an alternative site, just north of the Macombs Dam Bridge, which leads to the stadium. The Yankees rejected that offer and eventually ended up with the parking spaces they were entitled to—and the city relieved Arol of major obligations for construction and took on obligations of about $10 million. The law firm that represented Arol throughout those negotiations was Cunningham & Kamen.

Cunningham's role in these negotiations stirred some controversy. It was a triangular fight among the city, Arol and the baseball club, with each side opposed to the other two. Cunningham's interests, critics alleged, overlapped these lines of conflict. He was the lawyer for Arol and that the same time the Bronx Democratic leader—a power in city politics at a time when the city and the borough were committed to the Yankee Stadium deal at almost any price. It didn't help any when, on January 1, 1974, only three months after the Arol lease was amended, Cunningham was hired as general counsel of the Yankees.

With George Steinbrenner sidelined by Bowie Kuhn because of those illicit campaign contributions, Pat Cunningham became de facto head of the Yankee organization. It was Cunningham who represented Steinbrenner in July of 1975, at the "Dump Bowie Kuhn" meeting in Milwaukee; it was Cunningham who changed his mind overnight, voting to keep Kuhn in office for another seven years—and, perhaps, laying the groundwork for Steinbrenner's suspension to be reduced in the bargain. And it was Cunningham's political influence, in part, that helped prevent the Yankee Stadium project from suffering the heavy cuts inflicted on so many other projects during New York City's budget crunch.

255

The Rich Who Own Sports

Cunningham was also de facto head of the Yankees when, with awesome cynicism, the Yankees suddenly bit the municipal hand that had been feeding them. In November, 1975, the Yankees revived a suit against the city that had lain dormant in the courts for three years. This suit demanded payment from the city for damages the team claimed it had suffered because of the stadium remodeling. The Yankees wanted the city to pay for every item the city had torn up, or out, in the process of building the Yankees a new stadium—the playing field, batting cages, therapy tables, goal posts, pitching machines, flag and pennant poles, air conditioners, field lights, ice makers, football screens, the stadium organ, dishwashers, driers, chairs, the 64,850 old seats ripped out to make way for the new ones the city installed—even the 5,000 seats the Yankees had bought from New York City, at the end of the 1973 season, for $1 each, and had sold or given away as souvenirs. Cunningham was not with the Yankees when the suit was initiated, but he was acting general managing partner in November of 1975 when the Yankees suddenly asked for prompt payment for those "damages," accusing the city of "being dilatory."

By 1976, the cost of John Lindsay's "$24 million stadium" had swollen to nearer $100 million. And the indirect costs—for parking facilities, interest and tax exemptions—would probably add another $150 million to the city's bill over the next two and a half decades. Who would benefit most from this enormous expenditure of the taxpayers' money? Certainly not the people who lived—many in abject poverty—in the neighborhood around the stadium. Early on, to gain public acceptance and backing for the renovation project, city officials had emphasized that it would upgrade the neighborhood around the stadium, making the South Bronx safer and more attractive to live in. Then, in October, 1975, the $2 million earmarked to rehabilitate the neighborhood was dropped in an economy move, while the stadium renovation proceeded on schedule. Having "saved" $2 million in urban renewal, the city announced it would spend an extra $300,000 on the Yankees, including $215,000 for a tarpaulin to cover the playing field, $65,000 for security devices, $14,000 to strengthen the

256

supports of the scoreboard and $7,000 for carpeting in the Yankee offices.

Overall, by 1976, the city had spent—or was committed to spend—enough money to pay the salaries for a year of 400 average full-time municipal employees, or to house for a year 4,000 lower-income families. But it was the very rich who benefited from the city's largesse, not the very poor. A New York business conglomerate called Warner Communications, Inc., actually found three different ways to profit from the stadium project—from parking, from plumbing, and from the New York Cosmos of the North American Soccer League.

In 1976, the Cosmos signed to play twelve home games at the refurbished Yankee Stadium; Warner owns the Cosmos. But while Warner was paying the city rent with one hand, it was collecting rent with the other. A Warner subsidiary, Kinney Systems, Inc., built and owned several parking garages at the stadium, for which it would receive $2 million a year in rents from the city, plus tax exemptions worth another $2 million. Meanwhile, the city had to pay for repairs and maintenance on all those Kinney garages and parking lots.

Besides the Cosmos and the parking, Warner profited from the stadium plumbing. A Warner subsidairy, Wachtel, Duklauer & Fein, won a $2,520,000 contract to install new plumbing, when the low bidder, B,L&A of New York, was disqualified by the city. According to the New York *Times,* "The reason for the disqualification of B,L&A is obscure. Current city officials said they were not sure what had happened after B,L&A submited a bid almost $1 million less than Wachtel for the plumbing job."

No one seemed to know exactly why B,L&A's bid for the plumbing contract had been thrown out. The consensus among city officials was, as Herbert J. Simmins, the city's Commissioner of Public Works, phrased it, that B,L&A "couldn't cut the mustard."

Strangely enough, though, city records show that Wachtel later *hired* B,L&A to do a substantial portion of the stadium plumbing. Through October, 1975, B,L&A had been paid $342,000 for subcontract work.

●　　　●　　　●

The Rich Who Own Sports

By the 1976 season, in time to inaugurate the renovated Yankee Stadium, George Steinbrenner III was back at the helm of his ball club. He ordered his players to trim their hair. He turned free agent Andy Messersmith from a Yankee rooter into a Yankee hater by signing him to an agreement, then, according to Messersmith, reneging on some of the terms. Steinbrenner's own personal Watergate had cost him prestige in the world of high finance—he had abdicated the top post at AmShip, although he remained chairman of the board—but, overall, it didn't appear that his criminal record was going to do him any lasting harm. In September of 1975, for example, he had been granted a New York state license to race Thoroughbreds. Nor was Steinbrenner even a little bit repentant. "As I said before," he said again, "I have never fully agreed with the Commissioner's original ruling . . ."

Then Steinbrenner explained, as he had before, his antipathy toward long hair. "I have nothing against long hair," he insisted. "But I'm trying to instill a certain sense of order and discipline in the ball club because I think that discipline is important to an athlete.

"I want to develop pride in the players of the Yankees," the convicted felon added, without the slightest hint of irony.

When Steinbrenner's "committee of fifteen" purchased the Yankees from CBS in 1973, Deputy Mayor Edward Hamilton denied that the city's plan to renovate Yankee Stadium represented a multimillion-dollar windfall for an outside syndicate. He characterized it as an "investment" in the future of the Bronx, and went on to say: "Any landlord is delighted to learn that the tenant is hot property. We are delighted."

In contrast, only the year before, Mayor John Lindsay had called Wellington Mara "selfish, callous and ungrateful" when the Giants' owner announced he intended to move his franchise from Yankee Stadium to a sporting complex in New Jersey.

A George Steinbrenner would have been able to shrug off such criticism; Steinbrenner had, after all, shrugged off his very suspension from baseball. But, while other owners give mere lip service to the notion that their franchise belongs to a particular city or region, Wellington Mara is a true believer. It was with reluctance that Mara rejected in 1971 New York City's offer to move his Giant football team into a refurbished Yankee Stadium. But even a renovated Yankee Stadium couldn't match the facilities offered to the Giants by Sonny Werblin. The ex-owner of the Jets and current chairman of the New Jersey Sports and Exposition Authority was going to build, for a total cost of $50 million, a sports complex that included a 76,000-seat stadium and a race track for Thoroughbreds and harness horses.

Naturally, that initial cost estimate was absurdly conservative. Naturally, the public was going to foot the bill. Naturally, there were law suits by offended segments of the populace. Environmentalists and taxpayers groups brought to court fourteen major lawsuits challenging the Authority's right to develop its sports complex on 588 acres of meadowland. The taxpayers resented the fact that virtually all of the revenue from parimutuel racing conducted by the Authority would go to pay off the bond issue instead of being paid to the state. Proof of its political clout, the Authority won all fourteen court battles. More proof of its political clout, by the time Mara shifted his team into his new stadium, early in the 1976 season, the Authority had managed to spend $68 million on the project—$16 million more than Sonny Werblin's original estimate.

In 1975, New Jersey politicians refused to put the state's full support behind the construction bonds. The state declared it had only a "moral" obligation (not a legal one) to cover any of the complex's future debts. But even if the bondholders suffered losses, Wellington Mara was bound to come out ahead. In services, the Giants would get free office space, free watchmen, free maintenance staff, free cops, free scoreboard crew, free insurance, free water, free heating, free electricity, free sewerage and waste disposal, and free transportation for fans who have to park more than a quarter-mile away. In cash, the Giants would get 50 percent of all concessions, 25 percent of all parking fees (plus 400 free parking spaces), 50 percent of all advertising revenues from programs and souvenir books, about 75 percent of the gross ticket revenues, all membership fees in the Stadium Club, all radio and TV revenues, and up to 2,700 free tickets for each game.

The Rich Who Own Sports

Due to the renovation of Yankee Stadium, however, before Mara moved the franchise to New Jersey, he had to move it to New Haven, Connecticut. But after playing their 1973 and 1974 "home games" at the Yale Bowl, the Giants decided to pass up an option year at Yale and return to New York, sharing Shea Stadium with the New York Jets. That deal was worth between $400,000 and $500,000 to New York City in additional rentals, so to pave the way for the Giants' temporary return it had gone out of its way to discourage competition from the World Football League. As soon as the WFL Stars departed, early in the WFL's first season, the city started making anti-WFL noises. "We're not going to permit the WFL to come in and use the city to sell franchises outside the city," said Neil J. Walsh, then chairman of the Mayor's Athletic Community Task Force. Walsh, of course, turned out to be one of the key figures in arranging the agreement for the Giants' return.

"The Nassau Coliseum doesn't pay any tax," complained Donald J. Trump, a real-estate consultant for Madison Square Garden, in 1975, "and the Coliseum pays a low interest on its bonds. The Garden gets no help at all."

In 1975, the Yankees weren't the only enterprise in town trying to brew big-time sports and big-time politics into an intoxicant the taxpayers of New York City would swallow. While the Yankees and their political cronies were bleeding the city of millions of dollars, the Madison Square Garden Corporation was trying to sell an arena to the city for just one dollar.

The city was beset by job layoffs, near-default, a school strike, a wage freeze, a reduction of services, and a higher transit fare. The Garden and its political friends were attempting to negotiate a deal that would deprive the city of more than $50 million over the next ten years.

According to Jack Newfield, the *Village Voice* reporter who uncovered the scheme and publicized it, the deal was this: "The city of New York, through the OTB [Off-Track Betting] Corporation, would buy the Madison Square Garden building for $1 and lease it right back to the Garden Corporation. The point would be to take the Garden off the city's real-estate tax rolls, and save the

Garden from paying $2.5 million each year in real estate taxes. City-owned property is exempt from the real estate tax.

"The deal also calls for the city to pay off the $29 million outstanding mortgage on the Garden, held by Chase Manhattan Bank. This mortgage, at 7 percent interest, runs till 1992. The city would also have to pay $1 million each year to Penn Central for air rights [the Garden is located above the Penn Central railroad station]."

The major beneficiary, Newfield argued, would be Gulf & Western, which owned the largest share (37 percent) of Madison Square Garden Stock. The reason Gulf & Western was anxious to donate the Garden to the city, Newfield insisted, was to obtain a tax write-off of $20 million (the difference between the Garden's value and the mortgage value). The idea of New York City, with a total deficit of $3.3 billion, subsidizing one of the world's five biggest conglomerates struck Newfield as absurd. In 1974, he pointed out, Gulf & Western had reported sales of $2.3 billion, net earnings of $101 million, and assets of $2.7 billion.

As it turned out, the deal to sell the Garden to the city was part of the agreement (engineered in part by the ubiquitous Patrick J. Cunningham) which would bring the Democratic National Convention to Madison Square Garden in July, 1976. Madison Square Garden would accommodate the Democrats; meanwhile, local Democrats would convince the city to take over the Garden.

When Newfield broke the story, the local politicians argued that New York City had to take over the Garden; otherwise, the Garden would have to sell the Knicks and Rangers to keep from going broke. After all, in the fiscal year that ended on May 31, 1975, the Garden had registered a pre-tax loss of more than $7 million. Newfield replied that the Garden itself had, in fact, turned a $3.6 million *profit*. It had also earned $5.9 million from its racing activities. The overall deficit resulted from a $15.3 million loss in its real estate and hotel divisions, and had nothing to do with the profitability of its arena or its two pro franchises. Politicians and lawyers have learned there is a lot of money to be made from the control of sports in New York, Newfield wrote bitterly. "So, William Shea . . . is Mayor Beame's 'sports adviser.' Shea Stadium is named after him. His senior law partner, Milton Gould, is a director of the Madison Square Garden Corporation. Shea's client, Teleprompter cable TV [owned by Jack Kent Cooke], has the exclusive rights to the Nassau Coliseum. Roy Boe, the owner of the Nets and the Islanders, was on the board of Security National Bank with Shea."

Newfield went on to point out that Paul Screvane, the chief of the Off-Track Betting Corporation, and Pat Cunningham, the Yankees' "designated owner" in the absence of Steinbrenner, were two of the politicians lobbying hardest for the deal. One of Cunningham's cronies was Neil Walsh, the city's Deputy Commissioner of Public Events; Walsh owns an insurance company that sold a lucrative policy to the Yankees. "And Walsh was a principal organizer of the city's massive campaign to win the 1976 Democratic Convention for the Garden."

The incest between politics and pro sports didn't end there, either. One of the directors of the Garden Corporation was Leonard Hall, the former national Republican party chairman. Real-estate developer Donald Trump was on the Garden payroll for a reported $100,000 a year as a consultant, to help sell the Garden to the city. Trump's father, according to Newfield, had contributed $25,000 to Governor Hugh Carey's campaign in 1974, "funneled through fifteen different committees." Meanwhile, Howard J. Rubenstein, Mayor Abe Beame's closest adviser, was on the Garden payroll as a publicity consultant. Rebenstein was also getting $18,000 from Phil Iselin's New York Jets.

In the end, Newfield's revelations were picked up by other New York City newspapers. Newfield's outrage was echoed by other journalists. For Gulf & Western, the scheme suddenly became a public-relations liability; for the politicians involved, a public embarrassment. The idea of selling Madison Square Garden to the city for a dollar was dropped.

The politics of ownership, in sum, brings to the surface one startling fact. No only men of substance and ingenuity and wealth, but even multinational corporations (supposedly inoculated against the foibles of ordinary "men") take, as franchise owners, risks to their reputations that as sensible businessmen they would shudder at in the normal world of commerce. This raises a serious question. Who in his right mind would want to enter this world of political intrigue, dismal profits, prima donna performers and irate fans? The answer is, no one in his right mind; only someone who was crazy—crazy about sports.

Postscript

In 1976, after a fifteen-year absence, Bill Veeck returned to baseball as owner of the Chicago White Sox. Once upon a time, Veeck owned the Cleveland Indians (1946–49) and the St. Louis Browns (1951–53) and the Chicago White Sox (1959–61). The last time the Cleveland Indians won the World Series was under Bill Veeck (1948). The last time the Chicago White Sox won a pennant was under Bill Veeck (1959).

In those days, Veeck was baseball's P.T. Barnum, the one who originated "Bat Days" and "Cap Days" and exploding score-boards. He gave major league baseball the idea for promotional giveaways: a year's supply of sardines, 1,500 pounds of ice, 100 gallons of ice cream, a dozen squabs, a dozen lobsters, 6 ladders, a bird dog, rain capes for every customer on rainy nights—and all for the price of one admission. He gave baseball its first—and only —"Good Ole Joe Early Night," in honor of a night watchman named Joe Early, who complained that the only people who got special "days" and "nights" at ball parks were ballplayers who didn't need the gifts, anyway. It was Veeck, finally, who, in 1952, signed 65-pound, 43-inch Eddie Gaedel to a St. Louis Browns contract, and guaranteed Frank Saucier an entry in compendiums

267

of baseball trivia when he sent the midget up to pinch-hit for Saucier.

Back then, in the Forties and Fifties, Veeck was kind of a baseball pariah. He was good copy for the media, but a thorn in the sides of his fellow owners. In public, the other owners limited themselves, when describing Veeck, to words like "unstable," "erratic" and "opportunistic." In private conversation, though, many owners of that era rued the day they had co-opted a madman into their ranks.

Now, in 1976, fifteen years later, Bill Veeck came back into baseball, with a Pandora's box of subversive ideas tucked beneath his arm. He opened it even before the '76 season started. When, in spring training, the owners locked the players out of camp, Veeck slipped out in the dead of night and opened the door a crack. He introduced new uniforms for sweltering summer days: short sleeves and hot pants. He promised to put a bigger bang into his scoreboard to celebrate the Bicentennial. He promised to revive his old custom of sitting in the stands during a game, fraternizing with the bleacher bums.

And then, having opened that box full of subversion, this brownie of baseball, this leprechaun of the Louisville Slugger, sat back to await the howls of protest he was sure his mischief would arouse from fellow owners. After all, if baseball had been a serious business in the Fifties, it was a *big* and serious business now, in which players had become unionized and management corporatized.

Instead, he heard only a few weak whimpers. The truth was that in the decade and a half since Bill Veeck had last owned a franchise, men just as "eccentric" as himself had somehow infiltrated the sports establishment. Compared to Charlie Finley parading his pet mule through posh restaurants, and Ray Kroc screaming over the San Diego public-address system, and Al Davis with his allergy to clocks, and Bud Adams careening his fire engine crazily across the sage brush, and Gary Davidson conjuring up franchises out of thin air, and Jack Kent Cooke shouting at his players from midcourt, and P.K. Wrigley peppering his carefully manicured, multimillion-dollar sanctuary with potholes . . . and Clint Murchison's click-whirring computers, and Lamar Hunt's

Postscript

holey shoes, and George Steinbrenner's unlikely blend of apple pie and illegality—somehow, Bill Veeck's brand of maverick behavior had become, of all things, *respectable*. In the years between 1961 and 1976, it seems, the inmates had, without anyone realizing, taken over the asylum.

For an explanation as to why men of wealth and power and good judgment have been going crazy over owning sports franchises, we should, perhaps, turn back to the fiery fiddler himself, Nero, Emperor of all Rome.

When Nero was a child, he was passionately fond of horses —the way modern owners were passionately fond of baseball or football or hockey or basketball. Once he took the throne, he became a regular at the Circus Maximus, where the chariot races took place. The teams, remember, were distinguished by colors. Nero supported the Greens. He wore green in the Circus Maximus, and, just like a Ray Kroc might have, he had the track strewn with green copper dust. Then the charioteers went on strike and rioted. Officials of their league threatened to replace the charioteers' horses with common dogs. (Just as NFL owners, during the strike in 1976, would threaten to replace their players with "free agents" dragged in off the streets.) Nero was as concerned as a Wellington Mara about the "sanctity of the games." He ended that threat. Just like a Bill Veeck might have, he astounded everyone by awarding pensions to veteran charioteers. And, just like a Charlie Finley might have, he had veteran chariot *horses* dressed up in human clothes.

Nero began to spend more time at the business of chariot racing and less time at the affairs of state—a syndrome not unknown to our modern owners, who would much rather preside in the clubhouse than at board meetings. He had started out as a fan; now he had the urge to become a competitor. The way modern owners justify their involvement in sports in terms of "image" and "tax write-offs" and "civic duty," Nero defended his passion with a rationale no less transparent. "Chariot racing," he declared, "was an accomplishment of ancient kings and leaders; it was honored by poets, and closely associated with divine worship."

So Nero started his own private race course, where he could,

269

he said, drive his horses "remote from the public eye." That bit of pretense fooled no one. "Soon," says the historian Tacitus, "the public were admitted—and even invited. And they approved vociferously. . . . However, this scandalous publicity did not satiate Nero, as his advisers had expected. Instead, it led him on. He had definitely embarked on the slippery slope—a strange one for an emperor—of exchanging amateur for professional status."

We began with that prototype of Roman eccentricity, Nero. It would seem fitting to conclude with that symbol of modern eccentricity, Judge Roy Hofheinz. In particular, the peculiar circumstances surrounding Hofheinz's purchase of the Ringling Brothers' Barnum & Bailey Circus.

The day in 1967 the sale was to be consummated, Hofheinz flew to Rome, where the owner of the circus, John Ringling North, made his home. The first thing the Judge did when he arrived was to rent a lion cub for $80 per hour. He took the cub to Rome's Colosseum, where he had insisted North meet him to conclude their transaction. At that historic and hallowed site, after some preliminary wheeling and dealing North agreed to sell the Judge 50 percent of his circus. Then, as they were about to seal the agreement with a handshake, an altercation broke out between some of Hofheinz's assistants and the Colosseum guards. All Hofheinz had ordered his men to do was move a large building stone a couple of feet so the photographer he had hired to record this sublime event would have an uncluttered view.

The Judge seemed unable to comprehend what all the fuss was about—even after the guards had managed to make him understand how that particular stone had been placed on that particular spot some 2,000 years before, by an emperor named Vespasian.

DON KOWET is a free-lance writer who specializes in sports. He received a master's degree in economics from the London School of Economics, worked briefly as a social worker in New York, and served as managing editor of *Sport* magazine. He is the author of *Pelé*, a biography of the international soccer star, and a regular contributor to magazines. Mr. Kowet and his family live in New York City.